Exploring the Thought of Jane Jacobs

Exploring the Thought of Jane Jacobs

The Conversation of Cities

Richard Keeley

HAMILTON BOOKS

HAMILTON BOOKS

Bloomsbury Publishing Inc, 1385 Broadway, New York, NY 10018, USA
Bloomsbury Publishing Plc, 50 Bedford Square, London, WC1B 3DP, UK
Bloomsbury Publishing Ireland, 29 Earlsfort Terrace, Dublin 2, D02 AY28, Ireland

BLOOMSBURY and the Diana logo are trademarks of Bloomsbury Publishing Plc

First published in the United States of America 2026

Library of Congress Cataloging-in-Publication Data

ISBN: PB: 978-0-76187-489-8
ePDF: 978-0-76187-903-9
eBook: 978-0-76188-043-1

Typeset by Deanta Global Publishing Services, Chennai, India

For product safety related questions contact productsafety@bloomsbury.com.

To find out more about our authors and books visit www.bloomsbury.com and
sign up for our newsletters.

For Lou: constant champion, best critic, dearest love

Contents

Preface   ix

Acknowledgments   xiii

Introduction   1

1   Dreaming the City   11

2   The Existential City   27

3   City Talk: The Conversation of Streets   41

4   The Economics of Urban Life   67

5   Work in the City: Traders, Guardians, and Makers   97

6   Sustaining "the Whole Precarious Contraption": Education in the City   119

7   Further Conversations with Jane Jacobs   147

Appendix   175

Bibliography   177

About the Author   181

Index   182

Preface

As I stood on the porch of 69 Albany Avenue, Toronto on July 4, 1985, I was as nervous as a teenager on a first date. I hesitated to knock or ring. What would Jane Jacobs be like? What would she make of me?

I had been pursuing Jane Jacobs, via correspondence, since 1978, offering repeated invitations to visit Boston College. The invitations stemmed from my work. I was directing the university's PULSE program, a service-learning program that placed students in homeless shelters, schools, and homes for the emotionally troubled, as well as in advocacy and research roles for tenant and neighborhood organizations, consumer and legal aid groups all across Boston and its metropolitan region. The students played many roles: another pair of hands on the soup line, an ear for a teenager to whom no adult seemed to listen, a comforting voice on a suicide prevention hotline, a stout presence in a small claims court. They returned to campus brimming with questions: why did downtown Boston glisten with wealth while so many of its outlying neighborhoods felt crumpled and decrepit? Why did one feel safe in the Back Bay but wary on the streets of South Boston and Mattapan? How could anyone live in the housing projects on Columbia Point? What causes homelessness? What could anyone do?

Students and faculty alike grappled with many of those questions with the aid of *The Death and Life of Great American Cities* and *The Economy of Cities*. Jane Jacobs had thought about many of these questions and her work opened out toward farther avenues of understanding. Few of our students were city-dwellers: they were the children of suburbs and small towns. But the questions they posed required the tutelage of a keen observer of the dynamics of streets, neighborhoods, and districts. For many of those questions, Jane Jacobs was the tutor. Students began to bring "Jacobsian moments" to weekly classes and discussion. Understanding supplanted fear and incomprehension, energies refocused. There *was* something one could do. The next step seemed inevitable: bring Jane Jacobs to campus. And so, I wrote to her.

I hoped for a quick and positive response; I got the former but not the latter. Jane took my original letter, flipped it over, rolled it through her Olympia typewriter and replied: Mr. Keeley, PULSE sounds like a wonderful program.

But I am too busy writing to travel. Sincerely, Jane Jacobs. Jane Jacobs: recycler and homebound writer.

Disappointed but not deterred, I continued to write, but the response was always the same, a kind "no," with writing as the reason. (Once I overplayed my hand: noting a reference to a visit to Boston in a newspaper column, I wrote saying I thought she didn't travel. This was a mistake typical of a brash young man. She replied that a vacation was anyone's right. I went silent for a year.) The breakthrough came two years later. I forwarded her an illustrated study, done by a precocious student, analyzing Boston's South End. The neighborhood was leaning toward the upscale area it has now become and the student, herself involved with the poor and elderly there, saw what was coming. "She has it exactly right," Jacobs replied in a letter, and I thought our correspondence had new life. A while later, I sent her a letter with a raft of questions and a closing request: if she could not visit Boston, might I visit her? Yes, you may, she responded. And that led me to her front porch on the Fourth of July.

As I waited at the door, hopeful anticipation mixed with a little trepidation. Five years earlier, I had seen Jane Jacobs, from a distance, at the Great Cities of the World conference organized by Boston mayor Kevin White. She shared a panel with James Rouse, the acclaimed developer of Columbia, Maryland, and Boston's Faneuil Hall Marketplace; with Moshe Safdie, globally renowned architect and chairman of Harvard's graduate Design program; and the mayor himself. She spoke last, off the cuff, and delivered a trenchant criticism of Rouse and Safdie's remarks. On the spot, a celebratory event morphed into intellectual combat, and Jane Jacobs gave no quarter.

Jane Jacobs opened the door, and my fears were swiftly allayed. We met in her backyard and talked for two hours. Our conversation touched many points and made many pivots: at one point, I was wondering about using Herodotus to make arguments about economics, at another moment she was remarking on the wisdom of Canada's use of former immigrants as immigration judges. Not wanting to encroach further on a writer's time, I closed with an invitation to visit Boston College. She agreed.

Over the next fifteen years, Jane Jacobs made five visits to Boston College. She came as a Resident Author to PULSE, spending time in classrooms and entertaining questions from students. She was the centerpiece for *Jane Jacobs in Conversation*, a three-day conference involving architects, economists, philosophers, journalists, ordinary citizens, and Toronto city officials. At the Boston College Law School, in 2000, she was again the center of a conference

Figure P.1 Jane Jacobs, July 4, 1985 Toronto. Author photo.

titled *Jane Jacobs and the New Urban Ecology*. That was her last visit but not the most consequential.

That came earlier. In April of 1987, the university's Lonergan Workshop, an ongoing exploration of the thought of the late Jesuit philosopher and theologian, Bernard Lonergan, SJ, invited her to deliver two lectures under the title "Values and Ethics in Making a Living." She spoke on "Systems of Economic Ethics," a preview of the work that would become *Systems of Survival*. Her experience that weekend, rich in exchange with a host of interlocutors, prompted her to recast the emerging book as an imagined dialogue among a circle of friends. She said, in a subsequent letter, that she had learned so much in the interchange of ideas that it seemed fitting to create a replica of that exchange in the book.

That commitment to learning by exchange might have surprised some of her critics. Over the course of her authorship, not a few critics complained that she was a champion of no one's ideas but her own. Some saw her as a scold, a controversialist, the mistress of the repartee but someone lacking a rigorous and comprehensive perspective. One academic ethicist, reviewing *Systems*, sniffed that she misconstrued what ethics was all about.

The Jane Jacobs I came to know was no thin-skinned controversialist and self-promoter. She was the friend who sat on a folding chair and ate pizza with our bundled-up family and her son, Jim, as we prepared to move house in Worcester, Massachusetts. She marveled at the ingenuity of children, sending us a photo of a load-bearing toy bridge, constructed of linguine, by her granddaughter, Caitlin. She was the whimsical soul who sent our children a devilishly fashioned jug, with the challenge to drink from it without spilling. She was the matter-of-fact person who responded to a desperately eager student who asked, "but what can *I* do to help cities?" with "Ride a bike." She valued her work, not the honors that chased it. When I joined in the exploration of her basement files as she prepared for the donation of her papers to Boston College's Burns Library, I found a handsomely framed certificate noting her reception of the Britannica Award for "contributions to world knowledge." She was honored that year along with the Mexican poet Octavio Paz and the economist and diplomat, John Kenneth Galbraith. Surely, I asked, you'll want to keep this. She took it, turned it over, and replied, "Yes, I can make good use of this frame. You take the paper."

Jane Jacobs had a searching intelligence and a mind always alert for information that might be transmuted into knowledge. She was as eager for knowledge discrepant with her thinking as she was for confirming evidence. What counted was doing the subject justice. Jacobs is much heralded for her powers of observation, for what she saw, but her lasting importance is what she understood. Seeing is not thinking. Judgment intervenes between careful observation and repeated testing of hypotheses. Intelligence is restless with questions; good ideas come from paying attention to those questions.

Somewhere among my Jane Jacobs papers, I have tangible proof of that intellectual restlessness. It's a single sheet of graph paper, put to use as typing paper, introducing a chapter from *Cities and the Wealth of Nations*. It's a noisy and crowded page. The typeface squeezes in among the boxes, there are handwritten changes in two colors and pencil. These nudge up against words, phrases, and whole sentences struck through. And all rest beneath a giant "X" that slashes across the page in full.

I often used this sheet as an object lesson with students. Look at all the corrections, explanations, emendations, and the final dismissal, I'd urge. Here is a mind at work, trying and failing to do justice to an idea. Go and do likewise, I'd conclude.

If she were with us, Jane Jacobs would be undertaking a kindred re-visioning and rethinking of her work. What in that work might help us to understand, and affect, the world we struggle with now? That's what I hope to assist with in this book.

Acknowledgments

I have incurred many debts during the writing of this book. But I owe most, of course, to the late Jane and Bob Jacobs. Perhaps suspecting that if she allowed an interview with the importunate young man from Boston College, she might be free of his persistent letter-writing, Jane Jacobs welcomed me into her backyard at 69 Albany Avenue in Toronto on July 4, 1985. What ensued was a friendship that lasted until her death in 2006. I thank Jim Jacobs, Pat Brom, and Caitlin Brom-Jacobs for their hospitality and encouragement on my several visits with them. Their support and friendship mattered greatly as I pursued this work.

At Boston College, which now houses a Jane Jacobs collection in its Burns Library, four faculty members stimulated my thinking about Jacobs: the late Joseph F. X. Flanagan, SJ, and Patrick Byrne of the Philosophy department, Francis McLaughlin of Economics, and Fred Lawrence of Theology. They were full of fresh insights that enlivened my understanding and led me to think about Jacobs's work in much broader terms. Robert O'Neill, former director of the Burns Library, and Christian DuPont, its current director, have championed the Jacobs collection and made it a much-consulted reference and destination for scholars.

I am not alone in having felt the profoundly positive influence of the Jesuit community at the university, especially the teaching, scholarship, and friendship of Joseph Appleyard, SJ, David Gill, SJ, Bill Barry, SJ, and Robert Daly, SJ. Among the many other Boston College faculty and staff who have offered encouragement, comment, and critique are Ben Birnbaum, Mary Cronin, Carol Hurd Green, David Quigley, Joe Quinn, Carlo Rotella, and James Rurak. David Manzo was the first reader of my first draft and his enthusiasm quieted my misgivings and kept me at the wheel.

The Carroll School of Management at Boston College was my home for the latter stages of my career and played a significant role in the relationship between BC and Jane Jacobs. Jack Neuhauser, its longtime dean and a native New Yorker, orchestrated the funding for the university's 1993 conference, *Jane Jacobs: In Conversation*, with the assistance of Lori Egan and Nancy Samya. Richard Nielsen of the Management and Organization department contributed important research on managers and ethics, which Jacobs cited in *Systems of Survival*. I am indebted to Bill Bole for the suggestion that led me to my publisher. And I am grateful to Andy Boynton, current Carroll School Dean, for arranging an administrative sabbatical which allowed me to begin work on the book. Robert Taggart, Professor of Finance emeritus, has been constant in his support of my work.

While serving as Senior Associate Dean in the Carroll School, I enjoyed the friendship and support of Amy Donegan, Erica Graf, Amy La Combe, Kristen Nervo, Sara Nunziata, Terry Rezzuti, Ethan Sullivan, and Josephine Xiong. As Director of the university's Winston Center for Ethics and Leadership, I relied on the efforts of Brooks Barhydt, Jonah Berman, Monetta Edwards, and Ian Rogan. Among her other duties, Director Edwards now curates an annual Jane Jacobs lecture for the Center.

David Warsh of *Economic Principals* and former columnist for the Boston *Globe* taught me a great deal about the current state of economic theory and Jacobs's relations to it. He is not in the least responsible for whatever hash I have made of that discussion in this book. Mark Feeney, visual arts critic for the *Globe*, read a first draft of the manuscript with great care and patience, pointing out solecisms, anachronisms, questionable assumptions, and errors. I dared not ask him to review it once more, so failings of those kinds, and others, are entirely my own fault.

I first came to appreciate Jane Jacobs's work through the PULSE program. Patrick Byrne, now emeritus professor of Philosophy at Boston College but then a graduate student, and the late Joseph F. X. Flanagan, SJ, cofounded the program in 1969. College campuses, at that time, did not lack for students interested in engaging the crucial issues of the day—the Vietnam War and the civil rights struggle chief among them—and Byrne, a veteran of such commitments, developed a program model at the urging of the student government president, Joseph Fitzpatrick, and with the full backing of Flanagan. From its outset, PULSE would couple student engagements in the community—as tutors, advocates, researchers, counselors—with a curriculum anchored in Philosophy and Theology. That coupling struck many as unusual: surely, sociology, political science, psychology, and economics were more natural partners. What were those philosophers thinking?

It took time to figure that out: for several years, students enthused about their community placements but were (politely) disappointed in their classroom experiences. Faculty taught from a variety of syllabi, often salted with current, topical works—R. D. Laing's *The Politics of Experience* and Theodore Roszak's *The Making of a Counter Culture* featured in several courses—and struggled with how to relate texts to the rich texture of student experiences.

The experience of both faculty and students changed dramatically when Byrne, Flanagan, and Robert Daly, SJ, realigned the PULSE curriculum to track elements of a successful "great books" program at Boston College, Perspectives. The questions raised by the ancient philosophers, Plato and Aristotle; the Gospel writers; "modern" philosophers, like Locke and Machiavelli who disputed with the ancients and the Christians; and near-contemporary thinkers like Simone Weil and Dietrich Bonhoeffer; became the questions students posed when thinking about their roles, the people with whom they worked, and the city itself. If the early days of PULSE reflected some of a too-confident, self-righteous criticism of the social order, its tenor changed under the influence of these authors. Not a few students resonated with Bonhoeffer's claim that "we have once learnt to see the great events of world history from below, from the perspective of the outcast, the suspects, the maltreated, the powerless, the oppressed, the reviled—in short, from the perspective of those who suffer."[1]

And Jane Jacobs figured prominently as students sought to understand the city qua city. As I have argued throughout this book, while her work avoids cozy pigeonholing, its connections to the ancient thinkers is strong.

Throughout the book, I have emphasized Jacobs's understanding of the city as an organism, persisting through time due to the fidelity of generations of residents and citizens. I have seen this in Haley House, founded by John and Kathe McKenna, and I have come to think about PULSE in similar terms. The commitments that students engaged in as undergraduates have persisted in many forms. I know of at least two instances where a relationship that began as a college student befriending a troubled youth persisted over forty years and several instances where former PULSE students became leaders of the organizations which they first served as undergraduates. One led United Way programs in several large American cities; another rescued an agency under state scrutiny from potential demise; a third grew a single residential treatment house into a many-pronged, city-spanning network of organizations. They have become psychologists and counselors, doctors, nurses, physician assistants, teachers, lawyers, public defenders, priests and ministers, founders and leaders of schools, college and university professors, champions of community college education, poets, and novelists. One became a film producer, another was welcomed into the American Academy of Arts and Sciences, a third became a Google executive.

So let me now praise (some) men and women famous to me for their courage, fidelity, gumption, and cheerful persistence. They are not famous in any ordinary sense. Indeed, they put me in mind of the narrator's closing observation in *Middlemarch*: "for the growing good of the world is partly dependent on unhistoric acts; and that things are not so ill with you and me as they might have been, is half owing to the number who lived faithfully a hidden life."[2]

The list is long, but my memory is short, and so I offer apologies to those whose names do not appear. They, too, belong with Joan (DeNapoli) Byrne, Richard Gingras, Pat Hanehan, Jere Kelly, Dave Pellow, Richard F. X. Reagan, Mike Schippani, Mary White, Gordon La Sane, Tom Zlatoper, Mike Durkin, David Manzo, Mary Ann Nelligan, Matt Melvin, Linda Clark, John Tenerow, Ron Hobson, Tim Broccolo, Sarah Smith, Dennis Gilligan, Emilee Crowell, Kathy Rentsch, Jean Arcuni, Joe Bonito, Steve Calogero, Lori Campana, Mary Kate Costantino, Peter DeBiasi, Michael DeWinter, Jennifer Grumhaus Daly, Maureen Dumser, Karen Kelleher, Lori Havrilla, Peggy Heffernan, Marie Esposito, Avis Hoyt, Kim Kates, Kevin Kearney, Joan Kwiatkowski, Tricia Leonard Pasley, Kerry Maloney, Kerry McGowan, Suzanne Mettler, Diane Bella, Dave Mulhane, Anne Kimmerling, Tess James, C. J. Schoenwetter, Jennifer Pepi, Jan Reale, Jane Kelley Rodeheffer, Jon Scott, Heidi Sia, Steve Tumolo, Judy Kostka, Mary Stavrakas, Liz Wright, Peggy Bedevian, Cindy Kang, Sheila Lynch, Sara Marcellino, Jim Forbes, Nancy Soohoo, Cindy Bevivino, Mary (Donley) Swindal, Geralyn Vasile, Joe McLaughlin, Julie Fissinger, Kelly (Rush) Sanborn, Ginny Aultmann-Moore. Of these many, a special thanks to Richard F. X. Regan, who recruited me to become PULSE's Director, and Kerry Maloney, whose research project on the South End of Boston piqued Jane Jacobs's interest in PULSE.

My thanks to my editors at Hamilton. Brooke Bures was the first, and I hope her confidence has been well-placed. Zachary Nycum succeeded her. Both were kind and thorough guides to the thickets of rights and permissions, comforts to a fledgling author, and interpreters of Hamilton's formatting and production requirements.

I am very grateful for a grant from the Boston College Association of Retired Faculty, which allowed me to purchase the permissions for quoting from Jane Jacobs's work.

Finally, I cannot overstate the importance of my family to the undertaking and completion of this work. All of them—Lou, my wife, and our adult children, Matt, Austin, Tess, and Sean—met Jane Jacobs, and all of them encouraged—

and poked and prodded me when I languished—the undertaking. Our most recent family members, Angelina Keeley and Tom Bottkol have joined the chorus of supporters. Matt has been enormously helpful as editor: he knows an overreach when he sees it and picks up all the lost, or duplicate, spaces, thins out my overused words, wrangles with my syntax, corrects my grammar, and gently chides my pretensions. Lou, keen philosopher, has restrained my worst flights of rhetoric, always asking "what's the argument?" I leave it to them to judge whether the effort has been worth the candle(s).

Notes

1 Dietrich Bonhoeffer, "After Ten Years," in *Letters and Papers from Prison* ed. Eberhard Bethge (New York: Macmillan, 1978), 17.
2 George Eliot, *Middlemarch* (New York: Modern Library, 1984), 795.

Credit Lines

Introduction

If you are pausing over this book, it's likely that you are a lover of cities who has long known of the work and legacy of Jane Jacobs. You are in good, and wide, company. But in the years since her death, in 2006, Jacobs has gained even greater attention among an even wider public in surprising ways.

Take, for instance, the first season of Amazon Prime's *The Marvelous Mrs. Maisel*, set in late 1950s New York City. Midge Maisel, aspiring comedian and hassled wife and mother, stumbles upon an activist Jane Jacobs leading a rally against highway construction in Washington Square. She resonates to the message, piping up and joining in applause. In the company of Lenny Bruce, in the series' second season, Midge turns into the White Horse Tavern in Greenwich Village and finds Jacobs seated at the bar. Jacobs could be seen on stage, too. Off-Broadway theatergoers, if they were quick and so inclined, might have caught the rock musical, *Bulldozer: The Ballad of Robert Moses*. Moses, the master builder and public works commissioner of New York City, whose career is the subject of Robert Caro's *The Power Broker*, clashed famously, and repeatedly, with Jacobs. But the audience had to be quick: the show closed after a month and never made it to Broadway. *A Marvelous Order*, an opera by Jerold Greenstein, with libretto by US poet laureate Tracy K. Smith, which takes its name from a phrase from *The Death and Life of Great American Cities*, premiered at Williams College in March 2016. Like Matt Tyrnauer's documentary, *Citizen Jane: Battle for the City* (2016), the opera takes the Robert Moses-Jane Jacobs antagonism as its subject. This conflict figures, too, in a chapter of Pierre Christin's graphic novel, *Robert Moses: The Master Builder of New York City* (2014). Most recently, David Hare's *Straight Line Crazy* (2022), with Ralph Fiennes as Moses and Helen Schlesinger as Jacobs played to sold-out audiences in London and New York. Children can meet Jacobs in Susan Hughes's *Walking in the City with Jane* (2018). Most recently, Rebecca Pitts gave young adult readers a new biography in *Jane Jacobs: Champion of Cities, Champion of People* (2023).

Google kept me current with these moments and many, many others. Google launched its News Alert program in 2003; in 2004, I created one for tracking references to Jane Jacobs. In the subsequent twenty years, hardly a day has gone by without a notice pinging my inbox.

Alerts peaked in the months after her death, in April 2006. Admirers and critics, advocates and skeptics, public officials and ordinary citizens, friends, and countrymen (and countrywomen) took their measure of the woman and her achievement. Notice was taken worldwide: in Toronto, of course, her adopted city, and many other Canadian cities, but also New York, London, Tokyo. The range of countries spanned the globe with attention paid in Australia, South Africa, India, and Germany to cite a few. Someone great had died, but what to make of her? She was identified, variously, as an urbanist, an urbanologist (a neologism that she despised), a journalist, a sociologist, an activist, a philosopher, some hyphenated concatenation of the previous terms and, most acutely, an urban thinker. Jane Jacobs thought, and felt, the city. Both of those verbs are important.

Throughout her career, Jacobs was hailed, and chastised, for the depth of feeling she brought to writing about the city. Those who loved big cities and their abundant energies, peoples, places and occasions hailed her as a champion. Some professional critics, well-schooled in planning, architecture and governance, often dismissed her as a sentimental amateur. But Jacobs's love of the city was far from sentimental.. She loved the city fiercely and felt it deeply. But Jacobs "thought" the city, too, and did so with diligent attention to detail, leading to pointed questions, and tentative hypothesizing, and careful argument.

Without exception, the obituaries and encomiums highlighted her "first," and best-known book, *The Death and Life of Great American Cities* (1961)[1] It was, by these accounts, seminal, groundbreaking, a classic, required reading for all involved in urban planning, sharp, angry, wittily observant, profound. It *was* all of these things and its reputation eclipsed the notice taken of her following works, six of them (or seven or eight, depending on how one counts). The casual reader would be forgiven for assuming that *Death and Life* was the apex of a career.

That impression would be confirmed by a reading of my accumulated News Alerts: they are full of themes and phrases culled from *Death and Life*. Jacobs, for instance, had made much of "diversity" as crucial to city life, long before it became a charged cultural term. She thought that diversity of use, of building ages, and of people were avenues to successful city neighborhoods. She identified four interlocking factors as critical for successful city neighborhoods—short blocks; old buildings welcoming new and sometimes modest purposes; mixed usage; and dense population leading to eyes on the streets—and these factors often lead the articles and stories that Google brought to my attention. But the writers often deployed the four factors for purposes different from hers and, often, in ways insensitive to context, both immediate and historic, an insensitivity that Jacobs strove to avoid. Some singled out one factor, focusing, say, on the need for old buildings or a mixture of uses. She insisted that all four factors needed to be present to spur success: thriving neighborhoods resulted from the mutually reinforcing operation of the factors. Thus, a new venture in an old building faced failure if there were not sufficiently dense numbers of people on the street to catalyze further activity. Dark, abandoned warehouses at the edge of the city might offer the temptation of low rental prices, but their most likely occupants would be pigeons, absent the set of interlocking factors.

Critical as these factors are, and as important as they have been to the reception and practice of "Jacobsian" thinking, they are far from exhausting the richness of her work. Throughout her career, Jacobs focused on cities, but that focus, honed by careful observation, practical engagement, and wide-ranging reading, fostered extraordinary insights into cities' economies and governance, the relation of one city to another, cities' hospitality to difference, delight and beauty, and their precarious state as they pursued what she saw as the chief human enterprise: the building, sustaining, and transmission of culture. I intend to explore these often neglected elements of her legacy.

Jacobs wrote six major books after *Death and Life*: *The Economy of Cities* (1969), *The Question of Separatism: Quebec and the Struggle Over Sovereignty* (1980), *Cities and the Wealth of Nations* (1984), *Systems of Survival: A Dialogue on the Moral Foundations of Commerce and Politics* (1992), *The Nature of Economies* (2000), and *Dark Age Ahead* (2004).[2] These books will be the heart of my undertaking but there are other important sources. *Vital Little Plans* (2016), edited by Nathan Storring and Samuel Zipp, comprises previously uncollected talks, articles, interviews, and work left incomplete at her death. It is a precious sampler of her thinking and a tantalizing invitation for further exploration. Less readily available, but important for tracing subtle changes in her thinking as she approached *Systems of Survival*, is *Ethics in Making a Living: The Jane Jacobs Conference* (1989), edited by Fred Lawrence. It is the proceedings of a 1987 conference held at Boston College and contains two lectures and attendant questions and answers.

Best to say what my undertaking will *not* be. This is not an intellectual biography, a project well-realized in Peter Laurence's *Becoming Jane Jacobs* (2016), which traces the development of her thought, writing and arguments beginning with early days and her move to New York City in 1934. It is not a "biography of place," that field having been claimed by Glenna Lang's *Jane Jacobs's First City: Learning from Scranton, Pennsylvania* (2021). Nor will it be a biography, per se, a challenge met by Alice Alexiou's *Jane Jacobs: Urban Visionary* (2006), Lang's earlier *Genius of Common Sense* (2009) and most recently, and deeply, by Robert Kanigel's *Eyes on the Street* (2016). (Once, when I asked about the prospect of biography, Jacobs replied, "it's my ideas that you should pay attention to. I'm a very ordinary person.") I will not marshal a systematic response to her critics, or admirers, or a point-by-point defense of her positions or a lengthy verification or falsification rooted in current and recent history: scores will not be settled. But I will attend to thoughtful criticisms and suggestive elaborations of her thought. Recent comment, for instance, has wondered about gentrification as one outcome of Jacobs's work and worried about her understanding of diversity. Some of this notice will occur within the text; a select bibliography will point to other sources.

This is a generalist account and one with a "genealogical" interest. I am concerned with the lineage of themes that animate her work. Where do they originate? How do they recur and propagate? I hope to identify, retrospectively, the grand themes that root in small, particular places only to branch and blossom in surprising directions. I will give prominence to streets, neighbors, the pulsing of economies in venues large and small, problems of education, practical morality, and the preservation of cultures.

I hope also to place Jacobs's work within a much broader context than thinking about cities and their development. That is, of course, a broad context in itself, but I have an even wider horizon in view. Jacobs's work represents a profound meditation on the human condition. Deep questions underlie her thinking. What do human beings need? What do they seek? How do they fashion a life together? Who bears responsibility for sustaining civilization? What are the roles of art, nature, and family in securing the human enterprise? These questions place Jacobs far above the controversy that her work sometimes occasioned—is she an anarchist? a leftist? a libertarian?—and aligned, I think, with the concerns that the ancient Greek philosophers, Plato and Aristotle, raised in thinking about the *polis*. With Plato she acknowledges the power of dialogue—note that she employs a dialogic structure in two of her later works, *Systems* and *Nature*—and with Aristotle, she insists on the need to know the particulars of the circumstances in which human beings must act. Although she would never claim the title, she is, perhaps, a philosopher in spite of any disavowal.

I hope, finally, to be a guide to an interested reader. At a crucial moment in Augustine's *Confessions*, the not-yet saint hears a voice saying "tolle lege," take up and read. He opens the Bible and is never the same again. Taking up and reading Jane Jacobs has been a moment of "conversion" for many: suddenly, one sees and, later, understands cities in a wholly different fashion. But there are other reasons to take up and read her works: the direct but supple flow of her prose; delightful catalogs of items, cities, and processes that would make Homer proud; and, running throughout, the beauty of a mind at work, thinking in and through situations to produce an understanding that abstract theorizing can rarely attain.

As to my subtitle: when I broached it, some years ago, to a friend of Jacobs, the response was quickly dismissive. "No, you need to focus on economics. She's way beyond cities." I didn't engage with the friend at the time, but I thought that she missed something very important in Jacobs's work.

In 1995, on the occasion of a dinner thanking Jane and her husband, Bob, for the gift of her papers to Boston College, the then president of the university, J. Donald Monan, SJ, cited a letter from the early history of the Society of Jesus. Since their founding, the Jesuits have been great educators. In that letter, St. Ignatius of Loyola, the order's founder, wrote to a Jesuit brother planning the opening of a new school somewhere in Europe, advising him to "Be not far from the conversation of cities." Ignatius meant conversation in the older and broader sense of the Latin. It points to familiarity, intimacy, company: that well of human feeling and interaction that vivifies human life. Ignatius knew that cities were the place where ideas were born, people learned to govern themselves, societies evolved, art was created, and new enterprises emerged. The conversation of cities was life itself, and education needed to be alive to all of this. Ignatius wanted his schools to engage in the conversation of the city, not regard it from the outside.

Jane Jacobs knew this, too, and the evidence is everywhere in her work, although the attention given to her four factors for enlivening urban diversity can obscure these emphases. In cities, human beings learn the tasks of governance, first of self in the context of family, then with others, in the context of the street and neighborhood, then with unfamiliar others—those strangers who populate the city—through the means of formal representation or direct participation, and so on. In cities, the communal task of education thrives or withers. It withers if education is understood as purely formal instruction, conducted within classrooms, and rigidly sequenced. It thrives where teachers within that framework attend to, and nurture, the learning potential of the student. (The best teachers, she told me in an interview, are those "at the service of the students"[3]).

But education must thrive, too, in the collective transmission of culture, craft and citizenship. At its best, the city is a school for virtue where its inhabitants learn the costs and privileges of citizenship and the stakes for its sustenance. These are not small challenges and failure to rise to them has severe consequences: the city devolves into pockets of self-interest and transient commitments. Jacobs holds no brief for a perfect city, some version of utopia. She knew that cities are always problematic and the most successful cities stay abreast of problems by virtue of attention, sacrifice, innovation and perseverance. Cities prove worthy of that sacrifice and commitment to the extent that they answer to what every person needs: care, work, delight in beauty, and friendship.

Those needs are real, deep, and enduring. How does a city manage to provide these answers? Can it be traced to accident of geography? Luck? Money? Extraordinary characters? The ordinary character of people? Some combination of the preceding? To pose the question as I just have is to betray Jacobsian principles for understanding the city. It substitutes easy speculation and a string of seemingly apt questions for the difficult tasks of understanding what needs to be done in the light of history, studied observation of present circumstances leading to knowledge, and careful assessment of likely consequences. In the chapters that follow, these principles will shine through.

"City" is a small word, but the reality contains multitudes. "The city," announced Le Corbusier, "is the grip of man upon nature,"[4] the vigor of the metaphor suggesting human struggle against the wild and untamed, and suggesting, further, that the city is not "natural" to the human being. It is man-made, the triumphant artifice of its creators, their greatest achievement. To some small part of this, Jane Jacobs would assent: the city *is* the great human accomplishment, all the more marvelous for the myriad ways in which it continues to burst with life, work, beauty. But it is also, contra Le Corbusier's suggestion, wholly natural to the human being: in the city, the human community realizes the fullness of human potential. This will be the focus of the succeeding seven chapters.

In the first chapter, I will explore the richness of Jacobs's understanding by beginning with dreams, visions, and "myths" of the city. Like Le Corbusier, many entertain dream visions of the city. There are personal dream visions but there are also underlying cultural dreams, often religious at their sources, that guide a community. They are found in sacred texts across the world, and, in the West, especially in the Bible. They permeate the visions of founders of new societies and animate exploration. They influence the writing and practice of architects and urban planners.

If dreams are fanciful, Jane Jacobs was no "dreamer" of the city. In the next chapter, I explore her characterization of the city as "wholly existential." Cities are always in process. Jacobs helps us understand that cities emerge from constant choices, made by citizens, governments, businesses, families in constant interplay with each other and in response to developing questions.

That interplay happens on the street, the focus of the following chapter. No aspect of Jacobs's thought is more remarked upon than her concern with the street and its life. The chapter revolves around four different streetscapes, varied in time, scale, and complexity. Each is seen to offer elements of Jacobs's understanding, though none realize all of its complexity. I also explore the pitfalls of distorting or overgeneralizing Jacobs's focus on the street. The celebration of "eyes on the street" as the key to her understanding of urban success leaves too much out of her account and courts unhappy experiments in small towns, suburbs, and cities.

That flawed accounting extends to what Jacobs considered her most important contribution, the understanding of the economics of urban life, taken up in the next chapter. Jacobs wrote three books—*The Economy of Cities, Cities and the Wealth of Nations, The Nature of Economies*—focused on economics, and the fourth chapter takes up the threads that knit them together. Early skepticism of her work in economics, typified by a condescending *Time* magazine review of the first volume, gave way to growing affirmation and recognition from professional economists. Jacobs insisted on the difference between *growth*, as measured by such indices as Gross Domestic Product, and genuine economic *development*. She criticized the assumption that *nations* create wealth and insisted that *cities* were the genuine engines of economic life. She offered ways to measure new economic development and encouraged small-scale innovations in lending. At a moment when stock markets improve even as employment fluctuates and jobs become gigs rather than permanent positions, her insights may suggest what a vigorous economy might look like.

Exploring economies led Jacobs to think about the people and institutions that populate the marketplace. Just as a city is "wholly existential," economies are not machines operating blindly. People create economic life; and their interests, capacities, and functions differ. In the fifth chapter, I follow her provocative assertion in *Systems of Survival* that, despite its variety, economic life occurs within a framework bounded by only two ways of making a living. One is attuned to inclusive exchange, where people meet freely in markets; the other relies on force and law to govern those people and markets. Broadly speaking, these are the realms of commerce and politics. Adam Smith had noted the human inclination to "truck, barter and exchange,"[5] but Jacobs has something deeper and broader in mind. Exchange of goods, funds and, most important, ideas, powers economic life, but these may falter, or die, absent the protective work of government and regulation. But as Jacobs well knew, government and regulation might stifle economic life, rather than protect it, or might assume, mistakenly, the economic roles best left to individual innovators and enterprises. When those Jacobs calls "guardians" play at being "traders," terrible consequences may follow. I find examples of such overreach and role reversals in the history of Venice, a city Jacobs loved, and in a set of contemporary business scandals. Further, I pursue a modification of her schema by distinguishing "making" from trading and guarding, and I explore the difference between institutional ethics and an individual's ethics.

Becoming a trader, maker, or guardian means learning a way of life. How does this occur? In the penultimate chapter, I note a lacuna in Jacobs's thought, the lack of analysis of formal education. In her last book, *Dark Age Ahead*, she lambasted the contemporary situation where receiving a proper credential, a degree, counts as education.

But while Jacobs has little to say about schools, and much of that, critical, knowing and learning everywhere draw her attention. Learning, for Jacobs, occurred in many sites other than formal classrooms. Some of this had personal roots. Glenna Lang's recent work[6] underlines the role of the Butzner family in encouraging Jacobs's independent learning, tested by continuing dialogue with her parents, especially her father. Later, as a young working woman in New York, Jacobs was happily pursuing an independent course of study at Columbia's evening program, investigating economics, anthropology, history, and other subjects when a dean called her in, said that she was not doing things the right way, and told her she must conform or leave. She left. In sketching a Jacobsian philosophy of education, I note the convergence of her thought with two contemporaries. John Holt, who drew attention, reverently, to how children learn and Ivan Illich, whose forceful critique of schooling as enslaving, rather than empowering, are clearly her kindred spirits.

I conclude by trying to think along with Jane Jacobs about our present circumstances, taking her as an imaginary friend. As Glenna Lang wrote in *Genius of Common Sense*,[7] Jacobs herself, from a young age, conducted intensive, imaginary discussions with Thomas Jefferson and Ben Franklin as she walked the streets of her hometown. She favored Franklin, who was an inveterate questioner: why do they do things this way? Is there another way of looking at things? Our times call for similar undertakings. If density is crucial to urban vitality, how can that be realized in the wake of Covid? How do we rehabilitate public conversations and build back the structures of civic life, given the deterioration of civil discourse? What forms of new economic vitality will promote and sustain cities? What forms of learning best correspond to our changing circumstances? How do we use the wisdom of the past to shape the future?

But I begin with visions and dreams that influence how we think and feel about cities.

Notes

1 Her barely known, genuine first effort, *Constitutional Chaff*, was published by Columbia in 1941 while Jacobs, then Jane Butzner, was a part-time student there. It analyzed the losing arguments at the nation's constitutional convention.

2 She also wrote a children's book, *The Girl on the Hat*, published by Oxford, in 1990 and edited the diary of her aunt, *A Schoolteacher in Old Alaska: The Diary of Hannah Breece* for Random House in 1995. The former collected stories told to her young children and was written at their (adult) behest, the latter fulfilled a promise made years ago.

3 Richard Keeley, "An Interview with Jane Jacobs," in Fred Lawrence (ed.), *Ethics in Making a Living: The Jane Jacobs Conference* (Scholar's Press, 1989), 12.

4 Le Corbusier, *The City of Tomorrow and Its Planning*, translated from the 8th French Edition of Urbanisme by Frederick Etchells (MIT Press, 1971), 1.

5 Adam Smith, *An Inquiry into the Nature and Causes of the Wealth of Nations*, Book One, chapter two.

6 See Glenna Lang, *Jane Jacobs's First City: Learning from Scranton, Pennsylvania* (New Village Press, 2021).

7 See Glenna Lang, *Genius of Common Sense* (Godine, 2012).

Dreaming the City

In Italo Calvino's *Invisible Cities* (1974), the Venetian explorer Marco Polo beguiles the great Kubla Khan with tales of cities he has visited on his travels to the East. When the Khan loses interest and begins to spin his own descriptions of imaginary cities, Marco Polo responds with a reflection on the relation between cities and dreams. "With cities,"he begins, "it is as with dreams: everything imaginable can be dreamed. . .cities, like dreams, are made of desires and fears. . .cities also believe they are the work of the mind or of chance, but neither the one nor the other suffices to build up the walls."[1] Cities are no accident, born of whim or chance. They originate, Calvino suggests, in dreams and visions. Their persistence and prosperity will require much more than dreams, but the dreams will continue to exercise influence.

Does history confirm Calvino's view? I think so. Cities have been the stuff of dreams for centuries and the dream visions have at once spurred and complicated cities' development and, sometimes, led to difficult, unanticipated consequences. But to be clear: if dreaming implies an all-points perfect vision of a harmonious life, Jane Jacobs was no dreamer of cities. Perfection-seeking is utopian dreaming and utopia is, literally, a no-place. Real cities, Jacobs knew, are disharmonious places, where human beings search for work, love, friendship, esteem, and respond to the unpredictable, but wholly normal, problems these searches entail. Cities and citizens struggle to make the good concrete, not dream about it.

And yet the dreams persist and they continue to influence the ways in which we think about cities. To situate Jacobs's work, I will explore some of these dreams first, beginning with dreams connected to religious impulses.

Deep Dreams

In the deeper dreams of the city lie tangles of myth and legend. Romulus and Remus, twin founders of Rome, are raised by a wolf. Aeneas, a warrior returned from Troy, settles in Italy whence his great grandson, Brutus, is expelled by the goddess Diana, who commands him to seek a western isle. He lands in England, and founds London. Venice reveres Saint Mark who, legend tells, was adrift in the Venetian lagoon when an angel appeared and bade him peace and the news that he would find rest in the city. The Venetians took this story seriously, stole his bones from Alexandria, and bundled them back to the Basilica San Marco—where they disappeared, so the story goes, only to be rediscovered miraculously some years later.

The religions of the Near East—Judaism, Christianity, Islam—are replete with visions of the city. The epic of Gilgamesh, which predates all three, focuses on Uruk, oldest of all cities, the site of contests among human beings, demi-gods and gods. In the Bible, Babel, Babylon and Jerusalem become, respectively, archetypes of human insubordination to the will of God, exile imposed as a result of falling away from Israel's covenant, and the promise of glorious restoration to God's favor. For Islam, Jerusalem, Mecca and Medina become the lodestars of faith.

What is it about the city that commands the attention of shamans, priests and priestesses, prophets, and ordinary folks? The brief answer is that cities respond to abiding human concerns: the need to know about our origins and why we came to be here, the need to forge a common destiny from competing individual desires. Questions of identity, destiny, safety, and purpose course through both mythic and religious dream visions of the city and these have been explored by anthropologists, depth psychologists, and cultural historians, to name but a few of the searchers. I have found three twentieth-century thinkers especially helpful in illuminating these needs and questions.

The first is Mircea Eliade, a historian of religions, who devoted his scholarship to understanding commonalities of religious experience. His scholarship ranged over centuries and cultures across the globe. He was as interested in the stories of the earliest societies, fragmentary and arcane as they might be, as in the narratives of modern messianic and millennial movements. In archaic societies, he determined that cities and temples reflected a "celestial archetype."[2] Cities were founded on the spot reckoned to be the center of the world, the meeting place of heaven and earth. Shamans and priests found and marked this spot. What was there, in that special place, below the sky and above the nether regions of the earth, was the mirrored traces of the divine realm above. City founders paid tribute to the gods they could not see, or invested the mountains, the stars, the sun with divinity. Sites were selected, lines drawn, structures erected with an eye toward replicating, in microcosm, how things stood above, below and beyond this special patch of earth. The site of the temple, or the city, was sacred. It marked the very axis of the world, the centering place upon which the world turned.

If Eliade was correct about archaic societies, might a similar, atavistic influence be at work in the founding of historical towns and cities? The earliest towns and cities begin from a center. Take, for instance, a rendering of Paris before it was Paris. The Romans called it Lutece.

This map, dated 306 AD, depicts the city already established at a center, on what will become known as the Isle de la Cite, with roads leading to and from it. Countryside lies close by, as well as a temple to Ceres. Situated on an island, protected by the Seine which functions as a moat, Lutece is a small, secure settlement. If we were to consult a speculative rendering from 508, we would find the temple in ruins but development afoot. Agriculture now begins to dot the landscape where trees and forest stood before. The city has grown beyond the isle, and growth spurs further growth: buildings and thoroughfares emerge adjacent to the city. Over the centuries, the pattern will change but the centrality of the original city will remain. The city will grow in all directions but the center will hold its place in the imagination.

In books depicting medieval and Renaissance towns and cities, the bird's-eye view almost invariably shows enclosure, clustering and centering of buildings. A wall or fortification encompasses houses, churches and a public square: nothing sprawls or elongates.

Eliade would not have been surprised by the early Parisian renderings. He was insistent, further, that the influence of the ancient, center-seeking and world-defining urge persisted to this day and he warned against dismissing that ancient symbolizing urge as a relic of our nonage. Technical and scientific and decidedly rational as our society may be, the mysterious pull of the center still obtains and the hope for a deeper order and coherence persists. His suggestions were taken up by the twentieth century Norwegian architect and theorist Christian Norberg-Schulz.

In a series of books including *Existence, Space and Architecture* (1971), *Meaning in Western Architecture* (1974), *Genius Loci* (1979) and *The Concept of Dwelling* (1985), Norberg-Schulz explored the abiding human yearning to find and make a welcoming place on earth. Norberg-Schulz knew Eliade's work, and cited it. He drew out its implications by focusing on how human beings experience space. Norberg-Schulz drew further inspiration from the brooding

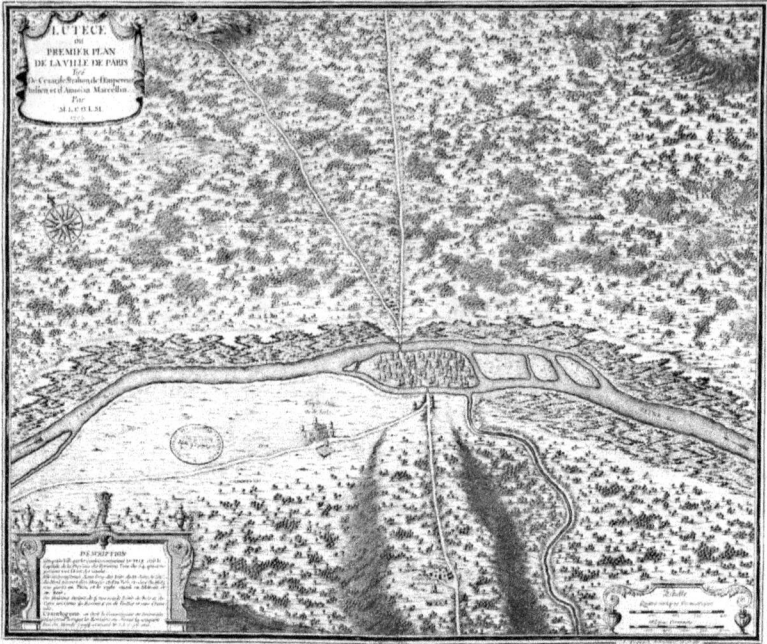

Figure 1.1 Lutece (early Paris). Public domain.

meditations of the philosopher Martin Heidegger. From Heidegger, Norberg-Schulz took the notion of "dwelling." Dwelling describes the relationship between the human person and the natural environment and the private and public realms. Dwelling involves "orientation and direction,"[3] and this applies to the private space of the home, the natural landscape in which home and settlement are located, and within settlements themselves. Further, the building of houses and the founding of settlements concretize the meaning of the universe. In a powerful analysis, Norberg-Schulz unfolded a progression of insights beginning with the individual person and extending to landscape, settlement, urban space, houses and institutions. The person standing erect upon the earth joins herself to the canopy of heaven. There she stands, a link between above and below, a first point of orientation and direction. How she shelters herself provides a second point: houses with floor, wall and ceiling mirror the enclosure one feels in the natural environment, or offer respite from its challenges.

Forms of dwelling differ according to the spirit of place. Places are defined by their situation within a landscape. Norberg-Schulz identified three distinct varieties of landscape—romantic, cosmic, and classical—and argued that they created a special "spirit" which, in turn, exercised profound influence on human beings. That spirit touched them individually but also shaped a collective expression of their understanding of the world, thus shaping distinctive forms of settlement.

To typify the *romantic* landscape, Norberg-Schulz drew upon his own experience, looking to the Nordic landscapes of fjords, mountains, snow and ice. Romantic landscapes are wild, mysterious, rugged. They are replete with forests, rivers, mountains, and glens. In legend and tales, they are the domain of trolls, fairies, and magical creatures. If life is to persist there, humans must make strenuous accommodations to carve out shelter from threatening rocks, to ensure access to water, to buffer homes from wind, rain, and snow. Homes are organized around the hearth, whose fire offers respite from the cold, light in the darkness, and sustenance from the oven. Towns and cities huddle together for collective warmth.

For Norberg-Schulz, *cosmic* landscapes reveal the yawning difference between human scale and the awful grandeur of the universe. The desert embodies the cosmic landscape. Beneath the dome of the sky, spangled with stars by night, seared by the relentless trek of the sun by day, human life seems cramped and insignificant. Such a landscape forces the human being to confront finitude when measured against the seeming infinitude of earth and sky, sun and moon and stars. Sand and rock and sun threaten life; the oasis becomes the shelter where life can bloom. Norberg-Schulz sees the architecture of ancient Egypt as an expression of the meaning of the world: the east, home of the sun, represents life: the west, death. The Nile forms the north-south axis and is the literal water of life. The arrangement of the temples and pyramids constitute a "geometrical" pattern organized by the sun's path and the river's flow.

The *classical* landscape marks a midpoint between the rigors of the romantic, where the person must seek out shelter amid the landscape, and the cosmic, where the vastness of the terrain and sky dwarf human scale. If cosmic landscapes carry a feeling of loneliness and potential menace, and romantic landscapes remind the person of the need to struggle for a foothold in the wild, the classical landscape evokes a harmonious relationship between persons and the natural environment. It welcomes habitation. Cities form in the shelter of hills and valleys, by the sides of rivers or the edges of lakes. The rendering of early Paris is a good example.

In classical landscapes or their towns and cities, Norberg-Schulz noted the importance of a center and paths for orientation. They are especially important within cities, helping a person to find a way and placing them together with others. These "others" are alike us in some respect, but quite different, too. "The city," he wrote, "is the place where *meeting* takes place. Here men come together to discover the world of the others. . .Meeting and *choice* are. . .the existential dimensions of the city."⁴ And within the city, through the contacts with so many who are other, one feels a mysterious kinship, even as one becomes more deeply aware of oneself. Jacobs was on to this: cities should create encounters with others, not offer a cocoon where sameness spins away. She wrote that "cities are by definition full of strangers"⁵ but she did not fear strangers: they were fellow dwellers in a shared world.

But dwelling within city limits, as natural as Jacobs and Norberg-Schulz suggest it is, appears suspect to many. In Western culture, the sources of that suspicion lie deep within the Bible. But there are counter themes as well. To trace these themes, I will follow the accounts of a third thinker, the Protestant sociologist and political theorist Jacques Ellul, who explored the Bible's deeply ambivalent attitudes towards the city in *The Meaning of the City* (1970).

Ambivalence was there from the start: the Bible's first book, Genesis, situates the ideal human existence not within a city but in a garden or, given the desert provenance of the Bible, and using Norberg-Schulz's term, within an oasis. When Adam and Eve, the original tenders of the garden, are expelled, they become the first homeless family. There is deep irony in the story: it is their decision to eat of the Tree of the Knowledge of Good and Evil, in the hope of becoming like God, that results in their banishment. In effect, they want to become self-sufficient, their own creators. This will become an undertone in the criticism of the city: city builders arrogate to themselves a power that belongs to God. Adam and Eve have to begin all over and this is no easy task. Expelled from paradise, human beings struggle to start anew. They seek safety in families and in tribes but this proves illusory: jealousy leads to fratricide as Cain kills his brother, Abel. The pointed moral of the tale: no one can be their own creator.

In such difficult circumstances, cities would seem a natural refuge. But, as Ellul points out, it is Cain, slayer of his brother, who is the first to found a city. From the outset, blood and violence stain the city. The city, Ellul writes, repeatedly, is a "man-eater."⁶ It is a monument to human arrogance, a collective attempt to become self-sufficient. In the Genesis story of the city of Babel, there is no need of God. Its people attempt to build a tower to reach the heavens, until God confounds the attempt by scrambling what had been a single language into many. Sodom and Gomorrah are proverbially iniquitous, home to every sort of evil and defilement and erased in a flash by God's anger. "The great city of Nineveh, in which there are more than a hundred and twenty thousand people who cannot tell their right hand from their left," [7] faces destruction as well until Jonah's reluctant preaching turns them to repentance. Babylon, likely the city inspiring the Babel story, is the preeminent "great" city, wealthy, luxurious, oppressive, and decadent. On Ellul's account, the great cities are proudly self-assertive and brazenly confident in their ability to succeed, without the help, or constraints, of God.

Suspicion of the city runs throughout the early history of the Israelites.[8] In the second millennium BC, Israel exists as a federation of twelve tribes. The tribes are pledged to a covenant with Yahweh: they are his people and they stand apart from other nations which rely on the protection of ruler-kings. At an annual event in the desert, at the shrine of Schehem, the tribes reaffirmed their covenant commitments. Far better to be a people of the wilderness and desert, accompanied by their God, than to be the subjects of an urban king. But eventually, and despite strong and continuing resistance, Israel becomes like other nations in seeking, and getting, a king. With kings come courts and palaces and the comforts of the city.

Israel is relatively fortunate in its early kings, David and Solomon. Under Solomon, Jerusalem, David's royal city, becomes resplendent. A glorious temple shelters the Ark of the Covenant. The city prospers. The challenge before Israel is clear: amidst the trappings of worldly success, can the people remain faithful to their God and his covenant?

Readers of the Hebrew Bible know how badly Israel failed that challenge, and the failure, though gradual, had catastrophic results. The prophet Zephaniah lamented "Woe to the city, rebellious and polluted, to the tyrannical city! She hears no voice, accepts no correction: in the lord she has not trusted."[9] Shortly after his outcry, the unfaithful people are led into captivity in Babylon. This is a painful and crushing irony: the holy city destroyed, its people dispersed, the evil city triumphant. "By the rivers of Babylon, we sat and wept when we remembered Zion," laments the Psalmist.

But the dream persisted. The lament over the wasted city found a counterpoint in the vision of a restored and glorious Jerusalem. While he sat in exile, the prophet Ezekiel urged Israel to return to covenant fidelity. The prophecies of Ezekiel chapters 40-48 presage the restoration of temple, land and priesthood, as well as the flowing of "living water." Israel could return to a renewed Temple and a New Jerusalem.

This fervent hope came to shape Christian belief as well. In the Book of Revelation, the last volume of the New Testament, a transformed Jerusalem marks the end of history. The ecstatic vision of Revelation 21 crests in these words:

> I did not see a temple in the city, because the Lord God Almighty and the Lamb are its temple. The city does not need the sun or the moon to shine on it, for the glory of God gives it light, and the Lamb is its lamp. The nations will walk by its light, and the kings of the earth will bring their splendor into it. On no day will its gates ever be shut, for there will be no night there. The glory and honor of the nations will be brought into it.

The destiny of all human beings—note that all nations are called to it, not just Israel—will be drawn to the heavenly city. Ellul writes: "when the Scriptures become more precise, it is always to describe the future under the aspect of a city. So it is with Ezekiel and all the prophets, without exception, and so with Revelation. . . What is coming is the city, not heaven."[10]

But even if the heavenly city will be the ultimate home for all, the tensions identified by Ellul in the Bible continue to affect subsequent Christian theology as it thinks about unheavenly cities. In its early days, the Christian religion rooted itself in cities throughout Asia Minor and, eventually, in Rome. Though a seedbed for the early Church, Rome was not always welcoming; a history of persecution is inscribed in the catacombs. Even when Christianity loses its outlaw status, with Constantine's proclamation of it as the religion of empire in the fourth century, the suspicion remained. When Rome fell to the barbarians in 410 CE, Roman critics identified Christianity as the remote source of the city's dissolution. These were old charges, taken on earlier by the Christian apologist Tertullian in the second and third centuries, and others. But it was St. Augustine who mounted the most prominent refutation of these claims in *The City of God* (ca.413-426). Writing in response to those critics who traced the fall of the empire to the disappearance of the old gods and the emergence of Christianity, Augustine argued the contrary. There were two Cities, one of God and one of Man, and they were intermingled. It was the City of Man, rooted in selfishness and sin, which led inevitably to the downfall of society. Only a city governed by a yearning for the one true God provided the possibility of an enduring community.

Human beings must live in the City of Man, argued Augustine, while hoping that traces of the City of God would peek through. Centuries after Augustine,

St. Thomas Aquinas would follow in this vein, seeing the Cities as intermingled. Aquinas was influenced, too, by the Greek philosopher Aristotle's understanding of the human being as a social and political animal whose life could not reach its fulfillment unless it lived with others. Aquinas affirmed this yearning for fulfillment, a human striving for happiness, even as he was duly aware of the sin and selfishness endemic to human beings which sabotaged efforts at perfection. In Aquinas's Christian understanding, grace and providence were the redress for these human failings.

If Aquinas made peace with this intermingling, a later Protestant reformer, John Calvin, was impatient with it. He made the city of Geneva, Switzerland, his dubious experiment for realizing the City of God on earth with an emphasis on the Scriptures, righteous living, and punishment for offenses great and small.

The struggle to accommodate, or integrate, Christian commitments with city life persists to these days. In the US, Christian sects of various stripes— the Shakers, Amish and Mennonites, to name a few—rejected integration and chose a life apart from the city. In the early twentieth century, the Social Gospel theology would see in the contemporary American city all the injustices decried by the Hebrew prophets and called upon the churches to remedy them. Some mid-century theologians saw the city differently. In 1965, Harvey Cox's *The Secular City* pointed to the city not as a den of iniquity but as the place where God, Lord of history, continued to work. On the twenty-fifth anniversary of its publication, Cox wrote that one of his "main purposes in writing *The Secular City* was to challenge the antiurban bias that infects American religion (at least white church life.) How many times did I hear, as a child, that 'God made the country, but man made the city.'?"[11]

With the works of Eliade, Norberg-Schulz and Ellul in mind, I turn now to trace deeper meanings in the American national experience.

American Dreams 1: Living as "a City on a Hill"

New undertakings prompt new visions. In 1620, John Winthrop, who would become the first governor of the Massachusetts Bay Colony, delivered a sermon to a congregation of his pilgrims-to-be in Holyrood Church, in Southampton, England. Contemporary readers of this sermon are likely to blush and rankle at Winthrop's quietist theology—he said, for instance, that the poor are there to be the objects of the rich's charity—but this theme was not the concern of Winthrop's congregation. They were a people under persecution, like the Israelites in ancient Egypt. The congregants were to think of themselves as a chosen people, seeking renewed faith in exile. Like their remote biblical ancestor, Adam, they, too, would suffer an "expulsion," though not from Eden. They were leaving a society hostile to their religious beliefs and practices. New possibilities for a beleaguered people lay before them and Winthrop announced the challenge:

> We shall find that the God of Israel is among us, when ten of us shall be able to resist a thousand of our enemies; when He shall make us a praise and glory that men shall say of succeeding plantations, "may the Lord make it like that of New England." For we must consider that we shall be as a city upon a hill. The eyes of all people are upon us. So that if we shall deal falsely with our God in this work we have undertaken, and so cause Him to withdraw His present help from us, we shall be made a story and a by-word through the world.[12]

This sermon, "A Model of Christian Charity," has exercised a powerful influence on American political thought ever since. Ronald Reagan, for instance, invoked the metaphor of a shining city set on a hill in his farewell address to the nation. "I've spoken," said Reagan,

> of the shining city all my political life, but I don't know if I ever quite communicated what I saw when I said it. But in my mind it was a tall, proud city built on rocks stronger than oceans, wind-swept, God-blessed, and teeming with people of all kinds living in harmony and peace; a city with free ports that hummed with commerce and creativity. And if there had to be city walls, the walls had doors and the doors were open to anyone with the will and the heart to get here. That's how I saw it, and see it still.[13]

The influence of the sermon extends beyond politics. Alex Krieger's masterful *City on a Hill: Urban Idealism in America from the Puritans to the Present* (2019), calls back Winthrop, too, finding Winthrop's influence shadowing hopes and plans for cities and towns.

The muscular confidence of Winthrop in God's providence and his people's capability infused faith and politics in early New England. Later generations of historians would detect the roots of an early warrant for American "exceptionalism" here—Reagan's theme—the notion that America has been singled out, by Providence or fate, for moral leadership in the world. What Winthrop had hoped for, Reagan, and others, saw realized.

Not everyone was so hopeful about the American prospect, especially with reference to cities. Thomas Jefferson, writing to Benjamin Rush well over a hundred years after Winthrop, and probably influenced by his experience of European capitals, as well as by love of his verdant Virginia, said "I view great cities as pestilential to the morals, the health and the liberties of man."[14] He thought that the city threatens what is best in the human being, whether body, soul, or politics. Instead of the city, Jefferson championed the vision of a nation of yeomen farmers, small landholders close to the land and the presumed moral benevolence of nature. (Other contemporaries disagreed. Alexander Hamilton, for instance, argued that cities were needed for America to prosper.)

Jefferson was not a lone voice. A book published a year after *The Death and Life of Great American Cities*, Morton and Lucia White's *The Intellectual Versus the City* (1962) chronicled the range of disaffection, disapproval, and fear, occasioned by American cities. They found a valorization of agrarian life in J. Hector St. John de Crevoceur's *Letters from an American Farmer* (1782), which bemoaned the constraints of formal European society as it extolled the natural virtue of the American farmer, and they extended it to Frank Lloyd Wright, whose vision of the ranch house open to the rolling plains was an antidote to the crush of the city. The city skeptics identified by the Whites field a formidable roster—Ralph Waldo Emerson, Herman Melville, Nathaniel Hawthorne, the brothers Henry and William James, Jane Addams. The critics have many complaints: cities pull people away from beneficent nature, they concede place and importance to commerce, they pile people upon each other in substandard housing, which is itself a function of the rule of manufacture and trade, they imperil the well-being of children and families, they corrupt our better angels. Not all of the critics objected on every count and not a few saw the advantages of cities, but the overall tone is sobering and cautious.

American Dreams 2: The Garden

Generations of American Studies scholars have explored these veins of thought. Henry Nash Smith's *Virgin Land* (1950), which predated the Whites' work, connected the country's westward expansion to the deep longing for a return to the garden. What to make of the city? Smith argued that the city was dreamed differently according to the region of the country. While the East, for example, could make a kind of peace with commerce and manufacturing, the South wrestled with a hybrid urban agrarianism. Fields, farms and plantations lay in comfortable adjacency to commercial and capital cities.[15]

Leo Marx pushed the analysis farther in *The Machine in the Garden* (1964). "If all America somehow could be transformed into a garden, a permanently rural republic, then its citizens might escape from the terrible sequence of power struggles, wars and cruel repressions suffered by Europe."[16] Marx saw the abiding tension between the technology we insist upon and the threats it poses to natural, untechnical life reflected in the nation's literature. He identified three modes of responding to the emerging struggle between the symbols of machine and garden. Emerson typified what Marx called a transcendent mode. While affirming progress, and nature, Emerson disparaged cities. Hawthorne and Melville took the tragic view: the machine will have its roaring day at the expense of the garden. Mark Twain represented a vernacular response, an easygoing accommodation, on Marx's terms. Huckleberry Finn floats on down the big river, the Mississippi, using or avoiding the city/machine when he must, but keeping always close to the natural. All of this amounts to what Marx calls a modern primitivism: we want all that our marvelous machines can provide but we rue the loss of "the garden."

These various attempts to interpret the relation between machine and garden, between city and countryside, might seem merely a retrospective and literary reading of American history. But these themes and images were on the mind, and influencing the practice of nineteenth-century businesspeople, too. In *Nature's Metropolis: Chicago and the Great West* (1991), William Cronon found that the "boosters"—apologists—for the city's development saw the railroad "less as an artificial invention than as a force of nature. . .Railroads were more than just natural; their power to transform landscapes partook of the supernatural, drawing upon a mysterious creative energy that was beyond human influence or knowledge."[17]

Jane Jacobs on Dreams

Jane Jacobs never theorized about dreams, myths, and symbols, but she knew the acute influence they could exert on workaday life and thinking about the city. In citing the Gilded Age Chicago architect Daniel Burnham's dictum— "Make no little plans, for they have no magic to stir men's blood"—she acknowledged the motive power of what I have been calling dreams. And when describing the ruinous effects of "cataclysmic" money where more judicious spending is called for, she wrote "First comes the image of what we want, then the machinery is adapted to turn out that image."[18]

While Jacobs never created her own dream vision, the introduction to *Death and Life* does identify three governing visions of the city—Radiant City, Garden City, and Radiant Garden City Beautiful— and excoriates their proponents. Chief among these are Ebenezer Howard and Le Corbusier. Although neither was an American, their thought was congenial with aspects of American dream images of the city and their influence upon thinking about cities and regions was pronounced.

Howard, Jacobs notes, was a nineteenth-century English court reporter who came to city planning as an avocation. He was appalled "at the living conditions of the poor in late- nineteenth-century London, and justifiably did not like what he smelled or saw or heard."[19] But the proposed remedy, Jacobs thought, was, unwittingly, the source of greater problems. Howard proposed the creation of Garden Cities, town-scale settlements where work and living were neatly sorted out, not jumbled together. The commitment to town-scale tips his hand, Jacobs argued: these principles, adapted as urban guides, actually describe suburban or small-town living patterns. For the "intricate, many-faceted, cultural life of the metropolis," Howard substituted a static and paternalistic—"if not authoritarian"—town society.[20] The real harm of these principles, Jacobs asserted, were the unwitting ways in which their advocates mapped them, mistakenly, to urban forms in thinking about housing, economy and society. Later thinkers influenced by Howard, including Lewis Mumford, reveal the power of the dream, or nightmare, of the city. In Mumford's *The Culture of Cities*, Jacobs points out, "The great city was Megalopolis, Tyrannopolis, Nekropolis, a monstrosity, a tyranny, a living death. It must go."[21] Or be reduced: sorted, contained, condensed—these are the operative actions to realize Howard's dream-vision. They embody an unacknowledged bias that Jacobs uncovers in her argument for the need for dense concentrations of people. "People," she suggests, "gathered in concentrations of big-city size and diversity can be felt to be an automatic—if necessary—evil. This is a common assumption: that human beings are charming in small numbers and noxious in large numbers."[22] And beneath that assumption sleeps the garden dream. In small and simple communities, close to the natural environment, goodness lies. In large, scruffy and complicated cities, goodness is at risk. This is a sweet and beguiling dream for the suburban dweller, but a threatening one for thinking about cities.

The French architect Le Corbusier touted the Radiant City, a dream-vision that, in one sense, squared the circle of bucolic comfort and dense concentrations of people. The Radiant City achieved this by erecting skyscrapers in parks. "The skyscrapers," Jacobs observed, "would occupy only 5 percent of the ground. The high-income people would be in lower, luxury housing and courts, with 85 percent of the ground left open. Here and there would be restaurants and theaters."[23] Le Corbusier had disparaged the aimlessness of medieval Paris—streets laid out "the pack-donkey's way"—and called for rectilinear, Cartesian order.[24] Highways would twine between the towers. Le Corbusier's formulations are striking. When he writes "the city! It is the grip of man upon nature,"[25] he reveals an entire philosophy. Cities are technological devices—he had famously called houses "machines for living"—poised to grapple with raw nature. Nature must be tamped down, or brought to heel like a dangerous animal. But, still: "The whole city is a park."[26]

Take a cab from Toronto's exurban airport to the city's center or enter Manhattan along the East River and evidence of Le Corbusier's influence sprouts before you: high-rises line the roadsides and automobile traffic, not pedestrian, dominates the scene. "The city which can achieve speed, will achieve success," he had written.[27]

Curiously, Jacobs does not mention Frank Lloyd Wright and his influence. In *Urban Utopias of the Twentieth Century* (1982),[28] Robert Fishman links Wright with Howard and Le Corbusier. All three were interested in the ideal city. All three were repulsed by the nineteenth-century metropolises they saw going awry in Europe and this country. All were confident that technology promised hope for bright urban futures. Le Corbusier exalted a new metropolis; Wright wished for extreme decentralization, ideally each family with its plot and a view towards the horizon; Howard split the difference, placing, to borrow Leo Marx's formulation, machine and garden each in its proper place.

As Jacobs concluded, Howard's and Le Corbusier's ideas were profoundly anti-urban. Yet they have also proved powerfully attractive. Confronted with the complexity and confusion that urban life can generate, the urge to simplify, to tame, to quiet discomfort by minimizing the strange, the tangled and the unpredictable is understandable. This is not to argue against all planning; there is a place for plans, but finely-tuned considerations of scale and scope and local ownership are all core components of appropriate plans.[29]

The city dreamers are Utopian thinkers, sometimes unawares. Jane Jacobs was no dreamer of cities but their seeker. I mean that designation this way: Jacobs always looked to understand what was given, and emerging, in the city present right before her. It would not do to prescribe by way of formal planning. That would be foolish: "Cities are not preordained—they are wholly *existential*."[30] We turn to what that might mean in the next chapter.

Notes

1 Italo Calvino, *Invisible Cities* (Harcourt, 1974), 44.
2 Mircea Eliade, *The Myth of the Eternal Return* (Princeton, 1971), 12.
3 Christian Norberg-Schulz, *The Concept of Dwelling* (Rizzoli, 1985),7.
4 Norberg-Schulz, *The Concept of Dwelling*, 51.
5 Jacobs, *The Death and Life of Great American Cities* (Random House, 1961),30.
6 Jacques Ellul, *The Meaning of the City* (Eerdmans, 1970).
7 Jonah 4:11.
8 To supplement this all-too-brief and selective account of Israel's history, see John Bright, *A History of Israel*, 4th edition, (Westminster: 2000).
9 See Zephaniah, 3:1-2.
10 Ellul, *The Meaning of the City*, 159.
11 Harvey Cox, *The Christian Century*, November 7, 1990, 1025 ff. Or see https://www.religion-online.org/article/the-secular-city-25-years-later/.
12 See https://www.gilderlehrman.org/sites/default/files/inline-pdfs/Winthrop%27s%20City%20upon%20a%20Hill.pdf.
13 See https://www.reaganlibrary.gov/archives/speech/farewell-address-nation.
14 See https://founders.archives.gov/documents/Jefferson/01-32-02-0102.
15 See Henry Nash Smith, *Virgin Land: The American West as Symbol and Myth* (Harvard, 1950).
16 Leo Marx, *The Machine in the Garden* (Oxford, 1964), 138.
17 William Cronon, *Nature's Metropolis: Chicago and the Great West* (Norton, 1991), 72.
18 Jane Jacobs, *The Death and Life of Great American Cities* (Vintage, 1961), 313.
19 Jacobs, *Death and Life*, 17.
20 Jacobs, *Death and Life*, 19.
21 Jacobs, *Death and Life*, 20, 21.
22 Jacobs, *Death and Life*, 220.
23 Jacobs, *Death and Life*, 22.
24 Le Corbusier, *The City of Tomorrow* (MIT, 1972), 11.
25 Le Corbusier, *The City of Tomorrow*, 1.
26 Le Corbusier, *The City of Tomorrow*, 21.

27   Le Corbusier, *The City of Tomorrow*, 190--191.

28   See Robert Fishman, *Urban Utopias in the Twentieth Century: Ebenezer Howard, Frank Lloyd Wright, Le Corbusier* (MIT, 1982).

29   For an especially helpful overview of planning styles, see Wade Graham, *Dream Cities: Seven Urban Ideas that Shape the World* (Harper, 2016).

30   Jane Jacobs, *The Economy of Cities* (Random House, 1969), 138. Emphasis mine.

2

The Existential City

What did Jane Jacobs mean by characterizing the city as "wholly existential"? Today, the adjective "existential" has a wide and sobering currency. Some political commentators in the United States fear an "existential threat" to democracy both at home and abroad. In the Middle East and Ukraine, leaders of sovereign nations and displaced persons alike fear for their very existence. "Existential," in these usages, points to the matter of survival.

When Jane Jacobs uses "existential," I think she has something less immediately dire, but no less important, in mind. She is thinking about the importance of understanding the city as an ever-developing organism, not an immutable object, something alive, hence "existing." What might she mean?

A long-standing tradition of philosophy in the West addressed the question of "essences." Imagine yourself visiting the San Diego Zoo, accompanied by your granddaughter. This is no veldt: you cross the asphalt of the parking lot, striding across manufactured materials, cars to your left and right. Within the Zoo domains, there is much more to see and a simulacrum of a veldt: the gathering of rocks, grasses, water, and trees to form the animals' various habitats. The rocks, inanimate objects, will never be anything else. The grasses and trees, are different, capable of growth and development, and needing nourishment to survive. The many marvelous animals are different from the rocks and the vegetation, : they move, they take in nourishment, they reproduce, and they die. They are animate life, different in complexity from inorganic material, but they, too, will never be anything other than their original species: a snake is a reptile; a bird is a bird. Everything, on this view, has a given essence, an unalterable core, which will be expressed in a particular way as life unfolds. And as for you and your granddaughter? You, too, have a distinctive essence. You both began as infants, toddled into childhood, learned to talk and communicate, thought and imagined many things, grew, in your case, through adolescence into adulthood and proud grandparenthood, but through all these changes, all these becomings, your essence, human being, has remained the same. Mineral, vegetable, animal, human being: each has a distinctive essence.

In the twentieth century, a branch of philosophy made a turn away from this line of thinking. Jean-Paul Sartre and his fellow "existentialists" attacked the notion of an immutable human essence. Human beings, they argued, do not have a predetermined essence: they *create* their essence via their choices. What any one human being will become is not the realization of some common "essence" but the consequence of her choices. In the case of the human being, existence trumps essence.

Thus Jacobs could see cities as "wholly existential" because they result from myriad, interlocking, and concatenating choices made in response to the particularities of time and place. In cities, the novel and the unanticipated can erupt in any quarter and at any time, defying the best-laid plans. City planners, on Jacobs's view, were heirs to an "essentialist" understanding. They did not understand that the city was an organism and thought of it, instead, as a single object fit for manipulation and regulation. Jacobs saw the city bursting out all over because this is what human energy does.

"All is flux," wrote the pre-Socratic philosopher Heraclitus. Cities, too, are in constant flux, a churn of contingency. My local newspaper runs a popular feature that dramatizes the flux that marks the history of Worcester. A period photograph captures a now-transformed site. The accompanying text drops a few hints and asks, "do you know where this is?" A week later, the answer follows. Thus, we learn that a small, ethnic market in Webster Square once hosted the city's first supermarket and that the empty lot, which was a sprawling car dealership itself squatted over several acres of a former farm. No one foresaw these changes, the city just "happened."

City life develops in response to contingent events: accidents and windfalls, luck and misfortune, the arrival of new peoples and technologies, the exits of others. The pace of change is inconstant. It may come in a flash or may emerge only after long gestation. The pressure of remote forces, unknown, unsuspected, or undetected can play havoc with the local and familiar. I discovered this at a young age from an unlikely source.

As a middle-school student, I took inordinate pride in the wastebasket that stood in the bedroom I shared with my brothers. One embossed panel of the wastebasket featured a colored contour map of the United States and another listed the country's fifty largest cities. I was proud: there sat Rochester, New

York, number 38 in the top 50, with a population of 318,000. Not bad, I thought: maybe we can catch Buffalo.

My boyish boosterism was heedless of the economic and social changes already underway. The influence of the extended US highway system would propel migration and growth in unexpected places. Eastern manufacturing moved south, west, and eventually, offshore. Retirees would swell the growth of communities fresh with warmth and sunshine. (When the 2010 census was taken, Mesa, Arizona, with a population of 439,000, occupied the 38th position; Rochester's population—210,000—and rank—number 99—had both declined.) Cities formerly well below Rochester—St. Paul, Miami, El Paso, Tampa, Toledo, and Austin, for example—were ascendant. No one saw this coming but, in retrospect, the change seems obvious and unavoidable, the effect of forces both far afield and close to home. "We live forward," wrote Soren Kierkegaard, "but understand backwards." This is a sentiment that Jacobs thought escaped planners.

Jacobs knew that one couldn't hope to eliminate contingency. The attempt to anticipate it, via the formulation of "contingency planning," might have seemed prudent, but also reflected not a little hubris, leading to a fundamental misunderstanding of the existential city. Cities are the human place; and human beings, in constant pursuit of their dreams and ambitions, are always making new things. To be sure, these are not dreams and ambitions pursued haphazardly. They, too, require plans. But they are not plans on the grand scale such as envisioned by Daniel Burnham. Burnham, as we saw in the last chapter, wanted "big plans" that might "stir men's blood." Rely on the passions, Burnham suggested, gin up expectations, get people excited, and grand things will result. Jacobs challenged this thought in print and in the streets. Over against the predilection for big plans, Jacobs championed what Samuel Zipp and Nathan Storring highlighted in *Vital Little Plans* (2016), their collection of Jacobs's articles, addresses, interviews, and unpublished pieces. In the hands of ambitious planners, big plans will restrict choice, argued Jacobs. The master planners assumed that ordinary citizens, left to their own devices, would make a hash of things. Thus they worked to limit choices, the better to mitigate the damage wrought by ordinary people. But ordinary people want to make their own choices. Contra the planning mentality, "The point of cities is multiplicity of choice,"[1] wrote Jacobs. And once one allows for choice, for the freedom of the city, innovation, upset, alteration, not to mention surprise and external shocks, all come into play.

Jacobs's insistence on the play of contingency in the development of cities offers no comfort to those who seek grand, onetime solutions to city problems and little consolation to city champions of a more modest bent. The closing pages of *Death and Life* offer this sober assessment:

> Being human is itself difficult, and therefore all kinds of settlements (except dream cities) have problems. Big cities have difficulties in abundance, because they have people in abundance. But vital cities are not helpless to combat even the most difficult of problems. They are not passive victims of chains of circumstances, any more than they are the malignant opposite of nature.[2]

If large numbers of people mean correspondingly large numbers of problems, they also carry the potential for resolving those problems. Jacobs knew that cities are inherently messy and that their problems ramify in unexpected ways. Some of her ardent supporters miss this accent. They assume that once the boxes for lively and diverse streets have been checked, for instance, the city can relax and its night watchmen call "all's well!" But good cities are not problem-free. Good cities ensure their success by constant vigilance, and they succeed if they stay abreast of their problems.

Admittedly, that is a big "if." Keeping abreast of problems means a careful attention to current prosperity coupled to a keen understanding of its sources. Keeping abreast also requires people vested with the authority to make appropriate corrections. In *Cities and the Wealth of Nations*, Jacobs concedes that "from time to time an existing city falters and doesn't correct its economy, which builds up further instabilities and stresses in the nation as a whole. Even if nations were run by selfless geniuses or by angels, stresses and instabilities from missing or arrantly contradictory feedback would accumulate; they are built into the situation itself."[3]

Note the casual echo, and intensification, of *Federalist #51* in Jacobs's caution—"If men were angels," wrote James Madison, "no government would be necessary"[4]—coupled to the acknowledgment that stresses and instabilities accumulate no matter the best of plans. One may hope for the best but fear the worst. Luck may run bad; external shocks may damage the city irreparably; good ideas, and the people to pursue them may disappear.

City problems may sprout overnight although their roots may be long in the ground. And expected success often falters. In *Economy*, Jacobs notes the surprising differences in economic success between "efficient Manchester" and "inefficient Birmingham,"[5] which eclipsed Manchester as a source of productivity and innovation in the nineteenth century. Smart money would have looked to Manchester to succeed but many good, small and seemingly unimportant things were afoot in Birmingham. Venice, a city which Jacobs analyzes in *Wealth*, offers an earlier cautionary tale. From the thirteenth through the sixteenth centuries, few cities could rival its power. It commanded an empire that spread down the Adriatic and into the eastern Mediterranean. Its traders opened Europe to the commodities—spices, silks, coffee, oils—of the Levant and Asia. Its bankers, like their Florentine counterparts, innovated financial instruments; its currency, the ducat, became the currency of choice. In its political traditions, the ease of social classes of vastly different financial means with each other, underlay a republic that seemed to promise social harmony coupled to extraordinary economic success. But as early as the thirteenth century, the foundations of its preeminence were cracking. Centuries later, William Wordsworth would lament its decay: "Once did She hold the gorgeous east in fee;/And was the safeguard of the west: the worth/ Of Venice did not fall below her birth,/ Venice, the eldest Child of Liberty."[6]

Once, but no more. To understand what happened is a complicated task, one that can benefit from Jane Jacobs's insights; they will be brought to bear later on such questions as these: How did Venice lose its economic power? What put liberty at risk? What combination of forces, events, people, and decisions were at play? And why did Venice fail to recognize what was emerging?

In the twentieth century, my Rochester was another city taken by surprise. At mid-century, its core civic and cultural institutions—the University of Rochester, museums, hospitals, The Eastman School of Music, to name a few—grew from the largesse of Eastman Kodak. The city's economy hummed with technological innovation. For Kodak, excellence in chemicals and film, and competence in associated goods like cameras and projectors, drove its success. It benefited, too, from an environment rich with other accomplished technical firms. There was Bausch and Lomb, with a thriving lens business, and Xerox would emerge from the Haloid Corporation. But something sputtered.

A fateful decision taken in 1975 looms large in the story of Kodak's decline. In that year, Kodak, always a technical leader, developed the first digital camera. This posed a conundrum. Film was Kodak's lifeblood. The idea of digital imagery threatened to choke off the blood supply. So, fearing that digital technology would kill its film business, Kodak put aside most further development of digital camera technology. When it reentered the digital market, it was too late. It had lost its early, first position, and its subsequent results were disappointing. If you return to the site of Kodak's industrial might today, you find empty acres of shuttered buildings lining the Ridge Road where Kodak achieved so much success.[7] Would angelic insight or genius have averted this outcome? Probably not. Stresses and instabilities were accumulating worldwide and rippling through many interconnected economies. But a dose of entrepreneurial courage, a willingness to risk the new technology, despite its hazard to the old work, might have yielded a somewhat different outcome.

Or consider any number of cities struggling with gentrification. Some critics have laid this problem at Jacobs's doorstep. In many cases, old buildings at a city's core have been put to new uses, as she had recommended. Jacobs had looked to these old buildings as nurturing places for new ideas to sprout, adventurous entrepreneurs to meet, and new work to develop. Instead, not a few cities have seen those new places populated by the wealthy few at the expense of the middle class. She made the city so attractive, the critics argue, that the well-heeled rushed to its center and, in the process, drove out the poor, those of modest means, and local businesses. Jacobs, by this account, unwittingly abetted gentrification. This is a serious charge, one with implications for understanding the sweep of Jacobs's work and the prospects for city life in our time. I will defer consideration until the next chapter when I explore the importance of streets.

For the time being, suffice it to say that Jacobs neither anticipated nor "planned" for gentrification. Nor, given its emergence, did she despair that nothing could be done. Jacobs never "dream[t] of a [city] so perfect that no one would have to be good."[8] Recognizing and responding to the challenge of doing the good is the ordinary task of politics, as practiced by ordinary citizens as well as elected officials, in Jacobs's city.

I witnessed the tension between planning and the surprising unexpectedness of the city the first time I saw Jane Jacobs in person. It was 1980, and Boston's then mayor Kevin White had convened a "Great Cities of the World" celebration in Boston's Faneuil Hall.[9] I was keen to attend a plenary session titled "Tools for Urban Design in a Period of Constraints and Opportunities: Coping with Change," that featured James Rouse, the noted real estate developer and urban planner who had orchestrated the redevelopment of Faneuil Hall Marketplace and Quincy Market; Moshe Safdie, the visionary architect and designer; and Jane Jacobs. I was fortunate to obtain a pair of tickets to the invitation-only event. Not everyone who had an interest in this event would make it in: as I walked through the marketplace on that autumn day, I skirted a crowd assembled in protest. It was a gathering of local activists, notable among them Mel King, who besides being a longtime community organizer, had served in the Massachusetts State House as a Representative and was a lecturer at MIT. The protesters were calling for attention to be paid to the urgent problems of the city of Boston, here and now. Throughout the session, as I sat within the dignified meeting space that is the formal hall, the chants and murmurs of the crowd were a consistent undertone.

Why these panelists? In opening the session, Kevin White acknowledged the influence that each wielded in Boston: Rouse, through his development of the Faneuil Hall parcel, a formerly neglected and down-at-the-heels historic site now turned to fresh commercial uses; Safdie, head of the Urban Design program at Harvard's Design School for his leadership there and his role in the redevelopment of the North Station area; and Jacobs for her acute appreciation and advocacy for the latent strength of neighborhoods. White continued by offering a revisionist history of the new Boston. He lauded the urban design community for its efforts in building coalitions among government, business, and residents, and characterized, to warm applause, the mayor's role as "sworn enemy of the status quo."

Safdie spoke next. His portfolio at that time included clients the world over with notable commissions in Boston, Montreal, Singapore, Jerusalem, and Mexico City. Design, he argued, represents a corrective to the modernism of an architect like Le Corbusier. Le Corbusier, who had complained, as we saw, about the "path donkey's way" that accounted for the medieval streets of Paris, foresaw a city of tomorrow with large skyscrapers soaring above green space—a marriage of machine and garden. Urban design will have none of this, said Safdie, since it must pay attention to the intricacy of particular places. But maybe there is too much particularity, he seemed to suggest when he noted that designers felt constrained working in Boston. There was so much community involvement. (I thought of the chorus of chanting protesters gathered outside.) Among his peers, Houston was a currently preferred site.

Rouse's work on the adjacent Faneuil Hall Marketplace, as well as on Baltimore's Harborplace, was well-known. Less appreciated was his work on the design of Columbia, Maryland, a planned community of 60,000 and a vindication, in his estimation, of the virtues of large-scale planning. In a voice echoing Burnham, he argued that "what we need is what I call the 'Big Human Plan,' a plan that sees the city as a system." References to new plans, new strategies, and new priorities studded his address.

As Jacobs assumed the podium, I thought she would have found much to agree with, apart from the Burnham-like braggadocio. I was wrong. Speaking off the cuff, apologizing for what might seem piecemeal, she quickly joined the issues. By the time big plans come to fruition, she asserted, they are already old or middle-aged. Contesting Rouse's claims about the historic importance of big plans, she traced the emergent success of Faneuil Hall and Quincy Market to the successful recycling of old ideas, tried on a very small scale, by architects like Ben and Jane Thompson in San Francisco. There is nothing startlingly new under the sun, she suggested. Small plans, undertaken at great and considerable risk by daring and creative "little people," are the drivers of change.

She pressed on. Big plans, with their prescriptive vision, stifle the emergence of future, alternative courses of action. They disregard the abilities of people to assume responsibilities for meeting the challenges of urban life and saddle them with enormous burdens. "We don't know what alternatives we'll need for the future," Jacobs maintained, "but if we think we know, we'll stifle them." Then, in a final, swift, and stinging rebuke: "believe me, cities are not going to be humanized by building new urban models at Harvard." And to hearty applause, she ended.

Her remarks captured the many elements of contingency and change that I have been trying to articulate. Overly prescriptive planning—those big plans enamored of a grand vision—proceeds on insufficient knowledge, since circumstances are always changing. The people best situated to detect those changes and provide the most apt knowledge are not country- and world-roaming planners and architects, no matter their skills, but people on the spot. Great cities of the world, in her view, depended on great persistence, courage, and insight from their people, not their formal leaders or the professionals they employ.

Jacobs was no fatalist, and she had no patience for determinism of any stripe. Geography, for instance, was not destiny. In her first book on Jane Jacobs, the author Glenna Lang relates the childhood story of the confident elementary school teacher who insisted that waterfalls always made for the growth of cities: no waterfall, no city. Not so, a young Jane Butzner insisted, look at Scranton! There were rivers and valleys but not a waterfall in sight and, yet, behold the city of Scranton![10] From a young age, Jacobs tested hypotheses with facts and a keen sense of history. She saw cities emerging as responses to challenges, not as captives to the accidents of geography.

Successful city neighborhoods, she would argue, are not the result of the presence of any one good thing. "It is fashionable to suppose," she wrote in *Death and Life*, "that certain touchstones of the good life will create good neighborhoods—schools, parks, clean housing and the like. How easy life would be if this were so! How charming to control a complicated and ornery society by bestowing upon it rather simple physical goodies. In real life, cause and effect are not so simple."[11] In subsequent work, Jacobs would expose a similarly wrongheaded determinism in thinking about the economic development of nations, regions, and cities. She termed it "The Thing Theory of Development," the notion that if one assembled, say, infrastructure, and enticed industries, and secured investment, city economies would thrive, automatically. Build it—dam, road, factory, ballpark—and finance it—with grants, private investment from afar—and development would come. But those assumptions often foundered.

In much of the preceding, I have followed Jacobs's concern to identify the genuine sources of city vitality with the constant work of many people pursuing many projects. Left unspoken, and perhaps unrecognized, is the most elusive contributor to the existential city: it's a matter of time. Time? We are back to philosophy, or science, here. What is this thing called time, where does it come from, what difference does it make?

The Time of the City

"Existential" time isn't mere clock time: you may not capture it by setting a timer to go and observing seconds slide into minutes and minutes pile into hours, days, months. Clock time is passing, of course, but the verb is suggestive. Passing time is *passive*, and its passivity breeds ruin in a city. Just letting things go may see a bustling corner slump into a shuttered and derelict set of buildings. "Existential" time is different. It is time fully lived, and it has only one measure: existential time is the gift of those who dwell in cities.

Jacobs first focuses on this kind of time in the chapter of *Death and Life* devoted to "the need for primary mixed uses."[12] She was writing about the wonderfully various people, each different in their interests and pursuits, who populated a district's streets. They pursued their work or activities throughout the day, creating a "time spread." "The significance of time spread can be seen especially clearly at the downtown tip of Manhattan,"[13] she argued as she contrasted the thronged streets of workaday Wall Street with the near emptiness of the same blocks during weeknight and weekend. Time spread is no abstraction: it corresponds to the actual presence, or absence, of people on the street. Empty time is time without people: there is no time without timekeepers. Human beings "make" time.

In a famous passage in *Death and Life*[14] where Jacobs describes her observation of the many, varied people who "used" her Hudson Street neighborhood in the course of a day and night, she dramatized this time-making. These people— residents and transients, merchants and customers, children and parents, public servants and idlers—are the time-makers who vivify the street. They do so without intending to play a special role. The good effects of their presence and activity—safety, conviviality, informal peacekeeping, economic liveliness— are unintended consequences. Jacobs's keen observation has often been cited and sometimes been pilloried, notably by Lewis Mumford. He dubbed her an amateur and scoffed at her suggestions of lessons to be learned. Like many, he was distracted by the poetic naming of the process as a "street ballet." One doesn't remedy serious problems with quaint thinking. Quaint and poetic visions offer no more than a "home remedy," sniffed Mumford, not the stuff of serious thinking.[15]

Mumford's criticism, and that of others, would be to the point if Jacobs remained fixed on the particularities of her one street over the course of one twenty-four-hour day. She might well be accused of offering nothing more than local color. But two chapters later, she moves far beyond the ordinary time of her street. She is writing about the need for aged buildings in creating vital cities, and she takes a very long view. The treatment here gives the lie to Mumford's dismissal. "We are dealing here," she writes

again, as we were in the case of mixed primary uses with the economic effects of time. But in this case we are dealing with the economics of time not hour by hour through the day, but with the economics of time by decades and generations. Time makes the high building costs of one generation the bargains of a following generation. Time pays off original capital costs, and this depreciation can be reflected in the yields required from a building. Time makes certain structures obsolete for some enterprises, and they become available to others. Time can make the space efficiencies of one generation the space luxuries of another generation.[16]

Consider what this implies. Measuring the economics of time by decades and generations spreads time far beyond a passing day or week or even year. These are not empty times where only compound interest or real estate values do their invisible work. Generations of active people fill those decades. The developments of decades are powered by people who turn passing decades into long moments of city building. These are the existential moments wrought by families who remain in a neighborhood or business owners who stick out hard times or new ventures spun off from original work. Just as each discrete city has an ancestry, a topic we will explore later, the streets, districts, and neighborhoods of any city inherit a collective bloodline. Whether each thrives or falters depends on the strength of that line.

When Jacobs wrote *Death and Life*, good intentions, powered by a vision of safe and clean streets and neighborhoods, sometimes led to awful consequences. Urban renewal policies, for instance, often led to the evacuation of people whose presence, over time, might have led to the revitalization of neighborhoods. Jacobs cited Boston's West End as a prime example of this mistake. Boston declared the neighborhood a slum, razed its buildings, and displaced its residents. No one, after all, would wish to live in a slum. But this judgment proceeded with scant regard for careful assessment of the facts on the ground. There was strong evidence, bolstered by the research of the sociologist Herbert Gans, that the West End was no slum but, instead, a healthy and well-functioning, if low-income, community that incorporated several ethnicities.[17]

The loss of the West End has been felt over generations. Today, a group of original residents publishes an occasional newspaper. They maintain the West End Museum, just a block away from the TD Garden, a sports and entertainment venue home to the Boston Celtics and Boston Bruins. A single building preserved from the original neighborhood stands like an overlooked sentinel amid upscale surroundings. When Jane Jacobs spoke at a 1993 Boston College conference, a group of amateur videographers captured a round of questions and answers with her about the West End. You can see that exchange on a looping video displayed in the Museum. Their loss abides.

The "redevelopment" of the old West End proceeded fitfully: the current usages came piece by piece as the master plan unfolded. What if, one might rightly ask? What if the West End had been given the time, capital, and political leeway to attempt its own development? "Time, in cities, is indispensable,"[18] writes Jacobs, but big plans are impatient with taking time. Time, after all, is money. And once residents are banished, existential time disappears.

Jacobs did not believe that movements of neighborhood "unslumming" would be swift, easy, or free of any missteps and failures. The West End was not a slum, but the observations she makes in her chapter on "unslumming and slumming" bear on the prospects of any neighborhood under siege. She writes

> The foundation for unslumming is a slum lively enough to be able to enjoy city public life and sidewalk safety. The worst foundation is the dull kind of place that makes slums, instead of unmaking them.
>
> Why slum dwellers should stay in a slum by choice, after it is no longer economically necessary, has to do with the most personal content of their lives in realms which planners and city designers can never directly reach and manipulate—nor should want to manipulate. The choice has much to do with the slum dwellers' personal attachments to other people, with the regard in which they believe they are held in the neighborhood, and with their sense of values as to what is of greater and what is of lesser importance in their lives.[19]

This quietly intense observation goes directly to the "existential" meanings of people's lives. It reflects as well the reverence with which Jacobs beheld the ways in which ordinary people made choices about their lives. They did not rely on expert guidance. Why would people choose to stay in less-than-ideal circumstances? If circumstances are bad and exit is an option, why not take it? They stay, in part, for friendship ("personal attachments"), the sense of well-being that friendship entails ("regard"), and both of these contribute to shape "their sense of values as to what is of greater and what is of lesser importance in their lives."

Jacobs was no sentimentalist, but she recognized the reasons of the heart. And the motivations she cites are the heart's reasons, bred on the streets and in neighborhoods. These motivations cut against the "rational choice" theory which assumes that self-interest, narrowly construed and often figured solely in economic terms, always drives decision-making. People can choose to act in ways that Jacobs terms elsewhere "ab-economic," but the costs may be substantial, and bearing them requires not a little courage.

Thus we should not underestimate the difficulty of these commitments and the courage and tenacity needed to sustain them. Neighborhood residents face difficult choices. In his recent book about South Shore, the Chicago neighborhood in which he grew up, Carlo Rotella writes, "but no matter how committed you are to your neighborhood, that commitment is limited, and you'll move on if the perceived rewards of moving are high enough or the penalties for staying severe enough. And the more resources you command, the more choices you have, the more easily the bond to neighborhood can be broken."[20]

In *Death and Life*, Jacobs saw community as a continuing human project, the sum of existential choices, not as a planned, predictable, and forecast outcome. This conviction animates all of her work.

The existential city does not operate on automatic pilot or conform to a posted schedule. It requires continual guidance as it navigates channels and avoids reefs. Its pilots are the people who live there. They must make constant adjustments and embody a host of virtues: patience, courage, perseverance, and fidelity to each other. A city full of transients cannot build what Jacobs elsewhere calls "love capital." A city reengineered to draw people to upscale housing and entertainment may succeed in both of those and yet still lack the energy imparted by those with deeper ties and stronger roots; a city that reserves power of decision-making to formal government and mutes the voices of the community will become a simulacrum of an existential city.

A moral ecology based on respect for others, the willingness to collaborate in defining and achieving common goals, and an abiding courage in facing up to difficulties underlie all successful cities. The moral ecology is not embodied in a formal charter, and you can't sign on to it by logging on and checking your assent. The moral ecology thrives on person-to-person contact and withers without it. The street, Jacobs knew, is the stage for that contact. But the kinds, purposes, and "meanings" of streets are extraordinarily diverse. How do Jane Jacobs's insights apply to the streets we walk or cycle or drive these days?

Notes

1 Jacobs, *Death and Life*, 340.
2 Jacobs, *Death and Life*, 447.
3 Jane Jacobs, *Cities and the Wealth of Nations* (Random House, 1984), 208.
4 James Madison, Federalist 51 in Alexander Hamilton, James Madison and John Jay, *The Federalist Papers*, (New American Library, 1961),
5 Jacobs, *Economy of Cities*, chapter 3.
6 William Wordsworth, "On the Extinction of the Venetian Republic, 1802."See www .poetryfoundation.org/poems/45539/on-the-extinction-of-the-venetian-republic.
7 See https://archive.nytimes.com/lens.blogs.nytimes.com/2015/08/12/kodaks-first -digital-moment/ for an account of Kodak's history with the digital camera.
8 This is an allusion, with alteration, to T. S. Eliot, "Choruses from the Rock.", in *The Complete Poems and Plays, 1909–1950* (New York: Harcourt, Brace & World, 1971), 106.
9 In what follows, I rely on my notes for that day.

10 Glenna Lang, *Genius of Common Sense: Jane Jacobs and the Story of The Death and Life of Great American Cities* (Boston, MA: Godine, 2012), 11.

11 Jacobs, *Death and Life*, 112–113.

12 Jacobs, *Death and Life*, chapter 8.

13 Jacobs, *Death and Life*, 154.

14 See Jacobs, *Death and Life*, chapter 2.

15 Lewis Mumford, "Mother Jacobs' Home Remedies," *The New Yorker*, December 1, 1962, 148.

16 Jacobs, *Death and Life*, 189–190.

17 See Herbert Gans, *The Urban Villagers* (The Free Press, 1966).

18 Jacobs, *Death and Life*, 133.

19 Jacobs, *Death and Life*, 279.

20 Carlo Rotella, *The World Is Always Coming to an End* (Chicago, IL: The University of Chicago Press, 2019), 193.

3

City Talk

The Conversation of Streets

"Eyes on the street" is the phrase most often identified with the work of Jane Jacobs. The hundreds of commentators, from journalists and academics to politicians, community organizers, and ordinary citizens, who populate my Google news feed seize it regularly, sometimes linking it with "new ideas need old buildings." Robert Kanigel chose it for the title of his biography of Jacobs. Everyone looks for eyes on the street. Why?

The ubiquity of that brief phrase has everything to do with the streets on which *we* live. People are worried about their streets. But those streets are very different from the streets on which Jane Jacobs lived. In *Death and Life*, Jacobs saw the vigilance provided by eyes on the street as crucial to the safety of her neighborhood. *Her* neighborhood was well-populated and dotted with shopfronts, restaurants, and various street trades. *Her* street's residents were the best guarantors of safety because they were committed to the neighborhood. When people were close at hand, and attentive, mischief and problems could be addressed quickly. Remote surveillance—think of the growth of closed-circuit television monitors—is a poor substitute for real eyes. CCTV presumes streets are hazardous zones. Keeping watch over streets becomes a police function, reserved for public authorities or paid private security.

So when journalists and commentators seize on "eyes on the street," they are looking about the streets on which they live or the streets of their towns and cities. They want to find eyes that are engaged, not averted, and if they are absent, they wonder how they might be encouraged.

But Jacobs had an argument to make, not a catchphrase to fashion for understanding the street. She insisted that no street stands alone but must be seen in relation to neighboring streets. Hudson Street did not generate vitality on its own. It drew on the people and resources of other streets and of the city as a whole. Her street was but one kind of neighborhood and it nested within two others: the district neighborhood and the encompassing city.

Casual commentators often miss another emphasis. Jacobs was explicit that she was writing about *great*, as measured by size and population, *American* cities. Dense concentrations of people, engaged in a variety of activities—work; parenting; enjoying the sights, sounds, and beauty of a place—made for thriving neighborhoods. Population numbers and density mattered greatly to Jacobs. Thus, while she has been read and cited all over the United States and throughout the world, she was not writing about small- or medium-size cities or towns or suburbs. You can find streets in all of these locales, but they cannot be expected to function in the same way as a New York City street, whether in 1960 or now. Regardless of the time frame, the streets of Greenwich Village are very different from those of Greenwich, Connecticut or of a small Midwestern town.

Further, Jacobs underlined the importance of the sidewalk—and a wide sidewalk, at that—in fostering the kinds of behavior that made for safety, cooperation, and strong public life. In suburbs and towns, roads matter more than streets and sidewalks. Roads lead you to streets and houses. And the houses are often clustered in *cul-de-sac* planning, where sidewalks count for little or for nothing at all.

A macro analysis of American patterns of living confirms what I have suggested about our streets. Most Americans don't live in the core of great American cities, although many live within the orbit of a greater metropolitan area. The National Center for Health Statistics characterizes US counties under three headings. Urban core counties, which include fifty-three counties with a metropolitan area of at least 1 million, account for 31 percent of the country's population. Suburban and small metro counties are a majority at 55 percent; rural counties include the remaining 14 percent. The United States may be a nation fortunate in its great cities, but relatively few of its citizens reside within their formal boundaries. One must therefore be cautious in applying Jacobs's work. Shorn of its context, "eyes on the street" becomes a slogan, not an insight for understanding the city.

If the streets on which most Americans live are not the streets that Jane Jacobs analyzed so keenly, why do so many return to her analysis? I think there are several interrelated reasons, all of which bespeak a great hunger for community. The eagerness with which people throng to lively streets, no matter whether they live in a great or a small city, or are visitors from town or suburb, reflects a deep yearning for connection. Second—and despite my caution about overgeneralizations—there may be transferable insights which may map to places other than great city streets. After all, there was no greater champion of the wisdom of the astute observer than Jacobs: those who cite her may be on to something unique to their places. Finally, her analysis is a model for *understanding* city life. Chambers of commerce and civic boosters cheer and "discover" street life all the time; but understanding how and why some streets work and others falter requires hard and patient and enduring attention.

To understand the enduring power of her analysis, I'll begin with an overview of the streets as she knew them. Her streets—the plural is essential—were dense, lively, interconnected and home to long-term residents. By way of contrast, I will interlace, as examples, four sets of other streets. Each shows at least one aspect of her perspective on what contributes to healthy, thriving streets, sometimes by pointing to her emphases on diversity, density, old buildings, mixed uses, and short blocks, sometimes by virtue of their absence. I will be taking liberties, as her commentators often have, looking, for instance, at small cities as well as great, looking beyond America in one case, and looking via the medium of film in another. But the looking, I hope, is not the casual glance I have warned against, but something undertaken judiciously in the interest of appreciating what is unique in Jacobs's *understanding*. And I encourage the reader to think about places known to her or, better, visit them. This is not idle advice: in writing about two sets of streets, one in Venice, Italy, and the other in Worcester, Massachusetts, I did just that, repeatedly.

Streets and Their Uses: Safety

In Part One of *Death and Life*, "The Peculiar Nature of Cities," Jane Jacobs claims that "To keep the city safe is a fundamental task of a city's streets and its sidewalks."[1] Safety does not, she insists, depend upon the presence of "police, necessary as police are."[2] It depends upon the casual vigilance of a street's users.

It's not surprising that she begins with safety. When Jacobs was writing *Death and Life*, she was a parent in a challenging urban environment. Whether parent or child, human beings long for a homeplace, a safe and secure center, and for paths to that center. These are abiding concerns. Healthy streets and sidewalks offer answers to those concerns. Some early and recent commentators have seized on Jacobs's emphasis to suggest that she was preoccupied with crime in the city. Thus, the *New Yorker*'s Adam Gopnik, a fair and perceptive critic, gets it wrong when he writes that "her work, written in the late fifties and the early sixties, seems *obsessed* with crime, and with insisting that crowded streets don't make crime happen."[3] Her obsession, if such it can be termed, is not with crime but with discovering the elements that combine to make a city a fit home. Good street neighborhoods offer a hope of security in a potentially frightening world.

For Jacobs, sidewalks were the most important part of a street. Safety lives where people gather and talk. Conversation happens on the stoop, at the corner, in front of the hardware store. And conversation is essential: "streets," writes Gopnik, "are not a city's veins but its neurology, its accumulated intelligence."[4] But accumulated intelligence is embodied, not an abstraction. And bodies need room to move. Jacobs consistently advocated for shrinking *roadway* space to enlarge *sidewalk* space. Wide roads make for more traffic but diminish conversation. And a classic American film dramatizes this very well.

First Interlacing: Where the Road Matters More Than the Street

On a recent cross-country flight, I watched, on a cramped and tiny screen, a story celebrating the wide streets of a central California city, Modesto, in 1962. *American Graffiti* reckons with many other things, too—the anxieties of young people facing limited, or great, opportunities; the storm clouds of a looming war; the propulsive energies of young love and sex; the inscrutability and unknowingness of adults—all driven by the sounds of pop music on a warm night.

The "streets"—streets, in this context, mean roadways—are full because the streets are where the action is. Sidewalks, so crucial to Jacobs, get little attention: they are important only as pickup or drop-off points. The roads are the stage for an automotive passeggiata, where boys cruise the street with their girls, or search for girls, and the bolder, boys and girls alike, look for drag racing thrills. On these streets, through and in their cars, the teenagers enact the rituals of adolescence. They see and are seen, they flirt and they taunt, they puff themselves up by stomping on their accelerator pedals, they commit minor acts of vandalism. On the streets—wide streets—the cars linger or prowl. The sidewalks and buildings themselves hold no interest for the young; in the movie, it's adults we see on the sidewalks or emerging from stores. The kids gather at the drive-in burger joint and flirt with the car-hops; social life doesn't require leaving the car.

Figure 3.1 Streets/Roads in *American Graffiti*. Used with permission, NBC Universal Archives.

The conversation of these streets is all about youth and young love, expectation and fear, and it is a conversation—back and front seat banter and teasing—but locked into their cars, the teenagers are locked into private adolescent chatter. The streets of *American Graffiti* are not city streets, where sidewalks might be important, but town and country roads and streets, and they are uncomplicated. Traffic rolls along at an easy pace under the guidance of traffic signals and observant drivers. There is no gridlock.

That was 1962, at least as George Lucas remembered it. Today, those relatively uncomplicated streets have a frenetic counterpart in contemporary suburban roadways. We know these kinds of roads well: they have multiple lanes, with special turn-off half-lanes, strings of lights hanging above all, and thicketed with every manner of signage, indicating routes and permitting or prohibiting turns. A drone's eye view would reveal the logic of all the signals. They promote easy access to chain stores, fast-food, outlets, motels, and multiplexes. They do not promote public pedestrian traffic and they need not. Exurban roadways, alive with commercial undertakings, are not places for neighborhood sidewalks. Apart from apartment or condo complexes, there's little residential life. You take these roadways to get home to suburban or small-town living on sleepy streets.

The Kinds of People a Street Needs

Jacobs saw a thrilling diversity of people filling thriving city streets. Not all these people lived on those streets, but she assumed that the primary users of the thriving street were its residents. A lively street needs a live-in community. A street given over to single nonresidential use may be important and successful in its function at the right time of day or night, but it can never be a place for full-on conversation. Residents are a necessary, if not sufficient, condition for a thriving city street. Thus, in the New York of her time, Wall Street had little to offer when night fell or the markets closed.

The need for residents, and especially those with a long-term commitment, poses an acute challenge for contemporary cities that wish for the kind of street Jane Jacobs celebrated. The challenge has many dimensions, occasioned by the interplay of several factors: the escalation of housing prices, which lock out low and middle income earners; the (related) proliferation of short-term rental properties catering to vacationers and transient workers; the resultant housing shortage; and the rise of a displaced or unplaced urban population. Transformations in the job market also play in the erosion of residential life. It was not unusual in Jacobs's New York time for wage earners and salaried workers to remain in the same physical place for a long period of time. Their jobs were close at hand and, for the salaried, prospects of advancement kept them close to home offices. But many factors have changed. Advancement in salaried positions may mean frequent changes of place. Young workers change jobs frequently; remote work encourages transiency in locales. Local hardware stores, and their owner-proprietors, give way to chains, local restaurants get priced out by changes in rent.

A Second Interlacing: A Historic "World City" Where Residents Can't Find a Home

45°26'21"N12°20'32"E45.4392°N 12.3421°E: Venice, Italy

Load these GPS coordinates into your navigation system and find your way to Campo San Giovanni e Paolo in the city of Venice, Italy. Let's assume you visit in May. The campo is open on all sides and there are many angles of approach. If you begin from the train station, and fancy a water view, you can take a seat on the 5.2 vaporetto, the water taxi that chugs along the city's northern edges. When you alight at Ospedale, you reach the campo by heading south along the

Fondamenta dei Mendicanti. If you eschewed the vaporetto and were to walk from the train station, you may have reached the campo by heading southeast through the Canareggio district, orienting by following the signs for Fondamente Nuovo and then veering across the small bridge on Calle Langa Giaconto Gullia. Or, in best Venetian serendipity, perhaps you started from a spilled-matchstick assemblage of streets originating in Castello which funneled, finally, into the Barbaria delle Tolle which left you on the south side of the great basilica that gives the campo its name.

What you will find in the campo depends upon the time of day. Day and night, the Ospedale draws walk-in traffic by foot and more serious cases via ambulance launch. By 7:00 a.m., the Rosa Salva Pasticerria will be readying for its morning opening, which will catch the come and go of parents and grandparents dropping children at school; flanking restaurants and shops will open somewhat later. At midday, all shops open, threads of ear-budded tourists in tow to their cruise ship guides will stop before the Colleoni statue. They will regard the baroque facade of the Ospedale—formerly the Scuole Grande de San Marco—and peek into the basilica. A gondolier or two keep a post on the canal, querying the passersby: "Gondola? Gondola?" By mid-afternoon, foot traffic swells as schools release the children; in an afternoon, you might see impromptu soccer games erupt. This is street soccer, begging for a photo: the children use the external, wall-mounted tombs of some doges, historic rulers of Venice, affixed to the basilica, as goals. By 8:00 p.m., the rhythm slows and the restaurants begin to chain their tables and fold their umbrellas.

Of the streets I have described so far, this campo, fed by a confluence of streets, seems closest to the daytime and nightly ballet of Jacobs's Hudson Street. (In fairness: it lacks the challenge of dealing with automotive traffic.) It makes the point that a neighborhood, collectively, not a street, singularly, enables the presence of vigilant eyes on the street. But resident eyes are more important than transient eyes; and in the campo and its many feeder streets, visitors and short-term residents command much of the space. Venice feels safe, but when you walk its streets by night, there's an emptiness that's disconcerting. Glorious in its history and beauty, contemporary Venice does not qualify as a great city on Jacobs's terms: too few people, too little diversity.

Why so few people? In the early sixteenth century, Venice was more populous than either London or Paris. The long-term decline of its population had to do with recurrent visitations of the plague and its eclipse as a commercial and financial entrepot as Atlantic trade routes opened up. In the early twenty-first

Figure 3.2 Approaching Giovanni e Paolo from the Castello district. Author Photo.

century, its resident population has slipped below 60,000. A different plague has driven that decline, forcing erstwhile residents to Mestre and other places on the mainland. The financiers and merchants who flocked to Venice in its heyday are now replaced by throngs of day tourists. Native Venetians have been priced out by the conversion of old buildings to multiple rental flats, even as luxury retailers and cheap souvenir shops, displace traditional businesses. This displacement of traditional residents by the accumulating pressures of tourism bears some resemblance to what in the United States would be called gentrification and not a few commentators would see it as an ironic revenge upon Jane Jacobs's ideas.

Jacobs and Gentrification: A Weighing of the Scales

As noted in the preceding chapter, there is no doubt that Jacobs's championing of the city renewed interest in its center among the formerly disaffected. But there is also no doubt that her work, properly understood, is a powerful argument *against* gentrification. In the States, gentrifiers, whose ranks included the wealthy young as well as affluent retirees, attracted more gentrifiers, "bourgeoisie Bohemians," bobos, as David Brooks termed them in *Bobos in Paradise* (2000), and thereby eliminated economic and cultural diversity. Brooks noted how both partisans of the left and right could keep company with Jacobs's views. To the left, she represented a congenial bohemianism, to the right, a defense of natural order. "Most important," he wrote, "Jacobs reconciles the bourgeois love of order with the bohemian love of emancipation."[5] For both, Brooks suggested, the Jacobsian city obscured the difference between town and country. Her city was tinged with soft, pastoral hues. Back to the gentle, urban forest! And many came running.

But Jacobs knew that there could be too much of any one good thing, like housing for the affluent, trendy cafes, or, for that matter, housing for the poor, because each threatened to make a diverse environment more uniform. How much of anything was too much couldn't be settled in advance. One needed keen knowledge of the local environment. But that knowledge needed power, too, whether informal or elected. She insisted on the need for good government at three levels, from the street neighborhoods to city districts and to city hall, to balance competing interests. The inherently problematic nature of the city required constant vigilance and unstinting willingness to engage with its problems.

Jacobs soberly acknowledged the prospects of failure. Trials would bring missteps and errors as well as success. In this sense, her work echoes the "creative destruction" which Joseph Schumpeter saw as endemic to capitalism. As newness crowds out some of the old ways, it will inevitably crowd out some established practitioners. Only those who can adapt and innovate escape the threat of obsolescence. And even strong and persistent efforts may fail.

A visitor in 2024 to Jacobs's former New York address at 555 Hudson Street finds a real estate company seated there and a plaque noting the time of her residence. Many years ago when I asked if she missed New York and her neighborhood, she admitted she did but remarked, "we'd never be able to afford living there now."[6]

Brooks's analysis of Jacobs, on the whole, is appreciative but other critics have been more stern. Sharon Zukin—see, for instance, *Naked City: The death and life of authentic urban places* (2010)—is a good example.[7] While extolling Jacobs's original analysis, she faults her for failing to anticipate what her work wrought. She, like others, argues that the unforeseen emergence of gentrification was an example of her lack of appreciation for economic inequality and racism. Jacobs, on this view, was blind to, or chose to ignore, the fraught realities of racial injustice. What resulted, the critics imply, was not what she wanted and was, to some degree, her fault. For all of her championing of close observation and judgments based on careful analysis, she was blind to the racism permeating the streets and naively unaware of the possible future outcomes of her recommendations.

If true, that last judgment would sting the most. Had the self-destruction of diversity, against which she had warned in *Death and Life*, been rooted in the very success of her celebration of urban life? In her final book, *Dark Age Ahead*, Jacobs addressed gentrification in the notes to the seventh chapter, titled, aptly, "Unwinding vicious spirals." "By the end of the 1990s," she writes,

> Gentrification was under way in what had been even the most dilapidated and abused districts of Manhattan. Again, the poor, evicted or priced out by the higher costs of renovating, were victims. Affordable housing could have been added as infill in parking lots and empty lots if government had been on its toes, and if communities had been self-confident and vigorous in making demands, but they almost never were. Gentrification benefited neighborhoods, but so much less than it could have if the displaced people had been recognized as community assets worth retaining.[8]

That paragraph acknowledges the facts on the ground: the poor *were* victimized, displaced because reckoned as liabilities, rather than assets, and the neighborhood *did* benefit, in physical terms, ostensibly because new paint and fresh uses of buildings replaced dilapidation and disuse. But there is something more in that paragraph, the suggestion of the possibility of "renewal with a human face," a neighborhood renewal that might have proceeded incrementally and valued the current residents. Note the several uses of "if": *If* there had been infill housing; *if* the government had been on its toes; *if* communities had been more vigorous, other outcomes were possible. But the government did not apply brakes, and communities did not exercise voice. *Dark Age* calls for an honest reckoning with things unforeseen or left unattended. Jane Jacobs was asking, in effect, "given these failures, OK, what do we do *now*?"

The pragmatism of that response gives the lie to a portrait of Jacobs as an urban romantic, the bobo of Brooks's coinage. A wry and persistent skepticism animates her work, and it originates in *Death and Life*. The opening salvos she directed against Ebenezer Howard and Le Corbusier in the Introduction point, as we saw, to underlying assumptions about how an injection of the "natural" into the unnatural city—via trees, parks, and zoning—would redound to its benefit. Jacobs saw this as reflecting a deep animus against cities, like those discussed in Morton and Lucia White's survey of American writers and thinkers, and a deficient understanding of what is natural. *Cities*, she insisted, are "natural" because of the requirements of *human* nature. Put simply, human beings are born into relationships and develop with the aid of others. To think that the pleasures of sun, water, parks, and green spaces were sufficient for realizing the fullness of human development reflected a sentimentalization of nature and a corresponding infantilization of human beings. Nature would mitigate the potential damage of close, urban living. This assumption reflected "a sentimental desire to toy, rather patronizingly, with some insipid, standardized, suburbanized shadow of nature—apparently in sheer disbelief that we and our cities, just by virtue of being, are a legitimate part of nature too, and involved with it in much deeper and more inescapable ways than grass trimming, sunbathing, and contemplative uplift."[9] Jacobs was no urban romantic.

Nor was she blind to the turnings of larger economic and social forces. As for race, its penalties and afflictions: Jacobs never ignored it, although she did not employ the language or assumptions of our contemporary discussions. Differences of language aside, she was keenly aware of systemic racism. In *Death and Life*, she identified "segregation and racial discrimination" as "our country's most serious social problem"[10] and connected it to the withering of social interplay on residential streets where only one color or culture was welcome. In the chapter on "Unslumming and slumming,"[11] she lamented blockbusting and the drastic discrimination against Black Americans by lenders. She held no truck with the "culture of poverty" notion that denied agency to Black Americans in the struggle to renew neighborhoods: it was the discriminatory denial of capital that rendered their efforts feckless. She continued this analysis in *Economy*, noting the persistence of discriminatory lending practices, and suggested that irregular, sometimes illegal, access to capital may spell a difference as it did for earlier immigrant groups. In *Nature*, she pointed out the catastrophic effects of denying free rein to the entrepreneurial energy of Blacks, women, and people of lower-class standing.

By her own admission, race does not get sustained treatment in her final book, *Dark Age Ahead*. That work focuses on five "jeopardized pillars" of society: family and community; higher education; science and technology; fiscal powers of government; and self-regulation by professions. "It may seem surprising," she writes, "that I do not single out such failings as racism, profligate environmental destruction, crime, voters' distrust of politicians and thus low turnouts for elections, and the enlarging gulf between rich and poor along with attrition of the middle class. . . . Perhaps my judgment is wrong, but I think these five are symptoms of breakdown in the five I have chosen to discuss."[12]

Jacobs is characteristically modest in that assessment. She does not suggest that there is one preeminent problem. She has no one solution. Alfred North Whitehead once remarked, "Seek simplicity, and distrust it." Jacobs, too, harbored a suspicion of what Whitehead termed "misplaced concreteness," the tendency to substitute abstractions for known facts on the ground. Both thinkers were committed to understanding messy, fluid realities. The way to that understanding required a patient and exhaustive exploration of interlocking and mutually conditioning factors. As we will see in the next chapter, Jacobs outlined a detailed and recursive process for exploring and explaining how economic development occurs or falters. "Gentrification," no matter how it is specified, strays into the category of abstraction. Jacobs wanted to see through that and act in ways appropriate to the situation. Act not alone, but with the contributions of many citizens and the instruments of their government.

A Third Interlacing: Down-at-the-Heels Streets and Upscale Neighbors in a Medium-Size City

In the existential city, change can sneak up on you. It did on me. I chose to visit Harding and Millbury Streets of Worcester, Massachusetts in the fall of 2019, and again in February 2021. Two ordinary streets, by any measure, but also close to an area flush with redevelopment money. The Boston Red Sox baseball team was relocating their Triple-A franchise to Worcester and building a new stadium to welcome them. I wondered how proximity to all that new money might affect the surrounding neighborhood.

When I first visited, here were my thoughts and initial findings, rendered in a reporter's present tense.

Harding and Millbury streets take some finding. The best landmark is I-290, which cleaves the city east and west. Millbury Street, taking its name from a nearby town, originates south of Kelley Square and tracks north, crossing through the square and changing names a little farther on. It becomes Water Street. Harding originates amid a skein of overhead passes, tracks, and nondescript streets behind Union Station, the city's railway hub, offering connections east to Boston and south toward New York City. It begins with modest ambitions, a simple, two-way street. South of Winter Street, it becomes one-way, a parallel north–south route to Millbury Street. As a one-way, it shoots out from the notorious Kelley Square. In Kelley Square, multiple streets cross, no lights regulate flow, and all who traverse it—by car, or bike, or on foot—pray or curse as they pass through. Locals shrug off the perils. They just keep moving. Some cars bear bumper stickers proclaiming "I survived Kelley Square."

Traveling through Kelley Square in 2019, you drive carefully. You can walk south on Harding but not drive: it's now one-way. Harding is narrow even for a one-way street; and if you have business there, well, the sidewalk often shades into a parking strip: wheels up and over the curb. The cars that roamed the streets of *American Graffiti*, rank on rank, would find no room here. They would find it two blocks east on Interstate 290, a north–south highway, three lanes in each direction, begun in 1957 and completed thirteen years later. When it came, many things went: churches, synagogues, bakeries, residences, ethnic communities. What came in their places was a southerly connection to the Massachusetts Turnpike, I-90, and, as it arced east past the center of the city, a connection to the outlying belt of I-495, which reaches north toward coastal New Hampshire and south toward Cape Cod.

If you walk Harding and Millbury Streets, you can find traces of what disappeared in the wake of the I-290 construction. A Polish social club remains. Several small ethnic restaurants, catering not to the vanished Finns but to those who like Asian and Chinese cuisines, are dotted among small enterprises—nail salons, and bars and a dusty, cluttered variety store. There's an early intervention program advertised in one storefront and a sizable restaurant supply store. Storefront churches—three on this visit—and body shops, auto detailing businesses, and auto repair are popular. To the west of Harding lies Crompton Park, empty when I visit, save for a solitary dog-walker. To the east, a block removed from I-290, Millbury Street turns its backside toward Harding. The backside spills out dumpsters, debris that missed the dumpsters, and parking lots, for customers or residents of second-floor apartments.

When I visit, there are few pedestrians on Harding, apart from two young men headed for Crompton's basketball court. The street is ill-kempt. Its casual neglect and down-market business uses might cause a pessimist to say "not much to see here, do your business and move along." A more optimistic person might say: here is a good place for very modest beginnings. If we traced our steps back toward Union Station, via Millbury, the signs of economic activity— bakeries, bars, restaurants—would appear the closer we got to Kelley Square. And in official circles, optimism runs high: the new ballpark will open in 2021. The city hopes a flush economy will raise the prospects for all neighbors. The fear, recently voiced in unofficial circles, is that displacement must follow. Even down-at-the-heels neighborhoods have their champions.

Figure 3.3 One view of Harding Street, Worcester. Author Photo.

One View of Harding Street, Second Visit

On a second visit, on February 28, 2021, Harding and Millbury Streets are easier to "find." The construction of the ballpark has triggered a host of changes. A traffic roundabout, complete with clearly marked lanes and traffic buttons for pedestrians, has loosened the threatening knots of Kelley Square. I park my car at the head of Harding Street, where all the spaces are metered, but it's Sunday and I get off free.

On the western side of the street, I note an immediate difference, the ongoing renovation of a five-story building at the corner with Winter Street. On both sides of the street, the sidewalks are wider than I remember, perhaps fifteen feet, a width that Jane Jacobs would approve of. As I approach Kelley Square, I see a gated, public parking lot serving the recently opened Worcester Public Market and a handful of other commercial places. The market fronts on Kelley Square but opens onto both Harding and Green Streets. A single homeless person sleeps on a bench outside the Harding entrance.

Standing at Kelley Square, I find its sharp and dangerous edges have been softened. Thanks to the roundabout, a pedestrian traffic island, ribbed crosswalks with flashing lights, and a mechanical voice urging caution, a walker can feel reasonably secure here. I set out for the south side of Harding.

Figure 3.4 A gentler Kelley Square. Mass Department of Transportation.

Had I stayed in the Square, and headed right, I would have been a long outfielder's throw from the Polar Park complex, opening in April to welcome the Worcester WooSox. It's clear that the impending opening has driven the regulation of traffic flow, the upgrading of sidewalks, and the sprouting of amenities like the Public Market. But it was Harding south of the Square that I wanted to see again. Would anything have changed there?

South of the Square, there are no fresh amenities. Harding Street is much as I found it before. The sidewalks are narrow and heaped with snow. Three-deckers, auto repair and detailing shops, and the back lots of Millbury Street enterprises string along its west side. Crompton Park remains lonely.

As I turn left onto Millbury and head north, I wonder if the ballpark's effects will have rippled down this street. After all, the street does have more commercial real estate space. But the effect seems to stop short of Kelley Square. The only exception, a two-story renovation, sits close to the junction with the Square. Farther away from the Square, there are many signs beckoning renters and inviting new business, but there seem to be no takers. Vestiges of the former neighborhood disrupted by I-290 remain: the package store with an Irish owner's name advertises a premium Polish beer and the European Pastry shop and café does a strong business. A parking lot mural pays tribute to Weintraub's Deli, on nearby Water Street, which lasted until 2018. Storefront churches—Hope and Deliverance, Kingdom of Grace, Iglesia Pentecostal, The Apostolic Church— continue to draw congregants. (And inspire business: I missed the name of that dusty variety store I noted on my first visit. It is El Arcana store, featuring a picture of the Ark of the Covenant, and advertising Libreria Cristana and Miscellanea—laundry soap, sneakers, Huggies, and flag-themed merchandise are stacked against the streaky windows.) I didn't notice the three hookah bars sprinkled along the street when I first visited. I am saddened by the closing of the previously remarked nonprofit, a storefront branch of Friendly House, a stalwart of the Worcester nonprofit community, serving youth and poor families. The sidewalks were lonely: I encountered only one person as I walked the blocks.

The Harding/Millbury neighborhood meets some of Jane Jacobs's criteria for success, and Polar Park has catalyzed some commercial investment. North of Kelley Square, the Public Market and nearby establishments invite foot traffic. The wide sidewalks welcome visitors who contribute to public activity. But this activity depends not upon residents, but transient visitors, who park their cars along the street, as I did, or in the public lot. The roundabout has easedtraffic at Kelley Square, but the roadways still function as borders to the area, not seams, to use Jacobs's terms, inviting exploration. Thanks to baseball, money has come to the neighborhood, but whether this represents economic development, understood as Jacobs does, remains to be seen.

The Unsuspected Roles of a Street's Residents

If a street is fortunate to have residents, Jacobs knew that residents did much more than tend their own gardens or mind their own windows and stoops. They opened a street's "gates" to outsiders, whether they were visitors, drawn to business, or people simply passing through. "Cities are, by definition, full of strangers" wrote Jacobs and, indeed, "even residents who live near each other are strangers."[13] The full conversation of the city, Jacobs suggests, involves a counterpoint between the familiar and the unfamiliar. Good streets, in turn, must incorporate both public and private spaces. No one, save an exhibitionist, wants to live in the public eye all the time but no one, as the Covid pandemic showed, wishes to stay home, shut-in, all the time. Both home and street must be "familiar," but both benefit from the touch of the novel and unexpected, which one encounters in public, on the street. Norberg-Schulz, we recall, saw the city as a place for meeting, the site where individuals, each unique, came together with others. In celebrating the role of diversity, Jacobs reminds us that it is difference—strangeness—that provides us with orientation in finding our way, both literally and metaphorically.

Apart from their safe-keeping role, residents provide two other essential functions on residential streets. They constitute, first, the foundation for incipient political life. As she turned her attention to the "uses" of city neighborhoods, Jacobs described them as "mundane organs of self-government,"[14] the place where ordinary citizens shape a local politics. For Jacobs, self-government begins with self-rule, not in the juridical sense, but in the sense the ancient philosophers meant. Self-rule means the capacity to see beyond the scope of one's personal interests and to realize that the good life together with others requires the restraint, perhaps sometimes the outright relinquishment, of personal wants and desires. Of course, restraint and relinquishment are difficult tasks in the arena of public life. Should my neighborhood bear the weight of new construction, or the provision of emergency services or the welcoming of migrants? Resolving such fractious question amicably and equitably presupposes that a street's residents are already engaged in conversations of much lesser consequence.

The topics of the literal conversation are not as important as the fact of exchange. In the ordinary conversations about noise and litter and kids nowadays or in the banter about sports heroes and villains or clashing tastes in music or the failings of formal government, residents fashion a basis for local civic life. Baseball may bore me and enthrall you, but if we live together on the block, we share a common interest in where we live. Aristotle saw the human person as a political animal, a member of the *polis*. People made the *polis* on the basis of shared commitments to it. When I once suggested to Jane Jacobs that her understanding of the city was essentially Aristotelian, she agreed. A street neighborhood in a great city can be a *polis* writ small.

As residents enact the rudiments of politics, they perform a second and related function on lively city streets. They help to establish a moral ecology. Streets and sidewalks, Jacobs argues, work to assimilate children into the life of the community. They are the stage on which children learn how to behave. What is acceptable conduct? Who is in charge? What do they expect me to do? These are some of the implicit questions to which children can discover the answers on the street. Adults are the keepers of the keys that unlock the codes of conduct for the neighborhood. Their examples are more important and effective, than hectoring. In the city, an environment both familiar and strange, children "need an unspecialized outdoor home base from which to play, to hang around in, and to help form their notions of the world."[15] The ordinary, casual street life and actions of adults play an important role here. Kith and kin or formal structures are not required. "People must take a modicum of public responsibility for each other even if they have no ties to each other."[16] And if the street is void of such adults or, empty of families, or, worse, populated with bad actors, the results are predictable.

Who wouldn't want to live on a street where business occurs, where children play and begin to understand the world, and where residents assume, and enjoy, a common responsibility for their lives together? But where to find such streets? How to make them? Jacobs understands the city as an organism, something that lives and breathes, expands and contracts, according to the actions of its citizens. Her understanding presupposes a vibrant public realm, a world of shared social spaces and face-to-face encounters. Without people on the streets, there is no "public" space. Harding and Millbury Streets, south of Kelley Square, lack such space because of their emptiness. Giovanni e Paolo in Venice has it at certain times, but not others, and the scarcity of full-time residents diminishes its capacity to offer a public realm. Suburban streets, if situated within "developments," won't offer any of these aspects. Nor will city blocks populated solely by transient workers.

There is a further complication for all neighborhoods, regardless of size or location. Digital technology has delivered an interconnectedness of people, institutions, countries, and cultures without precedent. They come right to our screens. But digital connectedness at our fingertips can crowd out physical connections at arm's length. Just about everyone has had the experience of stumbling into someone on a street who is transfixed by his or her phone. But there is a deeper problem here. Digital connections lionize the "preferences" of the individual "user," or consumer. We can see or read or listen only to what pleases us. We can dismiss or ignore the dissonance of contrary preferences. The language that I have used reflects another aspect of the cultural problem. It emphasizes "I" rather than "we"; it substitutes aesthetics (preferences) for ethics (judgments of moral worth); it regards me as an economic unit (user, consumer) rather than as a citizen, a friend, or a neighbor. The American experience has often invoked an ideal of fashioning one from many. Settling for "to each his own" has disastrous consequences for politics. This is an especially fraught topic, and I will return to it in the concluding chapter.

A Final Interlacing: 5th Avenue and E 51st

Where else could this be? This address immediately suggests New York City. What Harding and Millbury streets, or Giovanni e Paolo, or the streets of *American Graffiti* lack, New York has in abundance. Pinpoint this location on a map, if you are unfamiliar with the naming and numbering conventions of Midtown Manhattan, and you may be dazzled by the array of its near neighbors: Times Square, St. Patrick's Cathedral, Rockefeller Center, a quartet of museums, Grand Central Terminal to the south, and Trump Tower to the north. Step out onto the sidewalk and view vistas down the long stretch of blocks: just out of sight to the north, Central Park; lean south toward Greenwich Village—Jane Jacobs's neighborhood—and, farther, Wall Street and the island's tip. Walk along this street and enter the sweep of people. Voices in many languages fill the air: on a recent visit, I caught traces of Spanish, Italian, Arabic, German, and an unspecifiable Slavic tongue. Hotels, offices, restaurants, churches, synagogues, businesses, great and small, line the sidewalks. In a cacophony of horns, the grumbling acceleration of trucks, the wheezing of diesel buses, and the squish of brakes, traffic pushes by. Undaunted, pedestrians tread carefully, or stride New York boldly, across the intersections. A first-time visitor must be stunned: so many people, so much activity, so much life.

I wondered whether Jane Jacobs had anything to say about this slice of the city. Fifth Avenue gets four mentions in the index of *Death and Life*. Challenging "some myths about diversity," she found much to admire, on these streets and little to lament—save some tacky billboards. "Fifth Avenue in New York between Fortieth Street and Fifty-ninth Street," she writes

> is tremendously diverse in its large and small shops, bank buildings, office buildings, churches, institutions. Its architecture expresses these differences in use, and differences accrue from the varying ages of the buildings, differences in technology and historical taste. But Fifth Avenue does not look disorganized, fragmented or exploded. . . . The whole hangs together remarkably well, without being monotonous either.[17]

Those who suggest that Jacobs was the champion of only the small and quaint neighborhoods on a Greenwich Village scale should reconsider that opinion. Thriving neighborhoods come in many different shapes and sizes in the city that never sleeps.

On Not Drawing Hasty Conclusions and Listening to History

The diversity of our four examples should make clear that one can't simply wish for eyes on the street and its good effects. Their presence is conditional and their effects are not guaranteed. The streets and neighborhoods I have sketched all reveal some aspects of what makes streets and neighborhoods successful. Fifth Avenue checks several boxes—its users are many and diverse, its population dense with residents—even if the traffic and bustle challenge neighborhood peace and blocks are long. The campo Giovanni e Paolo frizzes with activity on a human scale, at least by day and early evening. Harding Street wants to be a vital meeting place, but it struggles with traffic and a lack of residential space. Even the car-captive kids of Modesto in the imagined streetscape of *American Graffiti* know that the street is where they get to see and be seen. But there is no one strategy applicable to all: if these areas are to thrive, they must do so in bespoke fashion, tailoring attention to their place and time. But there are principles common to all.

Size matters, as Jacobs well knew: that's why she wrote about great American cities. Diversity of function matters just as much, and that will be much more possible in a large city than in any middling city, let alone a commuter suburb. Whatever the size, the *history* of a place matters. Streets have a history, written by the choices of their citizens, and etched in names christening squares and pathways and buildings and monuments. In older cities, the current configuration of streets is a palimpsest of its antecedents. History is not determinative—Boston's Long Wharf, for instance, no longer welcomes richly laden ships of trade, but it does its own contemporary trade in luxury. Though dominated by modern merchandising, Venice's Merceria, the street that links Piazza San Marco to the Rialto today, recalls an earlier world of shops offering wools, linens, and the wares of tailors and seamstresses.

In thinking about the history and prospects of streets, Jacobs invokes the caution and skepticism that marked her comments at the Great Cities of the World conference. While there may be nothing new under the sun, the contrary boasts and enthusiasms of developers notwithstanding, there are great possibilities for tinkering, tweaking, and retrofitting. "We human beings are terrific copycats,"[18] quips one of her characters in *The Nature of Economies*. Streets and cities must learn from their counterparts without blindly copying and pasting their particular solutions.

This means paying attention to the physical forms of an area, the length of a street, for instance, and its adjacencies to other streets, features of its topography and the presence, or absence, of landmarks—parks and green space, water, plazas—and institutions of arts, commerce and government. Great cities do their work on the streets. A street neighborhood is constituted by a warren of adjacent blocks. In the most vital of these blocks, many different uses will intermix—businesses and residences and public spaces. This makes city neighborhoods different from what passes for a neighborhood in a town. A town can be self-contained, an island. If vital urban neighborhoods are a productive jumble of uses, town streets sort themselves out, some specializing in commerce, others in municipal functions. The diversity Jacobs envisioned for large cities isn't prized on such streets nor, given the physical constraints, could it be realized. In smaller cities, streets are likely to alternate between activity and hibernation. In towns, this is a given. Town streets need the fillip of special events—street fairs, town-wide celebrations, parades—to mimic the diversity of city neighborhoods. Such mimicry is an occasional occurrence, good for the time being, but no guarantor of the kind of street life Jacobs prized.

There are further consequences of the differences. A city neighborhood grows on cross-use, which builds bridges, both for economic life and for politics. "Differences . . . make for cross-use and hence for a person's identification with an area greater than his immediate street network."[19] Just as one street leads to another, walking the streets of one's neighborhood creates "a web of public respect and trust"[20] that animates the moral and political ecology. The walker's world enlarges as she realizes that there is more going on than whatever particular interest she is pursuing. The encounter with difference and the enlarged sense of the world does not automatically produce civic harmony—Jacobs was no romantic on this score, either. She thought respect and trust might emerge from such cross-use. But respect and trust are different from a mere tolerance or the homogenization of judgment and opinion. She knew well the rough-and-tumble of urban politics on streets, in districts and in the city at large. Cities breed disagreement. Interests conflict. When decisions are taken, grievances will remain, and conversations may be tough. But her hope was that the on-the-street encounter with difference might breed a measure of civic comity.

In *Dark Age Ahead*, Jacobs warned about the peril of widespread "cultural amnesia,"[21] a kind of willful forgetfulness of history. Learning, absorbing, and respecting the history of a place is the first step for an appropriate use of Jane Jacobs's thought, no matter the size of the place. Jettisoning history is pure arrogance, well-exemplified by Le Corbusier's disregard for the street map of medieval Paris, a tangle of small alleys and awkward corners suitable for the moseying of a domesticated animal but not for people. In the nineteenth century, Haussmann had already conjured a new Paris of wide boulevards, but Le Corbusier proposed to improve upon that by situating skyscrapers in parks interlaced by high-speed roads. Wiser heads prevailed. Venice avoided a similar fate: a futurist-modernist movement of the nineteenth and early twentieth centuries called for building rail to reach all the way to the Bacino, the waterfront near the Piazza San Marco, and argued that the Campanile, the hallmark tower of the Piazza which collapsed in 1902, should not be replaced. Know what you have, and work with it, is Jacobs's credo.

How might this translate for cities, towns, and suburbs today? Thinking along with Jacobs, rather than reducing her thought to a template, means thinking concretely, focusing on particulars, and avoiding a generalizing theory. But a few principles can guide that thinking.

Keep one's own Eyes on Streets, Plural, and Understand them in Relation to one Another.

A street is already defined, in part, by its own immediate neighbors. A street that stands alone is a dead end. Apart from those dead-end streets fortunate to terminate at some beckoning vista—a view of the harbor, a peak from which to regard a city unfolding below—dead-end streets will be dead to street life. As we noted, streets speak a language of mutual support, one offering "encouragement" where another falters. But proximity to activity won't guarantee success, as the Worcester example shows.

Nevertheless, streets are crucial to the conversation of cities. That conversation has been badly strained by the pandemic and its aftermath: cities once shut down were slow to recover business, visitors, and residents. Fewer people and fewer uses mean a faltering conversation. Matters are different for smaller cities, and certainly for towns, both of which are more accustomed to a rhythm which sees activity during the day but, apart from entertainment, little going on as the day wanes. But whatever the scale, Jane Jacobs would advise modest beginnings: judge carefully and work with what is at hand.

Take the Long View, but Take it with Caution

No matter how the questions may resolve in particular places, Jacobs alerts us to think historically about streets. Think like an archaeologist and sift through the records of the past. An archaeologist knows that what came before partially conditions what comes next, perhaps serving as a deep layer of support or indicating potential trouble. The ruins of ancient Mycenae in Greece sit atop even older ruins. Venice has fewer canals than at its peak, but their successors, the Rio Terras, former canals filled with rubble and overlaid with a new surface, convey passengers throughout the city. Via landfill, annexation, and private developments Boston grew its scrawny 780 acres of 1630 to its current size. Traces of its colonial configuration run throughout the downtown financial district and adjoining harbor. These examples underline the inevitability of change on city streets. Change often comes roughly and with destruction at its head. Jacobs knew this. "All city diversity grows, in part, at least, at the expense of some other tissue."[22] As we have noted, her frank realism on this point has eluded some of her critics who have cast her as a rosy optimist about the small, the quaint, and the timeless. If "adapt or die" is the byword for thinking about evolutionary development in biology, so too, for cities and streets. In *The Nature of Economies*, she insists upon the need for "constant self-correction" in economies,[23] noting that "in an ecosystem, a failed organism becomes food for more successful organisms or for newly arising life."[24] No wonder that Jacobs characterized the city as existential. Its rhythms are those of continually evolving life.

Resign Oneself to Unintended Consequences

Jacobs championed the new and renewed, as we have seen, but she would counsel a careful attention to context before the siting decisions foreclose even greater possibilities. Still, no one can foresee every consequence. The plazas which adjoin towering office buildings and banks are often the result of mandates to provide open ground space to offset a high-rise. But they are rarely welcoming spaces, inviting the passerby to engage. They are the first line of defense for the formal security one will encounter within the buildings' lobbies. If a city or town arranges a set of new shops to face each other across a shared parking lot, the configuration privileges auto transport over pedestrian access by turning a back to the street. Rehabbing a building rather than demolishing it is a good idea, but if it is designed for single use and single entrance it loses the opportunity to bring different uses, and users, together.

The natural cross-purposes in political life have counterparts in economic life on the street. Even as she extolled the magnetism of the street for vivifying the city, Jacobs saw powerfully contrary energies at work. The very success of a street in drawing people out—to commerce, friendship, and ordinary neighborhood life—might evoke unthinking, copycat behavior that threatened its existence. Diversity could self-destruct: success could breed failure. In considering "Forces of Decline and Regeneration" in *Death and Life*'s third section,[25] Jacobs foresaw the potential undoing of diversity by a profit-driven rush to cash-in, via imitation. A thriving restaurant nestled in a mixed-use neighborhood might soon find that its clientele had two or three rivals for its business as the mixed-use street transitioned to a "restaurant row." Brownstones reclaimed from desuetude by sweat equity might shoulder up against a string of row houses retrofitted by investors with deep pockets. In the rush to capitalize on success, repetition would crowd out diversity. Although Jacobs celebrated the ingenuity of imitators and entrepreneurs, she also bemoaned the lack of counterbalance from neighborhood groups or formal city government, who might ask, "should we?" and have the power to affect the answer.

Face Those Consequences with Humility, Not Anger

Failed or failing places are magnets for anger, blame, and finger-pointing. But remedies will depend on the kind of careful observation, judgment, and close to the ground experimentation that Jacobs espoused. Understanding the churn of people, streets, business undertakings, and emergent problems requires a fine-grained understanding of economies, already present in *Death and Life* but given full treatment in her later works. We turn to them now.

Notes

1 Jacobs, *Death and Life*, 30.
2 Jacobs, *Death and Life*, 32.
3 Adam Gopnik, "Street Cred," *The New Yorker*, September 26, 2016, 72.
4 Adam Gopnik, "Street Cred," *The New Yorker*, September 26, 2016, 71.
5 David Brooks, *Bobos in Paradise: The New Upper Class and How They Got There* (New York: Simon & Schuster, 2000), 126.
6 Keeley, "An Interview with Jane Jacobs," in *Ethics*, 28.
7 Sharon Zukin, *Naked City: The Death and Life of Authentic Urban Places* (New York: Oxford University Press, 2010).
8 Jane Jacobs, *Dark Age Ahead* (New York: Random House, 2004), 214.

9   Jacobs, *Death and Life*, 445.

10   Jacobs, *Death and Life*, 71.

11   Jacobs, *Death and Life*, chapter 15.

12   Jacobs, *Dark Age*, 24–25.

13   Jacobs, *Death and Life*, 30.

14   Jacobs, *Death and Life*, 114.

15   Jacobs, *Death and Life*, 81.

16   Jacobs, *Death and Life*, 82.

17   Jacobs, *Death and Life*, 226.

18   Jane Jacobs, *The Nature of Economies* (New York: Random House, 2000), 73.

19   Jacobs, *Death and Life*, 130.

20   Jacobs, *Death and Life*, 56.

21   Jacobs, *Dark Age*, 3–4.

22   Jacobs, *Death and Life*, 251.

23   Jacobs, *Nature*, 5.

24   Jacobs, *Nature*, 89.

25   Jacobs, *Death and Life*, Part Three.

4

The Economics of Urban Life

The Death and Life of Great American Cities will never go out of print: Random House added it to its Modern Library catalog. While Jacobs was justly proud of its enduring influence, she fretted over the neglect of her subsequent work, much of it focused, sharply, on economics.

Careful readers of *Death and Life* knew the obvious importance of economic activity to Jacobs—one couldn't imagine successful cities without the energy provided by all their citizens—and the urgency of understanding how and why it prospered, or faltered, was paramount.

Over the forty years following *Death and Life*, Jacobs wrote three books that foregrounded economics: *The Economy of Cities* (1969), *Cities and the Wealth of Nations* (1984), *The Nature of Economies* (2000). Though not her central subject, economics was fundamental to her analysis in *The Question of Separatism* (1980) and laced throughout *Dark Age Ahead* (2004). And more might have followed: at her death, as Samuel Zipp and Nathan Storring revealed in *Vital Little Plans* (2016), she was refashioning her earlier work into a systematic introduction to economics.

But Jacobs was not a traditional economist. Modern economic theory bristles with analysis driven by statistics and regression analysis. Graphs, tables, charts, and sequences of abstract equations are its units of logic and argument. You will find none of these in Jacobs's work, apart from an occasional, clarifying diagram. She had no formal academic training in the discipline. But what she did have was a formidable intelligence and a mind intent on understanding the actual to-and-fro of economic life. Her analysis of economies is as particular, concrete and historically minded as her thinking about streets and neighborhoods.

Perhaps it was the lack of formal academic standing that occasioned a bemusedly skeptical *Time* magazine review of the first book devoted to economics, *The Economy of Cities*. "Bless Jane Jacobs," it began, "Lively, lucid, blunt, original, she triumphs by being mostly wrong."[1] Professional snobbery was nothing new. Academics are sometimes quick to dismiss as amateurs those who lack the traditional intellectual regalia, and popular commentators sometimes follow in their wake. (Her husband, Bob, once related to me an exchange between Jane and an Oxford don. "Why should we think that a housewife has anything to say about these matters?" sniped the don to which Jacobs tartly replied, "why should we assume that a don knows anything about cities?") The presumption that only the academically credentialed could contribute to understanding the economy surfaced, ironically, at a Boston College conference in early 1993. As a member of a panel devoted to her work on economics, Jacobs grew increasingly exasperated as a fellow panelist, richly credentialed and widely published in the flagship journals of urban economics, repeatedly referred to her as "Professor" Jacobs. Finally, she blurted out, "stop calling me a professor! I'm not a professor! I barely finished high school!" The nonplussed professor went quiet for a moment and then resumed his commentary, still referring to her as a professor.

But, *Time* notwithstanding, there was a set of professional journalists and accomplished academics who discerned something important in her work. In 1969, the year *The Economy of Cities* appeared, Jacobs published "Strategies for Helping Cities" in *The American Economic Review*. The place of original publication is important: the *AER* ranks among the most prominent professional journals in the field. In this piece, Jacobs sketched the *good* role that government might play in revivifying city economies; we will see her skepticism about much government action in what follows. The formidable economic journalist David Warsh devoted several columns to her while writing for *The Boston Globe*. These would be included when Warsh later published *Economic Principals* (1993), a compendium of his articles on important economic thinkers. In his subsequent *Knowledge and the Wealth of Nations* (2007), Warsh went further, detecting connections in her work to the enlarging debate about how to understand processes of economic "growth" and "development" in underdeveloped economies.[2]

The pioneers of what came to be known as "new growth" theory included Robert Lucas and Paul Romer; Lucas won the Nobel Prize for Economics in 1995, and Romer, his student, in 2018. Lucas and Romer were both concerned with explaining what economists call the law of diminishing returns. In its basic form, economics highlights the interaction of land, labor, and capital in producing goods. None of these factors is inexhaustible: if land, labor, and capital are the factors involved in producing goods, the economist would expect that, over time, the investment returns, the output, would diminish. Physical resources wear out or are depleted, funds diminish, labor works harder and harder to create the next item. And with the gradual exhaustion, trouble would follow. This is something that Marx counted on in forecasting the inevitable decline of capitalism. Desperate for survival, capitalists would struggle against each other, to the ultimate demise of the system.

But contrary to these expectations, growth continued throughout the twentieth century and capitalism remained robust. Returns to capital were increasing: How to account for that? There must be, reasoned Lucas and Romer, some seemingly inexhaustible factor in production that traditional theory had missed. They found it in ideas. Unlike the traditional factors of production, ideas don't get exhausted. They passed from one mind to another, from one enterprise to another, and the passing often triggered new ideas and new results. Knowledge spilled over to a surprising effect. Jacobs had caught on to this in *Death and Life* in arguing for the potency of diversity of uses and users mingled together in thriving city streets, but her insight gained new potency when applied directly to thinking about economies. In a 1988 paper, "On the Mechanics of Economic Development," Lucas wrote, "I will be following very closely the lead of Jane Jacobs, whose remarkable book *The Economy of Cities* seems to me mainly and convincingly concerned [. . .] with the external effects of human capital."[3]

Not everyone would follow that lead.[4] Two other explanations for the persistence of growth in cities emerged to challenge the new growth theorists. The first explanation emphasized the power of concentration, suggesting that the clustering of big industries propelled growth by fostering competition for materials, talent, and markets. The vigor of competition *between* many different kinds of industry would propel growth. The second explanation, associated with Harvard Business School professor Michael Porter, argued for the importance of competition *within* industries. Car makers would compete with each other for large-scale mechanical engineers, tech firms would battle for coders and system architects, retailers would fight for the best marketing talent, and so on. Internal competition within an industry domain would have the beneficent effect of growth in the city at large. Both alternative explanations accented the importance of large-scale undertakings. The Jacobs hypothesis, by contrast, accented the importance of multiple, diverse enterprises, often small.[5] How to choose among them?

Three Harvard economists, Andrei Shleifer, Jose Scheinkman, and Edward Glaeser, tested Lucas's, and by extension, Jacobs's hypothesis against the two other explanations accounting for growth in cities. The conclusions they reached, wrote Warsh, were "consistent with Jacobs's view of the importance of a high degree of variety."[6] From that point on, observed David Nowlan of the University of Toronto, references to "Jane Jacobs externalities" became part of "the jargon of the discipline."[7] In his later book, *The Triumph of the City*, and in subsequent articles, Glaeser would make clear his disagreement with Jacobs on several points while acknowledging her influence on his thought and the "profound and prescient insights"[8] that recur throughout her work.

If not from graphs and mathematics, where did Jacobs's arguments originate? They lay in the combination of an unstinting willingness to question and be puzzled, a rich and disciplined imagination, careful observation, and a discerning judgment.

Accounting for Origins

Jacobs began *The Economy of Cities* with a single, simple question that led to startling suggestions. How, she asked, did cities begin? The common answer to that question presumed, she argued, that cities began after agriculture had taken root and allowed communities to gather and then expand. How could a city exist without a preexisting hinterland? First, hunt and gather; later, settle down and plant; still later, found a city. Not so, said Jacobs: cities must predate agriculture since only when people are together would they have the collective intelligence to break through to the thought of agriculture. This hypothesis has occasioned much comment, most of it critical, from anthropologists and historians. Only a small minority within these fields would credit her analysis.[9] But Jacobs added another twist to her story of the city which is harder to dispute.

At the Beginning(s)

In popular imagination, myth swaddles the birth of ancient cities: Uruk in *Gilgamesh*, Babel in Genesis, Rome in Vergil, and any number named by Eliade are good examples. The story of each city recalls a founding act, either in concert with the will of the gods or, as with Babel, in defiance of God. Each city is unique: its people know only one, true city, singular and exemplary. With the birth of cities comes work to be done: daily life to provision, walls to erect, temples to dedicate, deities and rulers to appease.

But history tells, and prehistory suggests, another story Jane Jacobs wrote in *The Economy of Cities*. A city does not emerge on its own in a single burst of life. Multiple, contemporaneous births—twins, triplets, quadruplets—are the rule in the emergence of cities. The birth of cities is a mutual begetting, the result of a contemporaneous coupling born out of need. "In modern and historical times, no creative local economy—which is to say, no city economy—seems to have grown in isolation from other cities. A city seems always to have implied a group of cities, in trade with one another."[10] Cities complement each other, and they figure in each other's development, an echo of the complementarity that marks the lives of successful streets and neighborhoods that Jacobs explored in *Death and Life*.

Reciprocal need spins webs of connections among cities. A city and its people can create many things, but not all things, and what they lack they must find elsewhere. In effect, incipient cities confront what business literature calls the "make or buy" decision. If a manufacturer needs a sprocket for the latest contraption, she can decide to make it herself or buy it from someone else. It's a similar case with original cities. Jacobs sketches an imaginary city, New Obsidian, modeled on a Turkish site, which illustrates the point. The imagined New Obsidian has a commodity, obsidian, in abundance but lacks many rudimentary goods that its near neighbors create. If the people of New Obsidian want these goods, how are they to get them? New Obsidian *could* devote time to acquire the raw materials *and* learn the crafts that would transform them into the sought-after goods, but that would be a lengthy and inefficient process. The New Obsidians want those goods right away. The ready-to-hand solution is to swap: trade obsidian for whatever the neighbors have that they want. Both sides win in this exchange. Later, a city might choose to develop its own versions of the traded-for goods, but the urgency of present need reveals the advantage of using what you already have. Exchange meets needs.

There is a refraction, here, of the theory of comparative advantage, first articulated by the classical economist David Ricardo (1772–1823). Ricardo argued that a country should not chase proficiency in all manner of economic processes. It couldn't hope to succeed in all things. It might lack labor or raw materials or available land. Instead, a country must recognize its strong suits and play those cards. One country might have access to exceptional ports and be rich in timber and grain; another might be flush with minerals and skilled metal workers. No one country can be the source of all the things its people need. Countries should exploit native advantages and see what they might garner in exchange. But Jacobs alters the Ricardian view by changing the accent: comparative advantage theory, even in its contemporary incarnations, focuses on *countries*. In *The Economy of Cities*, as elsewhere, chiefly in *Cities and the Wealth of Nations*, Jacobs focuses on the *city* as source of comparative advantage.

To make her case, Jacobs did not rely solely upon her thought experiment with New Obsidian. She found evidence in other quarters. In *The Nature of Economies*, a book cast as a series of conversations among friends, one of her interlocutors finds support for her position in the history of Venice. Venice began as a refuge for immigrants. Fleeing the depredations of the Huns as the Western Roman empire collapsed, the early Venetians sought safety in the marshlands at the head of the Adriatic. Their existence was sparse and perilous. An early Byzantine consul, Cassiodorus, wrote of them:

> You possess many vessels . . . [and] . . . you live like seabirds, with your homes dispersed . . . across the surface of the water. The solidity of the earth on which they rest is secured only by osier and wattle; yet you do not hesitate to oppose so frail a bulwark to the wildness of the sea. Your people have one great wealth— the fish, which suffices for them all. . . . All your energies are spent on your salt fields; in them indeed lies your prosperity, and your power to purchase those things which you have not. For though there may be men who have little need of gold, yet none live who desire not salt.[11]

Salt was not as good as gold, but it did not need to be: it had value for everyday cooks and chefs. Salt became the basis for rudimentary trade and offered Venice a comparative advantage. Trade in this simple commodity, later augmented by trade in fish, coupled with Venetian persistence and inventiveness, spurred economic development. Living on the marshes, over generations, the Venetii built competency in sailing and navigation. Those skills enabled them, shortly, to travel up the reaches of the rivers like the Po and the Brenta with goods in trade. Other goods and trade followed in the train of this early success. They carried modest goods, to be sure—salt and fish—but goods in demand in upriver markets. From such simple trading of commodities, the economic life of Venice gradually emerged.

But if a city needs other cities to grow, which were Venice's generative cities? Politically and culturally, Venice lay within the intersecting spheres of the great cities of Constantinople and Rome. Its history and architecture came to embody elements of both cultures. But in the early days of its economic development, Venice could not trade on equal terms with these great cities. Instead, it served as what Jacobs would call a "supply region."[12] It was useful to its powerful and sophisticated metropoles in providing simple staples. Constantinople and Rome had a taste for salt and fish, but if there were an emerging Venetian craft economy, it would find no takers in the big cities. Venice could not hope to trade finished goods on equal terms with flourishing cities, so it settled for trade in its commodities.

Commodity trade can take a city only so far. The sources of Venice's eventually emergent development lie elsewhere. Development relies upon human talent that learns by doing, by imitating, and by seeing through failures to innovation. Every society has beginners and aspirants. One can imagine the first stirrings of artisanship among some Venetians who might begin the long process of imitation that could culminate in skilled craftsmanship. At the outset of this long process, it was important for Venice to find trading partners of similar scale and scope if it hoped to trade in its humble goods. These partners would be what Jacobs termed "backward cities" in chapter ten of *Cities and the Wealth of Nations*. They engage in a symbiotic process of development, "developing on one another's shoulders."[13] Venice would earn revenue from its commodity trade with the great cities, but its economic development would spring from interchange with cities similar to it in scale, complexity and aspiration. Supply regions and backward cities can escape those classifications only by the combination of skill, luck, perseverance, and insight that one sees in the history of Venice.

With the commodities that were of interest to Constantinople—salt and fish, and eventually timber, harvested from the Dalmatian coast—Venice began to earn imports that it desired but could not yet produce. In the beginning stages of its craftwork, Venetian products would be cheap imitations, serviceable but undistinguished, and of interest only to similarly small and backward cities. There were plenty of these upriver from Venice. In the longer run, assuming persistent interest, rugged craftsmanship would grow into refined practice or perhaps be put to new uses. The elaboration of the Venetian economy reflects that. Its magnificent glass industry, for instance, began modestly, as did the expertise in the handling of textiles, which grew from its later trade with the East. The motives for such development among the artisans themselves were probably not chiefly commercial. "The practice of improvising, in itself, fosters delight in pulling it off successfully,"[14] writes Jacobs. Delight and aesthetic appreciation lie close to the heart of much economic innovation. Some create, apart from financial incentives, because the process, from idea to realized object, is beautiful.

Trade spurred financial innovation as well. The Venetians had no choice: as the city became a destination and transit point for merchants from many regions, it needed mechanisms for receiving, valuing, paying for, and exchanging goods and services. Although Renaissance Florence has a well-earned reputation for banking, Venetians were busy at this, too. They established correspondent banks in many cities and popularized the use of journal transactions rather than actual cash exchange in business dealings. Over time, the Venetian ducat became a preferred currency throughout the Mediterranean.

Thus, from an unpromising beginning in marshes, Venice became over many generations what the art critic John Ruskin (1819–1900) called the "paradise of cities." The descendants of fisherfolk and marsh-dwellers became river pilots, boat and shipbuilders, traders and craftsmen, bankers and financiers. These transformations were wrought over many years. They depended on a host of interlocking factors, chiefly the reciprocal relationships of cities—some already established, others yearning to join the ranks—as well as good fortune and perseverance. And, says Jacobs, they depended upon gifts, new twists, and old things just lying around.

Gifts, the New from the Old, Imports Coming and Going

"There is no such thing as a free lunch," goes the economic commonplace. Free things are deals too good to be true: the friendly barkeep has already priced into the drink the cost of the "free" victuals he sets before you. The "no money down" auto lot financier has tailored his interest rates to recoup any immediate losses. Nothing, it seems, is free. But with regard to a city's economic development, Jane Jacobs dissents. Cities enjoy "gift" resources, freely bestowed, or inherited without strings of obligation.

In *The Nature of Economies*, the last of Jacobs's economics trilogy, a group of characters drawn from various professions explores economic growth and development with insights gleaned from the natural sciences. One of the characters, Murray, observes that "initial resources for settlements' economies aren't earned by export work, but all the same they're earned in a different way—earned by combining gift resources with human effort."[15] He cites the example we have been exploring, the early Venetians who brought astuteness to their circumstances, concentrating "salt by cleverly directing seawater into series of evaporation ponds [. . .] probably at first to get salt for their own use, then subsequently for export, too."[16] Not everyone living near salt water realized the hidden bounty of the salt amid the tide or could figure out how to extract it—but the Venetians did. Persevering intelligence joined to gifts yielded good results. Natural resource endowments—rivers, tides, wind—can be gifts, but they must be understood as such and require careful tending. Traditions of craft and local knowledge can be gifts so ready to hand that they may be overlooked or undervalued. They, too, need care.

Although the identification of the gift dimension of the economy came later in her economic writing, Jacobs was always alert to the unexpected aspects of economic vitality. Beginning with *The Economy of Cities*, she explored how economies become dense with possibilities, ramifying in all directions, or grow torpid and stagnate. "Cities are places where adding new work to older work proceeds vigorously. Indeed, any settlement where this happens becomes a city."[17] This is a simple, functional definition of a city—the city is the place for intensive economic innovation. In Jacobs's view that innovation is not spun down from the top, whether from government or large enterprise, but something which bubbles up through the drive, curiosity and know-how of entrepreneurial risk-takers. Cities are organisms, and organisms need nutrients. In *The Nature of Economies*, Jacobs calls this nutrition-seeking "self-refueling." This is not a process carried on in isolation. It is neither automatic nor guaranteed. As at their beginnings, cities need one another, and, within cities, one risk-taker needs another. "Self-refueling" presumes a continuing process of diversification. By contrast, a settlement that does not add new work to older work remains, well, a settlement. It may be a comfortable place to live, perhaps, but not one to catalyze innovation and spur the growth of an economy. Suburbs fit this description: good places to live if one wants a comfortable peace and pace, but not the source of the competition and attendant innovation that will spur economic development.

Jacobs had explored this process of development in the second chapter of *The Economy of Cities*, "How New Work Begins."[18] The chapter is that rare case of Jacobs providing what passes for a mathematical expression. New work builds upon previous work, she argues, and the novelty requires the fresh insight someone brings to bear. Failure can often open new vistas. Jacobs recounts the early frustrations of the Minnesota Mining and Manufacturing Company, which we now know as 3M, in developing sandpaper. The sandpaper worked poorly, but the adhesives it employed to bind the grit to paper were another matter: they stuck well, and 3M stuck by them. Many kinds of tape followed, from Scotch to recording tape. She captures the process in this diagram

$$D + A\text{-------}>nD$$

where D represents an original division of labor to which something new, A, is added yielding an indeterminate, n, number of new divisions of labor. In turn, each new division of labor provides the possibility of additional innovation. Connected one to another, the new divisions branch out like spider webs. Older work coupled with human ingenuity and market savvy proves remarkably fertile. Jacobs knew that not every innovation roots and prospers. She modified her original diagram to include the term "nTE" to represent many iterations of trial and error.

$$D + nTE\text{----}> A\text{-------}nD$$

The engineers at 3M, for instance, fretted, fiddled, and tinkered before the adhesive qualities of their products became the focal point. Among small businesses, the Bureau of Labor Statistics reports that 20 percent of new businesses fail within a year, and perhaps one quarter survive for fifteen years. Jacobs was not naïve: new work is risky business.

How does human ingenuity discover new possibilities in the midst of established work and old ways? Jacobs explored some of this, as we saw, in the example of the primitive Venetian economy. In *Economy*, she provides another example in tracing the emergence of the Japanese bicycle manufacturing industry in the late nineteenth century. No government planning board or corporate executive team intended to establish a full-fledged industry by building bicycle manufacturing plants, staffing them, and then producing, financing, and marketing their bikes. The industry began from scratch, with small steps, and grew, first, from the work of skilled repair people who fixed imported broken bikes with imported parts, then learned to create spare parts, and, eventually developed the capacity for the wholesale manufacturing of bikes.[19] Market savvy was crucial here, too: early efforts could not compete with imported foreign bikes, just as early Venetian artisans could not compete with master Byzantine craftsmen. But at the right time, Japanese bike makers and Venetian artisans entered a wide and welcoming market.

Jacobs's emphasis on ingenuity, leading to innovation, and market savvy leading to economic vitality, counterpoints what she sees as a mistaken emphasis on the division of labor as a source of economic expansion. Adam Smith (1723–

90) first gave prominence to this idea in *The Wealth of Nations*, a title echoed in Jacobs's *Cities and the Wealth of Nations*. Jacobs cites Smith's justly famous description of the pin factory where "One man draws out the wire, another straightens it, a third cuts it, a fourth points it, a fifth grinds it at the top for receiving the head,"[20] before criticizing Smith's assumptions and conclusions. Smith advanced the idea that coordination of many hands along one assembly line yielded output that so far outstripped the efforts of a solitary pinmaker that one could not deny the propulsive force of the division of labor. Jacobs disagreed: division of labor does indeed yield extraordinary results in ordinary *production* work, but it has nothing to do with the process that leads to *development* of new economic energy. Put differently: the division of labor rationalizes preexisting production, making it more efficient. Efficiency is a good thing, but creativity is not one of its offspring. New work, and increased vitality, require something different. New work arises when someone, a person, not a process, realizes that the current division of labor might yield greater results with a break, a twist, a turn, a putting to new and previously unforeseen uses.

Economic life, in Jacobs's view, develops out of response to real needs, not fleeting wants and desires. As she has shown, in meeting those needs, a city can't go it alone. "No city by itself develops all the various goods and services required to overcome its complex practical problems . . . cities copy each other's solutions, by importing relevant goods to solve the problems."[21] But solutions taken off-the-shelf from one city will rarely fit circumstances on the ground in another city. Copying solutions requires trimming or enlarging to fit the local realities. Intelligent risk-taking and attentive trial and error are what cities need.

The exchange of goods, services, and ideas, as the Venetian and Japanese examples show, generates economic life; exports and imports are its roots. In the second chapter of *The Economy of Cities*, Jacobs focused her attention on the intricate processes whereby cities interact with each other to earn imports via exports. In turn, she followed the winding path where goods and services formerly imported by a city may become homemade and the processes whereby new exports arise, or fail to materialize, as a city seeks sustained economic growth. The goods which a city's economy produces serve to underwrite the imports it seeks from other cities. But simply gaining imports, via exchange, does not equate to economic development. Stockpiling the goods that exports have yielded in effect equates the presence of stuff on hand with economic vitality. Much "stuff" can be warehoused and set aside until someone puts it to use. But development is a process, and a complicated one. This is where Jacobs's several multiplier effects and what she calls import shifting and replacement come into play.[22]

She pays attention first to the "export-multiplier." Jacobs did not originate the idea of a multiplier effect. Economists had long identified the ways in which one kind of work generates another kind of work. If there are roads to be built, there is concrete to mix, rock to quarry, food and shelter for workers needed. She is unique in directing attention to export and import multipliers in the context of the city. Imagine an economy, writes Jacobs, that starts to grow by exporting local commodities or goods on hand. While "a young, small city necessarily has a meager economy,"[23] "when the exports of a settlement increase, the local economy of the city grows too. The local growth results from what the economists call 'the multiplier effect.'"[24] The basic idea, as I have noted, is deceptively simple: one job breeds another, whether in direct relation to the export work—supplies for manufacturers, food and shelter for workers—or sprouting a related line of work which may, in time, become itself exportable.

Complexity enters with the reciprocating system triggered by import-replacing, where a local economy begins to produce what it had formerly imported, and import-shifting, as the local community begins to import new and different goods. Though the systems are reciprocal, it is the import-replacing and import-shifting phase that leads, according to Jacobs, to "momentous consequences."[25] Why is this so?

"In the case of an export-multiplier effect, some of the new imports earned by the export growth go directly back into the export work," but "in the case of an import-replacing multiplier, however, none of the different (seemingly additional) imports go either directly or indirectly into exports from the city. All are added to the growing local economy."[26] In this instance, what happens in the local economy stays in the (enlarging) local economy. Locals get the benefit of the goods produced and the jobs that produced them.

I have used the word "phase" to describe the import-replacing and import-shifting movements in the growth of the local economy, but this is misleading, suggesting a serial, temporal sequence: first, replace, then shift. By contrast, Jacobs insists that the system must be a constantly flowing feedback loop, truly reciprocal, lest the economy falter: it is a coinciding process, not a sequential one. A city that settles for replacing and shifting imports, ignoring the exports that make those processes possible, or fails to recognize new export possibilities, will stagnate. "If a city stops generating new exports after an episode of import replacing, it will not earn any more imports to replace. It will not have the grist, so to speak, for another episode."[27] In effect, vibrant city economies depend on brave and intelligent risk-takers, be they entrepreneurs or astute city officials, who ask "What's next? What's the new, 'big' thing?" and who are encouraged, or, at least, not restrained, in pursuing answers to these questions.

In this regard, government may facilitate, safeguard, or obstruct access to opportunity. Jacobs's skepticism about government is well-known. In the closing pages of *Economy*, she notes, wryly, "the only possible way to keep open the economic opportunities for new activities is for a 'third force' to protect their weak and still incipient interests. Only governments can play this economic role. And sometimes, for pitifully brief intervals, they do. But because development subverts the status quo, the status quo soon subverts governments."[28] Jacobs here intimates a theme she will explore later in her work, the difference between those who make a living by exchange and those who become, as in government, the regulators or guardians of a society.

What might government do to protect "weak and still incipient interests"? Providing money comes first to mind. But Jacobs is cautious here. In describing government's role in providing financial capital, she notes that it most often is "imitative"[29] of private sector banking practices, not "innovative." Both banks and cities want sure bets, not risky business. In both cases, advantage accrues to the well-established enterprises, and nascent efforts scrounge for funds. Just as was the case for poor, redlined neighborhoods seeking mortgage loans, new enterprises in poor neighborhoods face similar challenges. "People at the bottom of a society customarily find it difficult to get capital for development work [. . .] social discrimination and unequal protection of people and their rights by the law (in actual fact, as opposed to theoretical equality of people under law) can effectively prevent many persons from developing their work."[30] Jacobs never offered a systematic analysis of racism in the city, but she was keenly aware of the damage done by discriminatory lending practices. She was sensitive to the undervaluing of women's work, wryly tolerant of the uses of shady money by immigrant groups and coyly applauding of the laudable uses of graft. But Jacobs prized novel, within-the-law approaches to financing as well. She was an early champion of Muhammad Yunus's Grameen Development Bank. Yunus, whose pioneering work in microfinance is well-described in his book *Banker to the Poor* (2008), used lending circles, chiefly comprised of women, to fund small enterprises.

His ideas grew from careful observation of the village craftspeople he passed on his way to his work as a formal economist. Local basket makers had skill but no capital reserves. Each day, they would produce one or two baskets, but they had to borrow money for the materials from the local moneylender. Even if the crafter were successful in selling the basket, much of the revenue would be returned immediately to the moneylender, who set exorbitant interest rates. But the crafter had no choice: she had no surplus funds to break the dependence and move out of the vicious circle. The cycle would renew each day: more money on loan, meager sales, and so on. The crafter could not get ahead. Lending circles offered a way out: poor people pooled their slim resources and evaluated the creditworthiness of borrowers. They took on a task that big banks refused since there wasn't sufficient payoff for them. The loans were very small, much too small to be of interest to commercial banks, and focused on local ideas without the constraints of commercial lending. The due diligence of creditworthiness resided in the circle itself: who better than the local people to judge the likelihood of repayment? Their own money was on the line. While microlending has endured many challenges, it has been a spur to economic development across the globe.

Kindred efforts, animated by close attention to the needs, desires, and possibilities of economic development among the very poor, are at the heart of The Massachusetts Institute of Technology's Poverty Action Lab, directed by Abhijit V. Banerjee and Esther Duflo. Conducting "randomized control trials" in desperately poor neighborhoods across the world, Banerjee and Duflo dispel many of the common assumptions about the very poor, accent their agency and point ways to foster development at a grassroots level.[31]

Given Jacobs's skepticism about government as an agent of change, one might surmise that it always plays the villain or the unwitting bureaucrat for her. But Jacobs always sought instances of government functioning well. Underlying all of her thought, though formally identified only at the last in *Dark Age Ahead*, was a commitment to the principle of subsidiarity. Put simply, the principle of subsidiarity insists that problems be resolved at the lowest, least complicated level. When an angry dog runs unleashed in a neighborhood full of young children, one is entitled to pick up the phone and call canine control. But the subsidiarity principle suggests that neighbors address the matter with the dog's owner, eliminating the need for formal recourse and, likely, building solidarity in the neighborhood. In *Death and Life*, her analysis of the three kinds of urban neighborhood—street, district, city as a whole—also reflects the subsidiarity principle. This is far from a laissez-faire or "she governs best who governs least" perspective; subsidiarity wants full-throated, good, and effective governance scaled to the appropriate level. Subsidiarity requires citizens to join in the ongoing act of governance. Problems that escape neighborhood resolution may be resolved at the level of the district. Problems that overwhelm districts suggest the need for the intervention of city hall or higher offices, as a last resort. While this may sound like a polished, civics textbook analysis, Jacobs knew that civic life was always a struggle. We will return to this theme in the concluding chapter.

Government, thought Jacobs, cannot be, nor should it aspire to be, the chief agent of economic development. In economic matters, it acts best when it guards the commercial sphere against force, intimidation, special interests, and influence peddling. But the temptation to ignore these proper roles is strong. Venice, again, offers a powerful example.

Although many historic shifts contributed to Venice's demise as a trading city and an economic dynamo—the rounding of the Cape of Good Hope, which opened new routes to the East, the opening of the Atlantic trade, which privileged Atlantic coastal countries, like Spain and Portugal—government entrenched with self-interest played an early, major role.

At its peak of commercial success in the thirteenth and early fourteenth centuries, Venice was effectively ruled by its Great Council, a body whose numbers had grown as the city prospered. Originally a preserve of Venice's aristocratic elite, the Council initially welcomed other, non-noble but rich, members. Venice had pioneered "the *commenda*, a rudimentary type of joint stock company,"[32] in which an ambitious young man traveled, at some personal risk of safety, with the cargo which belonged to an established, and stay-at-home, merchant. In turn, the young man received a hefty percentage of the trade. Ambitious young men made fortunes and an entry pass to the Council. As noble birth was no longer the privileged channel to the Council, the newly rich arrived in ever greater numbers, to the dismay of the old moneyed class. Success bred reprisal. The Great Council banned the *commenda* since "the *commenda* benefited new merchants, and now the established elite was trying to exclude them."[33] As Darren Acemoglu and James Robinson argue in *Why Nations Fail* (2012), the decision by the Great Council in 1297 to close membership to all but noble families—the so-called Serrata—frustrated the hopes of the economically successful non-noble class. This social and political closure carried economic closure in its train. The successful exclusion was one of a series of steps that wrought irreparable harm to the economy. Venice moved to nationalize trading monopolies and dampened private trading via excessive taxation. Its population shrank, its economic energy dissipated, and the city began its long decline. Today, there's still a little fish to trade, Acemoglu and Robinson comment wryly, as well as pizza and gelato to offer visitors, but Venice is otherwise a tourism-dependent shell of itself.

Government can fail, as in Venice, when greed, coupled with fear of losing personal advantage, leads to exclusion and diminished opportunities for newcomers. But it may also fail in subtler fashion by confusing, say, the rapid infusion of money or addition of "new" jobs with genuine economic development. Big government requires big money, and the prospect for greater revenue tied to new jobs is an enticing prospect. Small wonder that the promise of "new" jobs at the cost of tax cuts and other benefits proves so alluring, as in the courtship of Amazon by several American cities in 2017. While the rhetoric of the courtship touted the creation of "good jobs," Jacobs would have been skeptical. "Good" jobs, on her understanding, grow from innovation, respond to critical needs and, ideally, offer challenge and learning to the worker. Amazon wasn't innovating: these jobs were already part of a captive division of labor,[34] not new jobs created from the ferment of trial and error which spurs the export-import reciprocating system. Nor does the addition of these transferred jobs take into account the full range of costs imposed on the hosts: tax breaks and incentives, impacts on public services, such as education and safety, escalation of residential rents, traffic congestion, and so on. In the case of Amazon, those most likely to be affected—residents of local communities—did take account and their anger helped to drive Amazon away from some places. (But not in my hometown: less than a mile away from where I write, an Amazon warehouse arose—and sat empty—until just this round of editing.) Jane Jacobs would not have been happy with the process or the outcome, but she would not be surprised: economic expansion was confused with genuine economic development.

What does government need to know to foster economic development effectively? In "Strategies for Helping Cities," the *AER* paper cited previously, Jacobs proposed a new, difficult, and concrete approach to understanding the health of a city's economy. She identified two complementary strategies.

The first reflects her commitment to subsidiarity: federal tax dollars should be returned directly to cities, and cities should lead in determining how the funds can be directed. Federal aid to cities is not something new. But the means of dispersing the funds matters greatly. Jacobs was rightly suspicious of block grants, which were tied to nationally generated criteria. Local needs, preferences, and history suffer on this account. If, for instance, federal transportation grants feature highways, but nothing else, funds for providing or enhancing public transport go begging. Jacobs also saw a basic unfairness in the process: cities contribute disproportionately to national income accounts, but less populated farmlands and the countryside reap a disproportionate share of revenues.

The second strategy identifies what needs to occur if the returned funds are to be used wisely. The city must know how and where it is growing or lagging, and this knowledge will depend on exacting attention to the city itself. How to know this? Jacobs proposes the construction of development "rates" that are city-specific and that are assessed at five and ten year intervals. But "remedial" work must be undertaken, right away, even given scarce evidence, since a city cannot afford not to try new things as it waits for the five year results. Trial and error, response to contingencies, will rule this phase. As she said in an interview, this is a matter of "touch and go," risky but necessary business.

This is a daunting task, and Jacobs sketches it with some reluctance since it "might suggest that to collect that data is the salient task."[35] How daunting? Consider the paragraph of the *AER* article which forms a kind of mission statement for such work.

> To achieve a rather refined portrait of a city's economy and the processes at work there, one would need data on the following: 1. Which new goods and services (appearing since the last compilation) represented replacements of imports and, among these, which were transplants of production from elsewhere and which were locally originated; 2. Which new goods and services represented new input items; 3. What input items had been lost since the previous compilation; 4. Kinds and value of export work lost; 5. Kinds and values of work exported and which of these represented new kinds of exports; 6. The genesis of these new exports (that is, whether produced by organizations that had already been exporting, by organizations set up *de novo* for export work, or by organizations formerly producing only for the local market); 7. Numbers and types of new organizations created by breakaways from older organizations; 8. Kinds and sizes of new organizations being financed locally as distinguished from those financed from outside, and the terms of investment; 9. Changes in quantities and kinds of imports since the previous compilation.

"There is no substitute for knowing the particulars,"[36] concluded Jacobs in *Death and Life*, and economic development is full of particulars. Gathering, sorting, integrating, understanding, and acting upon these troves of data is a daunting task. And this is for but *one* city while Jacobs argues, as we have seen, that cities must be understood in relation to other cities.

Cities develop on each other's shoulders. They are reciprocal agents of each other's boom times. Still, not every city is a great city, and not every city is dynamically implicated in the growth of another. And beyond cities lie suburbs, towns, hamlets, farms, and the fringes of the wild. How, if at all, do cities affect these regions?

The Metropolitan Focus: Cities and Their Neighbors Near and Far

In the early pages of *Death and Life*, Jacobs warned, we recall, about the dangers of extrapolating her thought to "what goes on in towns, or little cities, or in suburbs which are still suburbs."[37] But a few pages later, she extols the "intricate, many-faceted, cultural life of the metropolis"[38] a first indication of her insights into the urban *region*. The caution against mistaken application of her urban principles to towns or small cities shouldn't be understood as a discounting of the region. Given her emphasis on reciprocal relations among cities and her commitment to an organic view of development, attention to the dynamism of the region beyond the city's borders has a prominent place in her thinking. What sparks and bubbles and flows in the city proper finds outlets beyond its juridical boundaries.

I am interchanging two phrases—metropolitan region and region—without the precision of professional urbanists and planners. I am using both terms to describe areas within the orbit, or field of force, generated by a city. For example, Boston's region, in my usage, would include southern New Hampshire and Portland, Maine; Worcester, Massachusetts; and Hartford, Connecticut. Each of these cities and areas, of course, is autonomous, but each benefits from the powerful Boston economy. Commuter traffic flows are one good indicator; spin-offs of relocated industries are another. Within Massachusetts itself, local pride notwithstanding, some cities are styled "gateways," with Boston the prized destination.[39]

Jacobs gives extended treatment to urban regions in her later works. As she addressed *The Question of Separatism*, she began by asserting that the dynamic interplay between Montreal and Toronto was "responsible for what has been happening in Quebec."[40] As it turned out, Toronto figured as the more economically vigorous city and Montreal, according to Jacobs, suffered from the history of Canada's "profoundly colonial approach to economic life,"[41] a tendency to remain content with a status as resource-provider, not economic innovator. But comparisons of the two cities aside, the initial point is clear: the province of Quebec bears the economic stamp of the two cities.

The region bears the stamp in another way: "the great growth surge of Montreal—was simultaneously undermining an old culture in the countryside and developing it into something new in the metropolis, and sending this new city-shaped culture back into the countryside."[42] Urban culture displaces, or transforms, rural culture. It alters contrary assumptions and imparts restlessness. Marx and Engels likely overstated the case when they dismissed the "idiocy of rural life" in *The Communist Manifesto*. But the mass migration from countryside to cities around the world is today's story. "How you gonna keep 'em down on the farm (after they've seen Paree?")" asked the First World War song. The global push toward cities suggests you can't.

Jacobs's extended treatment of urban regions continues in the second chapter of *Cities and the Wealth of Nations* by examining cities' own regions. Subsequent chapters explore supply regions and transplant regions, distant from an originating city but spawned by it. Neither type hums with the dense creativity sometimes found in a city's own region. "Some city regions are unique, being the richest, densest and most intricate of all types of economies except for cities themselves,"[43] avers Jacobs. But note the subtle qualifier: some. Not every city generates a region, and cities that do generate regions vary in richness, density, and intricacy.

Some regions, absent the catalyzing power of a local city economy, may become and remain "supply" regions. Some, as Venice did, can escape this state. To invoke a political metaphor: if the city economy is lord, supply regions are vassal states. They are "stunted and bizarre, economic grotesques."[44] If one had removed economic incentives and human ingenuity from historic Venice, a supply region, it would have remained useful for its salt and fish but never destined for greatness. Supply regions are "over-specialized and wildly unbalanced."[45] Some are dependent on the good fortune of their natural resources but subject to abandonment when resources run dry or alternatives emerge. Others have supplied cheap land and low taxes for military or corporate uses, but wither when these retreat.

Worse may come. Exhausted supply regions may become "regions workers abandon."[46] When opportunity fails to knock, the young seek possibilities elsewhere. Supply regions which fail to diversify, stubbornly relying on their initial advantages, sacrifice present gain for future vigor. Once bereft of the income derived from resources, jobs disappear and so, too, the workforce. (Departing from her emphasis on cities, at least initially, Jacobs details how Uruguay became a supply region during the Second World War, but lost its advantage as other countries recovered and Uruguay failed to develop city economies.)

Given the vitality of great city economies, and Jacobs's emphasis on exports, one might ask, "why not export whole industries far away and start the process once more?" Far from charity, this would seem to be in an enterprise's best interest: reach far to build greater strength. Jacobs concedes the possibility of the first point of that hypothetical question—"transplant regions"[47] do exist—but not the second. Some—that word again—

> enterprises that a city generates can move, but can't move far. They are tethered to relationships with other producers or consumers or both [. . .] Conversely, freedom from those relationships, the very freedom that makes an industry capable of moving to a distant region with a city, automatically creates transplant economies that do not produce much for themselves, no matter how successful at attracting industries.[48]

Transplanted enterprises take advantage of distant localities. They take up space and make demands on local infrastructure. They are creatures of efficient routine, but not the source of the improvisatory development that fuels the export-import dynamic. And "this is the nature of successful economic improvisation of any sort: if it works, it isn't because it is abstractly or theoretically 'the right thing' but because it is [. . .] practical for the time, the place, and the resources and opportunities at hand."[49] Transplant enterprises are free to pick up and plant a flag elsewhere: they are, to return to a civic metaphor, expats with no abiding ties. The regions need stay-at-home citizens.

Cities and regions need something else, too: capital. In accenting the reciprocal export and import relationship, highlighting risk-taking and trial-and-error development work, and noting the often problematic involvement of government in economic planning, I have given it scant formal attention. But attention must be paid.

Capital and Its Mysteries: Money, Material, Love, Sweat, and Brains

Capital is a word with many shades of meaning. Several years ago, Thomas Piketty's *Capital in the Twenty-First Century*, a 900-page exposition of economic theory and policy, enjoyed remarkable longevity on the *New York Times*' best-seller list. Piketty's title, of course, recalled Marx's *Das Kapital*. Concern with the injustice of inequality binds both books: Marx saw inevitable revolution issuing from it and while Piketty does not speak of revolution, he fears the social discord born of the widening of the gap between rich and poor. While revolution as Marx envisioned it may not be in the offing, class resentments and social distress will compound dangerously, thinks Piketty, as long as a wealthy class can enjoy a return on its investments that surpasses the growth of ordinary wages on which most people rely. Capitalism is a rough master on these terms. It rewards those who have the luxury of funds to invest and dividends to reap and ignores those who lack the same.

As we have seen, even in *Death and Life*, Jacobs had warned of the consequences of opportunity denied for access to capital. In the case of poor neighborhoods, often redlined by banks, lending was scant or nonexistent. But while some argued the need for government funds in massive amounts for large projects to resolve the problems, she offered caution. She worried about the source of the money, its volume, the knowledge of its dispensers, and its lingering effects.

Jacobs captured these reservations in her discussion of the perils of "cataclysmic"[50] money and the salutary effects of "gradual" money. Cataclysmic money—money on the grand and overwhelming scale—might come from private, commercial sources, the black market, or most usually, from government coffers. It worked dire effects on cash-starved cities since "these three kinds of money behave not like irrigation systems, bringing life-giving streams to feed steady, continual growth. Instead, they behave like manifestations of malevolent climates beyond the control of man—affording either searing droughts or torrential, eroding floods."[51] Jacobs, like Aristotle, would never suppose that unlimited money was good in itself: it all depends on ends and uses, on timing and means of conveyance. The subsidiarity principle applies here: too much money can overflow and flood local channels.

If the sheer volume of cataclysmic money threatens cities, so, too, does the vision that impels the flow. Whether the source be the government, wed to a vision that prizes the automobile, or private lending, which sniffs at thriving, if unkempt, neighborhoods, or shadow money, which sees apartments as income units to be flipped and maximized, problems follow the money. "The decay of cities [. . .] goes right down to what we think we want, and to our ignorance about how cities work."[52] Where there is no vision, the people perish, Scripture says, but not any vision will do. Visions divorced from local knowledge and shorn of respect for local residents are colonial visions. They come with strings attached, chains that link back to the colonizer.

The bonds often involve goods, sometimes materiel, as well as money; or, more precisely, they may fund the purchase of stuff that the grantee wants to push. In analyzing "Capital for Regions without Cities,"[53] Jacobs has this in mind. "Carried away by the power of money to finance great capital undertakings, many people seem to think of such investments as being development itself. Build the dam and you have development! But in real life, build the dam and unless you also have solvent city markets and transplanted industries, you have nothing."[54] This is the "thing theory of development,"[55] mentioned previously; and absent markets and industries, things will fall apart, despite the center's hopes.

To extend the metaphor: colonization can occur within national boundaries. Jacobs saw this in the rise of the "Sunbelt Cities," sometimes heralded as promising new forms of urbanization. Misplaced hope, she concluded: "the Sunbelt Cities are trade-off cities,"[56] fueled by the transfer of retirement incomes from one part of the country to another and, more ominously, sustained by what she calls "transactions of decline."[57]

Those transactions come in three forms—"prolonged and unremitting military production; prolonged and unremitting subsidies to poor regions; heavy promotion of trade between advanced and backward economies"[58]—and all are at play in Sunbelt Cities as well as in underdeveloped countries receiving foreign investment. Note the qualifying phrases: "prolonged and unremitting," "heavy" promotion. Committed to the subsidiarity principle, Jacobs recognized the need for one level of government to assist another. Poor regions do need help. But making them perpetual wards of government overseers does nothing to help them grow strong. If a city starved for capital settles for these transactions, always seeking more of the same, then no economic development will occur. "Military transactions," for instance, occur "at the expense of intercity trade and also at the expense of the import-replacing process."[59] To put it baldly, cities won't—can't—swap tanks and missiles with each other, nor will spin-off arms manufacturers be allowed. Military concerns are national concerns, and though financed with city dollars, they do not fuel the export-import systems that drive a city's economy. City economies dependent on transactions of decline always remain vassal economies.

Yet, even for cities strapped for conventional capital or remote from the engendering power of other cities, Jacobs saw hopeful signs. For the most important capital available to cities is human capital. This is the insight that first captured Robert Lucas's attention. Even as she describes the grim consequences of transactions of decline, Jacobs points to the possible sources of regeneration. Cities "require continually repeated inputs of energy in two specific forms: innovations, which at bottom are inputs of human insight; and ample replacements of imports, which at bottom are inputs of the human capacity to make adaptive initiatives."[60] Human beings make do, make the best of what's at hand, make some things new and some things different. Left free of interference, they are not inclined to settle for the same old, same old. They will stake a bet on themselves, and others, and use their own resources—"love capital," Jacobs calls it somewhere—to build a vibrant North End in Boston, say, while a blinkered government sees only a shabby surround, or develop a capacity for making pottery or ships or bicycles without waiting for permission. "Learned helplessness" occurs only when every innovative effort or personal sacrifice feels the blunt force of formal restraint or when the seduction of continuing economic subsidies causes an agent to become a vassal.

It is no surprise, then, that Jacobs sees the promise of allowing for "drift,"[61] rather than plumping for a confidently plotted master plan for encouraging development. To borrow the term of the development economist William Easterly, Jacobs is a "searcher,"[62] not a planner. She champions the efficacy of curiosity, drive, and energy as people strive to forge new solutions to new problems. And they will find a solution, given the rein, since

> It is natural for human beings to build new kinds of work and skills on earlier kinds because the capacity to do this is naturally built into us, like the capacity to understand and use a language in an open-ended way [. . .] Without the capacity to add new work to our earlier work, new skills to our earlier skills—as all human beings do individually starting in infancy, and as we do collectively in developing human economic life—we might be something else, but we wouldn't be human beings.[63]

In *Death and Life*, Jacobs had decried the "deep contempt for ordinary people"[64] she saw engrained in the assumptions of planners and bureaucrats. Since nonprofessionals couldn't possibly know what's best for them, it would be better to decide on their behalf. Nonsense to all of that, said Jacobs. Human beings are born problem-solvers. Each of us struggles, literally, to get a foothold in the world as we move from infancy to toddling. Each of us struggles to master the symbols encoded as language. With the aid of others, we come to a deeper understanding of ourselves and a purchase on the world at large. Collectively, we craft an economic life and a politics that respond to the contingencies we encounter. Facing those contingencies is our work, *is*, in fact, the basis of economic life. This is genuine economic development, not something "given. It has to be *done*. It is a process."[65]

Like infants, we learn by practice and support and not a little pain. Throughout her economic analysis, Jacobs returns to the idea of natural, organic development. Aristotle emphasized this, too: human beings have a natural capacity that they actualize by their own effort, and with the prodigious aid of many others—family, friends, neighbors, teachers, et al.—and which yields the possibility of community, something much greater than an assortment of the pooled interests of different individuals. This emphasis on organic development in Jacobs's work brings two other antecedents to mind.

The first is the great Victorian economist Alfred Marshall (1842–1924). In the preface to the eighth edition of his *Principles of Economics* (1920), Marshall asserts that

> The Mecca of the economist lies in economic biology rather than in economic dynamics. But biological conceptions are more complex than those of mechanics; a volume on Foundations must therefore give a relatively large place to mechanical analogies; and frequent use is made of the term "equilibrium," which suggests something of statical [*sic*] analogy. This fact . . . has suggested the notion that its central idea is "statical," rather than "dynamical." But in fact it is concerned throughout with the forces that cause movement: and its key-note is that of dynamics, rather than statics.[66]

For Marshall, economics was a preeminently human science, hence fraught with ethical significance. He wrote that

> The main concern of economics is thus with human beings who are impelled, for good and evil, to change and progress. Fragmentary statical hypotheses are used as temporary auxiliaries to dynamical—or rather biological—conceptions; but the central idea of economics, even when its Foundations alone are under discussion, must be that of living force and movement.[67]

At the end of his preface, Marshall acknowledged that the mathematicians, armed with sophisticated analytic methods, were coming to the study of economics and that their influence would be profound, but he did not see economics as reducible to quantitative analysis or utilitarian weighing of costs and benefits. Indeed, in sketching the hoped-for characteristics of the economist, he writes, "The economist needs three great intellectual faculties, perception, imagination and reason: and most of all he needs imagination, to put him on the track of those causes of visible events which are remote or lie below the surface, and of those effects of visible causes which are remote or lie below the surface."[68] A paragraph later, Marshall cites the advantage accruing to the physical scientist by virtue of his ability to return to "subsequent observation or experiment."[69] The emphasis on recurrent observation and experiment seems of a piece with the painstaking collection of data that Jacobs commended in her *AER* piece on helping cities. (By coincidence, Robert Lucas delivered his breakthrough paper on economic development as part of the Marshall Lectureship at Cambridge University.)

A second parallel for Jacobs's approach is contemporary: her commitment to organic order, indeed a reverence for the order that emerges from nature and human beings following their natural intelligence and insight, has remarkable similarity to the method and work of the geneticist Barbara McLintock. As Evelyn Fox Keller notes in her biographical study of McClintock, *A Feeling for the Organism*, (1983) "through years of intense and systematic observation and interpretation (she called it 'integrating what you saw'), McClintock had built a theoretical vision, a highly articulated image of the world within the cell."[70] Her methods were thought old-fashioned, particularly in the wake of the new experimental tack in molecular biology. McClintock's commitment to seeing and understanding—that work of integrating—in the plant world seems remarkably similar to Jacobs's methods. How does understanding develop? "Her answer," writes Keller,

> is simple. Over and over again, she tells us one must have time to look, the patience to "hear what the material has to say to you," the openness to "let it come to you." Above all, "one must have a feeling for the organism. One must understand how it grows, understand its parts, understand when something is going wrong with it. [An organism] isn't just a piece of plastic, it's something that is being constantly affected by the environment, constantly showing attributes or disabilities in its growth. You have to be aware of all of that."[71]

Marshall, McClintock, and Jacobs were all poised to "hear what the material has to say to you." This is not a poise easily attained, given the natural human inclination to meet any situation with a headful of preconceptions. It is a poise perhaps best described by the French social critic and philosopher Simone Weil as she reflected upon the phenomenon of attention. Faced with a person afflicted in mind and body and spirit, the very best that one can hope to do, said Weil, is to ask that person "what are you going through?"[72] That question gives reverent, central regard to the sufferer. Diagnosis and prescription give way to presence. So, similarly, with McClintock, Marshall, and Jacobs, attention to the organism allows one to sideline preformed theory and conjecture. To understand corn, or the economy, or city life generally, one must pay attention to it as something alive.

And the city is something alive, stretched across time, sustained by its makers. Consider the passage in which Jacobs describes, beautifully, the cumulative, if often unacknowledged, effect of human capital across centuries and cultures. As she draws her chapter on "Explosive City Growth" in *Economy* to a close, she writes:

> What I am saying is that every city has a direct economic ancestry, a literal economic parentage, in a still older city or cities. New cities do not arise by spontaneous generation. The spark of city economic life is passed on from older cities to younger. It lives on today in cities whose ancestors have long since gone to dust. New York, far from having sprung from the Erie Canal (a mere artifact of New York), is more likely the great-great-great-great-grandcity of Urartu, say, by a descent that traces back through London, Venice, Constantinople, Rome, and Vetulonia or Tarquinii, oldest of Etruscan cities. These links of life may extend—perilously tenuous at times but unbroken—backward through the cities of Crete, Phoenicia, Egypt, the Indus, Babylonia, Sumeria, Mesopotamia, back to Catal Huyuk itself and beyond, to the unknown ancestors of Catal Huyuk.[73]

All around us are the traces of the gifts of many, invisible city-dwellers throughout time. We should attend carefully—something new may be just around the corner—and be grateful.

Notes

1 "The City of Man," *Time*, June 13, 1969.

2 My sketch of new growth theory relies heavily on David Warsh, *Knowledge and the Wealth of Nations: A Story of Economic Discovery* (W. W. Norton, 2007).

3 For the Lucas paper, see https://www.parisschoolofeconomics.eu/docs/darcillon -thibault/lucasmechanicseconomicgrowth.pdf.

4 Sympathetic accounts of the explanatory powers of Jacobs's thought can also be found in the work of Pierre Desroschers and David Ellerman. See, for example, Desroschers on "Cities and the economic development of nations: an essay on Jane Jacobs's contribution to economic theory" in the *Canadian Journal of Regional*

Science 301: 119–134 and Ellerman in "Jane Jacobs as a Development Thinker," www.ellerman.org.

5   This discussion relies on Warsh, *Knowledge*, 306–307.

6   Warsh, *Knowledge*, 308.

7   David Nowlan in Max Allen (ed.), *Ideas that Matter: The Worlds of Jane Jacobs* (Ginger Press, 1997), 113.

8   Edward Glaeser, *Triumph of the City: How Our Greatest Invention Makes Us Richer, Smarter, Greener, Healthier, and Happier* (Penguin, 2011), 145.

9   "Jacobs's initial premise is certainly fallacious. . . .But while the opening premise of Jacobs's analysis proves faulty, and while her arguments do not prove that agriculture was invented in the city, the margin of uncertainty around that period is such that the hypothesis cannot be rejected outright." Paul Bairoch, *Cities and Economic Development: From the Dawn of History to the Present*, trans. Christopher Braider (Chicago, IL: The University of Chicago, 1988), 17. Robert Kanigel surveys scholarly contention on this issue in *Eyes on the Street: The Life of Jane Jacobs* (New York: Alfred A. Knopf, 2016), 295.

10   Jacobs, *Economy*, 33.

11   Roger Crowley, *City of Fortune: How Venice Ruled the Seas* (Random House, 2011), 5.

12   Jacobs, *Wealth*, 59ff.

13   Crowley, *City of Fortune*, 144.

14   Crowley, *City of Fortune*, 150.

15   Jacobs, *Nature*, 55.

16   Jacobs, *Nature*, 56.

17   Jacobs, *Economy, 48.*

18   Jacobs, *Economy*, 63ff.

19   Jacobs, *Economy*, 61ff.

20   Jacobs, *Economy*, 81.

21   Jacobs, *Economy*, 102.

22   See the Appendix to *The Economy of Cities* for a set of diagrams tracing the impact of interweaving exports and imports.

23   Jacobs, *Economy*, 125.

24   Jacobs, *Economy*, 134.

25   Jacobs, *Economy*, 145.

26   Jacobs, *Economy*, 158.

27   Jacobs, *Economy*, 160.

28   Jacobs, *Economy*, 247.

29   Jacobs, *Economy*, 206–207.

30   Jacobs, *Economy*, 217.

31 See Abhijit V. Banerjee and Esther Duflo, *Poor Economics: Rethinking Poverty and the Ways to End It* (Random House India, 2011) and *Good Economics for Hard Times* (PublicAffairs, 2019). Jacobs, who died in 2006, would have applauded this work.

32 Darren Acemoglu and James Robinson, *Why Nations Fail* (New York: Crown, 2012), 152.

33 Acemoglu and James Robinson, *Why Nations Fail*, 156.

34 Jacobs, *Economy*, 74.

35 Jane Jacobs, "Strategies for Helping Cities," in Samuel Zipp and Nathan Storring (eds.), *Vital Little Plans* (Random House, 2016), 186. Published originally in the *American Economic Review*, 1969.

36 Jacobs, *Death and Life*, 441.

37 Jacobs, *Death and Life*, 16.

38 Jacobs, *Death and Life*, 19.

39 Note: For Jacobs's own differentiation of these terms, see the Appendix to *Economy*.

40 Jane Jacobs, *The Question of Separatism: Quebec and the Struggle over Sovereignty* (Random House, 1980), 10.

41 Jacobs, *Question*, 16.

42 Jacobs, *Question*, 13.

43 Jacobs, *Wealth*, 44.

44 Jacobs, *Wealth*, 59.

45 Jacobs, *Wealth*, 63, chapter 6 passim.

46 Jacobs, *Wealth*, chapter 5 passim.

47 Jacobs, *Wealth*, chapter 7.

48 Jacobs, *Wealth*, 98.

49 Jacobs, *Wealth*, 101–102.

50 Jacobs, *Death and Life*, chapter 16.

51 Jacobs, *Death and Life*, 239.

52 Jacobs, *Death and Life*, 317.

53 Jacobs, *Wealth*, chapter 8.

54 Jacobs, *Wealth*, 105.

55 Jane Jacobs, *The Nature of Economies* (Random House, 2000), 32.

56 Jacobs, *Wealth*, 201.

57 Jacobs, *Wealth*, chapter 12 passim.

58 Jacobs, *Wealth*, 183.

59 Jacobs, *Wealth*, 189.

60 Jacobs, *Wealth*, 193.

61 Jacobs, *Wealth*, chapter 14.

62 William Easterly, "Planners vs. Searchers in Foreign Aid," *Asian Development Bank*, January 18, 2006.

63 Jacobs, *Wealth*, 224.

64 Jacobs, *Death and Life*, 82.

65 Jacobs, *Wealth*, 119.

66 Alfred Marshall, *Principles of Economics* (Macmillan, 1920), xiv.

67 Marshall, *Principles of Economics*, xiv.

68 Marshall, *Principles of Economics*, xv.

69 Marshall, *Principles of Economics*, 42.

70 Evelyn Fox Keller, *A Feeling for the Organism: The Life and Work of Barbara McClintock* (Freeman, 1983), 12.

71 Keller, *A Feeling for the Organism*, 12.

72 Simone Weil, "On the Right Use of School Studies," in *Waiting for God*, trans. Emma Craufurd (Harper, 1973), 115.

73 Jacobs, *Economy*, 176.

5

Work in the City

Traders, Guardians, and Makers

The vital city economies described by Jane Jacobs bubble with all kinds of work. Should anyone doubt the extraordinary range of work found in cities, she advised the doubters to consult their local Yellow Pages. Although largely supplanted by digital equivalents, print versions still exist, and as I flip through the first few pages of the Worcester, Massachusetts pages, I find accountants, addiction specialists, advertising, air conditioning contractors; and that is just getting started in the "A's."

Jacobs celebrates entrepreneurs, those who make their own way, but she well knew that all work is not of this kind. While solo practitioners—butchers, bakers, and candlestick makers—do populate small craft industries, most people report to do work not of their own making but at the direction of others. Assembly lines persist, even if without the stultifying routine that perplexed Charlie Chaplin in *Modern Times*; now, robots assist workers and vice versa. Building and restoring are always with us, so construction persists, perhaps without the heroic figures of the brawny men pictured in Thomas Hart Benton's *America Now* mural or the daring laborers on high steel or the women welders captured in the photography of Margaret Bourke White. In the contemporary American economy, services predominate, both the highly personal services rendered in spas, boutiques, salons, and restaurants, and the highly glossed professional services of the legal and health care industries and the services rendered at distance, and electronically, by banks, insurance companies, and retailers. Teachers and preachers, musicians, actors, and professional athletes all put their services at our disposal.

As Jacobs considered the seemingly unlimited number of ways to make a living, she delivered a surprising judgment in *Systems of Survival* (1992). There is a deep logic to the economies of human living, she argued, and at root there are but two basic ways to make a living, each with a unique moral orientation. Given the bewildering array of ways to make a living, one would rightly suspect a similarly bewildering set of codes, ethics, and guidelines to govern the conduct of work. How could one subsume factory workers and information technology specialists and cooks and lawyers and soccer players under one of two headings? The US Bureau of Labor Statistics[1] identifies twenty-five occupational groups, from Architecture and Engineering to Transportation and Material Moving; the Production category alone has fifteen subgroups, from Assemblers and Fabricators to Bakers and Quality Control Inspectors. The diversity Jacobs celebrated in the city seems vitiated by the suggestion that just two moral orientations govern our collective working life.

Order! Order!

Astonishing as this claim might be, there were foreshadowings of her analysis in earlier works. Beginning with *Death and Life*, Jacobs had insisted that a city's civic order emerged in organic fashion. As varied and complicated as a city's enterprises and politics were, as those Yellow Pages attest, "a marvelous order"[2] governed their emergence and interconnection. The order was not a master plan, orchestrated and imposed from without. One didn't wait for solutions to be administered. Neighbors and citizens, alone or together in small groups or through, when needed, the instrumentalities of government, addressed the problems at hand. Order might not appear immediately, nor was it always easily perceived. Jacobs took the long view. Cities and their economies struggle over generations. Nevertheless, the "innate, functioning order"[3] of the city was generated and sustained by dense networks which were, as in the case of sidewalks, "intricate, almost unconscious . . . [and which established] voluntary controls and standards among the people themselves."[4] What would organic order look like in the bustling interplay of people making a living? Conflict would seem inevitable: Wall Street's ways are not Main Street's; buyers still need to heed the caution of *caveat emptor*. How could so many different kinds of people be expected to compete, to cooperate, to concede, if need be, and live with their differences? Jacobs thought that they could, but she left it to her later work to specify how.

One finds a first glimmer of the later project in *Cities and the Wealth of Nations*. There, Jacobs began to worry about the persistence and durability of organically self-regulating systems in the domain of work. *Wealth* opened with fierce criticism of economists' failure to explain stagflation, and it continued the emphasis, developed in *The Economy of Cities*, on the indispensability of the import-replacement process for economic development. In its latter chapters, she had considered Sun Belt cities, like Dallas, Houston, and Phoenix, and other urban regions whose swelling populations were tied to the defense economy or benefited from a tide of Rust Belt retirees tired of the wet and cold. These regions, the sites of military bases, defense-related industries, and the enterprises that sprung up to serve both, had drawn migration from the Rust Belt and other deindustrialized areas. But military-related spending, though it swelled local coffers, she argued, was a poor spur to economic development as she understood it. The industries were comprised of "captive divisions of labor,"[5] within large organizations, not fertile nodes of innovation, cross-fertilization, and entrepreneurial vigor. Jacobs had a deeper fear: she sensed that military concerns and economic development forces were at odds. Development, as she understood it, organic and unpredictable, wants to bust out all over; military logic wants to eliminate outbursts. In describing "The Predicament,"[6] facing theorists who sought new patterns of economic development and their disappointment with various failed strategies, she noted that "military arts derive from the hunting and raiding life, economics from the making and trading life. Many assumptions, institutions and virtues that work very well in the one serve badly in the other."[7] Hunters and raiders inhabit a moral ecology different from that shared by makers and traders. Makers and traders use things found at hand or via gift or exchange and their own good energy and insights to meet human need. Hunter-raiders seize what they need: they are *opportunistic*. Makers and traders seize *opportunities*. Habits that ensured success in the hunting and raiding life might prove disastrous if transposed to the making and trading life, and vice versa. Designing a more efficient bow or more lethal sword is not the same as enjoying the strength and skill to employ them. Departments of commerce and departments of defense don't share quarters. The alternatives were stark: one either traded or raided. Traders, it seemed, were the genuine economic innovators. Raiders pillaged what others had made. But Jacobs was not satisfied with this formulation.

Hunters and Raiders, Makers and Traders Reconceived

The "hunting and raiding" versus "making and trading" distinction would issue in what Jacobs termed the distinction between guardian and commercial "syndromes," the heart of *Systems of Survival*. *Systems* was a dramatic departure from Jacobs's customary style. Instead of a straightforward exposition of a position, she created a kind of Platonic *Symposium*, where a cast of characters probed "the web of trust upon which so much business depends."[8] The participants were a varied professional lot: Armbruster, a retired publisher and the symposium's convener; Kate, an animal biologist; Hortense, a lawyer; Jasper, a crime novelist; Quincy, a banker; and Ben, an author and environmental activist. They meet occasionally over good coffee, fine wine, and dessert. (In *The Nature of Economies* (2000), there is a partial reunion and another set of symposia where Kate, Hortense, and Armbruster are joined by a father and son team of ecologists, Hiram and Murray.) As the late reference to raiding and trading in *Wealth* suggested, Jacobs's project had been long in the making. But before she unfolded her idea at length, she took an important, largely unknown, step that deserves notice for the light it sheds upon *Systems* and the longer trajectory of her work.

The occasion was a conference, held on April 10 and 11, 1987, under the auspices of the Lonergan Workshop at Boston College. (Bernard Lonergan, SJ, was a Catholic philosopher and theologian whose masterwork, *Insight* exercised profound influence in both disciplines. Lonergan had once quipped, "if you want to understand what insight is, read *Death and Life*. There is an insight on every page." For her part, Jane Jacobs would also read Lonergan's then unpublished treatise on economics.) The conference topic was "Values and Ethics in Making a Living," and Jacobs offered two lectures and engaged in conversation with respondents. Jacobs later confided that her enjoyment of the back-and-forth of the workshop discussion prompted her to recast *Systems of Survival* as a conversation among peers.

In the first lecture, Jacobs elaborated on the raider-trader distinction mentioned in *Wealth*. We can make a living in one of two ways, she argued: "we can simply take what we need or want without by-your-leave" and "as a kind of shorthand, although I am not fully satisfied with the term, I shall call this approach and its many later derivatives and offshoots, 'raiding,' its ethics and value code the raiding system."[9] At the same time, "we can assemble or produce certain items, or provide a service, and by voluntary negotiation and agreement, exchange what we have for other things we need or want [. . .] I shall call this approach and its many derivatives and offshoots 'trading.'"[10] Each system has distinctive elements, and they could be captured in a table.

Table 5.1 The original table. Boston College Lectures.

The Trading System	The Raiding System
Shun force	Shun Trading
Come to voluntary agreement	Exert Prowess
Be honest	Be obedient and disciplined
Collaborate easily with strangers and aliens	Adhere to tradition
Compete	Respect hierarchy
Respect contracts	Be loyal
Use initiative and enterprise	Take vengeance
Be open to inventiveness and novelty	Make rich use of leisure
Be efficient	Be ostentatious
Promote comfort and convenience	Dispense largesse
Invest for productive purposes	Deceive for the sake of the task
Be industrious	Show fortitude
Be thrifty	Treasure honor
Security	Be exclusive
Compromise	

There are subtle differences between the brief comment in *Wealth* about raiders and traders and the theme as announced in the lectures. In *Wealth*, Jacobs had seemingly confined economic life to the making and trading life; the hunting and raiding life yielded no economics, only the military arts. Now, she recognized both raiders and traders pursuing economic life: it's the form that differs. If economics is about making a living, everyone, hunter and trader alike, has to make a living. Nor is it the case that hunter-raiders need to be at constant odds with maker-traders: each has a living to make and each must pursue it on their own terms. Of course there can be aberrations within the systems—hunters who despoil their hunting range, traders who tamper with the scales—and between them—the hunter-raider next door might decide that the neighboring maker-traders are easy pickings and snatch away their goods; traders might adulterate goods for sale. But hunter-raiders, should they seek a stable base of operations, would do well to make peace with maker-traders and protect their common interest in survival. And maker-traders might well beware the implicit threat of force.

The distinction between the raider and trader systems proposed in the lectures undergoes further revision in *Systems*. Terms and format change. Hunter-raiders are now guardians. Maker-traders share the commercial syndrome. Items come and go from the original table as noted below. Format undergoes a startling

Table 5.2 The table revised. *Systems of Survival.*

The Commercial Syndrome	The Guardian Syndrome
Shun force	Shun Trading
Come to voluntary agreement	Exert Prowess
Be honest	Be obedient and disciplined
Collaborate easily with strangers and aliens	Adhere to tradition
Compete	Respect hierarchy
Respect contracts	Be loyal
Use initiative and enterprise	Take vengeance
Be open to inventiveness and novelty	Make rich use of leisure
Be efficient	Be ostentatious
Promote comfort and convenience	Dispense largesse
Dissent for the sake of the task*	Deceive for the sake of the task
Invest for productive purposes	Show fortitude
Be industrious	Be fatalistic*
Be thrifty	Treasure honor
Be optimistic*	Be exclusive
[Security]**	
[Compromise]**	
*First appears in *Systems*	**Included in Boston College lectures, omitted in *Systems*

revision: the straightforward expository prose of the lectures gives way to an imagined conversation conducted among a diverse set of characters.

The alterations can be ambiguous. In the preface, for instance, Jacobs says that all animals can find and pick up things and make territories, but only the human animal trades and produces for trade. It's hard to escape the suggestion that the hunter-raider system, now called the guardian syndrome, falls far short of human potential at its best. Still, Jacobs was judicious in explaining how guardian culture may guard well.

There is a further ambiguity to note. When one of the dialogue's characters, Kate, presents the commercial syndrome—formerly the maker-trader prototype—she omits mention of making or producing, although she presupposes *trading* "our goods and services."[11] Where do these goods and services originate? Where do traders get them?

In a question-and-answer session during the Boston College conference, one conferee pursued the idea of "making" as a form of "making a living" separate and distinct from trading. Jacobs replied, "I think they use the same system, if they are successful. Producing *organizations* [emphasis mine] use the same system of ethics and values as trading organizations. They are not distinct. Successful banking uses the same system."[12]

Her response shifts the focus to the case of organizations, but a question remains: does Jacobs's commercial syndrome adequately capture the "making" undertaken by an individual working alone or in a small group? Or is a third syndrome required to account for these kinds of work? Jacobs's syndromes table suggests, I think, that making *does* occupy a third space, one that incorporates elements of the other two.

Consider a furniture maker. He must learn his craft, and that will require guardian-like attention to tradition. As he progresses from apprentice to master, struggling to perfect his craft, he demonstrates prowess. He must be obedient and disciplined, knowing the measure of his tools and the quality of his materials. In all of this, he acts as the guardian.

But trading precepts are of equal importance in his "making." He must bring initiative and enterprise to his project. As he employs his tools and materials, he must discover solutions to problems—the knot in the grain, the limits of his technical skills—via invention and the realization of novelty. And in all of this undertaking, he must be industrious. He has chosen his own devices; no one else will make the items for him.

I was the beneficiary of this kind of craftsmanship. A friend presented me with a cherry side table modeled on a Shaker design by a famous New England craftsman. Before I had a chance to comment on its elegance, he turned it over and began identifying flaws: a less-than-perfect join here, a slight imperfection there. He had learned his craft by apprenticeship to a master and developed it— he would not say "perfected" it—by continuing practice, the production of one item after another. And when he presented my wife and me with a Shaker dining table, modeled on the same craftsman's design, it was clear that his industry, initiative, and prowess had reached a very fine level. His making blended elements of both syndromes.

Or consider the writers of literary fiction, lionized (or denounced!) for their daring creations. They, too, must know their tradition, their chosen language, even as they innovate within it. They must submit to the discipline imposed by the language even as they coax novel possibilities from it. An innovator at their writing desks, they are also heirs and guardians of a rich tradition.

The furniture maker and the writer are but two examples of the hybridization of the commercial and guardian syndromes. Scholars, teachers and preachers, stage actors, and jazz musicians also qualify. While Jacobs did not allow for a third way for making, as I am suggesting, she was attuned to art and to other anomalies. Lawyers, she suggests, may onetime play the trader, another the guardian.[13] And art stands apart: "its independent provenance from both taking and trading does seem to make it sui generis, and its difficulties different from those of commerce and guardianship,"[14] concludes Armbruster, the symposium convenor.

Nor did Jacobs insist that every aspect of life be accounted for between the two syndromes. Kate pleads, "maybe personal love in all its aspects—friendship, love among family members, sexual love, the intensely personal love of the artist for the art or the scholar for the subject—is too profoundly important to us to be governed by something so extraneous to love as the structures of commerce and guardianship."[15] That Jacobs would allow for exceptions is not surprising. Unlike a certain kind of system builder who would brook no exceptions to his carefully wrought designs, Jacobs was always, as in her observations of cities, alert to the flaws in the pattern, the rough edges, and the unexpected event. Each human action, said Aristotle, is unique and unrepeatable. Hence, he and Jacobs insisted on knowing the particulars of the circumstances in which one acts. Embedded human action—this decision, here and now, taken in this way—overflows the strict dimensions of idealized ethical systems.

Working "With" and Working "For"

Setting aside art and leaving the question of making as a hybrid syndrome apart, what of the work of organizations? In response to the interlocutor's question at the Boston College conference about making as distinct from trading and raiding, recall that Jacobs focused on *organizations* in her response. Jacobs's persistent attention to the creativity and energy of the individual entrepreneurs and the self-organizing group often draws the charge of romanticizing the work of individuals and small groups. But it is clear that she appreciates that large-scale, organized efforts differ in size and kind from cottage-scale efforts. Organized work, as distinct from solo effort, evokes a new set of questions. These involve the roles that exist within an organization, the persons who fill those roles, and the overarching work or purpose of the organization.

If an organization is to achieve its goals, it must be clear about who does what and the details of that doing: where, when, how, and with whom. Roles restrict or deny the freelancer. The interlocking of roles, when an organization functions well, should produce optimal results for the operation.

One qualifies for a role by virtue of achievement or promise. Once occupied, the role fixes a person's function within an organization: she does numbers, he leads design, they staff both. Within their spheres of competence, so the theory goes, workers are left to their own, supervised devices. By doing their parts, the employees contribute to the success of the larger organization.

The diversity of roles required within any complicated organization suggests that most will need a mix of makers, traders, and guardians. There need not be a strict correlation of person to type to organization. I may be serving a guardian role within a relentlessly trading organization, or vice versa. A technician at a station in a laboratory works independently but in concert with others and under the supervision of a lab director. And an organization's ethos, or culture, may differ from any one individual's commitments. Still, when I work for an organization, I affirm, either implicitly or explicitly, its way of doing business. This can make for personal friction when personal values, commitments, and virtues seem at odds with one's workplace.

The world of work is so varied that we should not be surprised to find traders and guardians intermingled, even if their formal role definitions and areas of responsibility pull them apart. Not every employee of a mutual fund company, for example, is a trader, though it is itself a trading organization. Nor is every government employee a guardian writ small: she may be a trader in her tasks even as she staffs the guardian organization. The "dancers" in Jacobs's celebration of the "ballet" of Hudson Street in *Death and Life* were a varied cast: a butcher, locksmith, delicatessen owner, laundry owner, baker, longshoremen, business executives, a tailor, and a barkeep. In these ranks, most, if not all, would have worked within the commercial syndrome, but executives and barkeeps alike have to play the guardian role, too. In the city, formal guardians are often a silent, background presence, important in preserving public order by formal policing, but they are at work in bureaus and offices, too: behind a desk supervising public health, updating the voting rolls, and so on. Sometimes, they are dangerously, if softly, overweening in drawing up regulations and bureaucratizing city life. In the worst case, guardians act violently under the auspices of their role.

Thus it is clear that the two syndromes do not exhaust all possibilities, nor are they strict binaries. They can function symbiotically. Commerce, after all, drives the economy and guarantees, at one remove, the taxes that will sustain the operations of government. But trade needs the shelter guardians provide: adjudication of disputes, securing of place, setting rules—just enough as needed—to ensure a fair and open marketplace.

And whether trader, guardian, or some hybrid, there is a common set of principles and virtues, a shared moral substrate, Jacobs asserted. Common to both are "universals—cooperation, courage, patience, and so on."[16] (In the Boston College lectures, Jacobs unfurled a somewhat different list: "courage, responsibility, competence, good judgment, and so on."[17]) On the basis of these universals, and in response to the exigencies of commercial and guardian life, she suggested, the two syndromes emerge.

By arguing for a universal *core* of moral principles while further identifying differing *expressions* of these in the two counterpoised syndromes, Jacobs was addressing the problem of moral relativism in what I think is an Aristotelian manner. She assumed that all people, given a proper upbringing, seek to do the right thing even as their capacities for thinking clearly and acting with insight and courage will vary enormously. Anthropologists have chronicled the enormous differences in cultural practice across regions, nations, and ethnicities. But the observed range of variations does not in itself entail a vindication of moral relativism.

In this matter, Aristotle again provides a helpful perspective. He famously described moral virtue as an act consisting in finding a mean relative to the actor. He insisted that no matter how varied or problematic the circumstances, one could discover the one right way to act. For Aristotle, moral virtue consisted in finding a mean between extremes of feeling and acting. Courage, for example, has to do with the feeling of fear. The courageous person, he argued, was not fearless: the person without fear was reckless, an extreme, just as a person paralyzed by fear—the other extreme—was cowardly. The courageous person had the right amount of fear, for the right reason, and in the right way. What was the right way? Here, Aristotle appealed to the example of a person known to be courageous. Be like them, as best you can, said Aristotle. The qualifier "as best you can" is crucial, for no one demonstrates courage in exactly the same way. Circumstances and human capacities differ. To clarify, Aristotle offered a humorous example of finding the mean relative to oneself. The Olympic wrestler, Milo, must necessarily consume much food and drink to sustain his strength. If I, a sedentary writer, were to follow his example, disaster—obesity, hypertension, elevated cholesterol—would ensue. Aristotle relied on the measure of the person of practical wisdom as a guide to right action, and he supposed that one would recognize such a person from one's own experience. Today, we might identify such a person as a mentor, a good example to follow.

To place this in Jacobs's terms: on the spot and in the midst of one's business affairs, the virtuous trader will know how to conduct herself. She will have learned what is appropriate and what violates the norms of the commercial syndrome, and she will do her best to pursue that right course. The determination of the right course, and the will to pursue it, will often be difficult—and she may fail, at times, since fear or circumstances might combine to deter her from doing what needs to be done—and others might dispute the decision taken, but the good trader knows what will sustain the integrity of the system. She is a casuist, in the good sense, someone sensitive to the particular challenges of acting in particular cases but appreciative of guiding principles. And her example can shape the tone of an organization. Others similarly situated will look to her. When we know a person of practical wisdom, we find ourselves wondering what she would do in our own circumstances.

Similarly, those entrusted with guardian powers face concrete decisions about how best to exercise them. Governments exercise power through their bureaus and, for many, a bureaucrat is, by definition, an unreflective rule follower, the unhelpful person at the end of the government helpline, the person in the iron cage, himself encaged by a welter of prescriptions. The bureaucrat, the popular conception goes, goes by the book and doesn't peer above his place in the hierarchy. But those who exercise their powers well know the importance of seeking equity in circumstances that are complex and hard to untangle and can find degrees of freedom in which to operate fairly. To take an industry I know well: in the bureaucracy of higher education, academic rules say that everyone must complete all assignments before a grade can be determined. But in the face of student illness, family distress, or tragedy, many a dean has relaxed that requirement and still served both the person and institution with equity. For the sake of fairness, the dean upholds the rule of law but knows when to lift its burdens.

In the Boston College lectures, an interlocutor observed, "there are similarities in your list of courage, tenacity, responsibility, competence and good judgment to what we know classically as the cardinal virtues."[18] St. Thomas Aquinas, the great philosopher and theologian of the Middle Ages, identified these as prudence, justice, fortitude, and temperance. The Boston College interlocutor paired Jacobs's terms in this way: he connected good judgment with prudence, tenacity with fortitude, competence with temperance or moderation and responsibility with justice. Jacobs welcomed the suggestion, and I think it animates her discussion of wisdom in chapter five of *Systems*. As Jasper and Kate concluded outlining the guardian syndrome, Kate says, "there are no substitutes for wisdom, either in commerce or guardianship.... Without wisdom everything limps along or breaks down. But wisdom is a complex quality, a combination of common sense, foresight, judgment, awareness, and moral courage."[19]

Kate offers, here, a condensed explanation of the character of the person Aristotle described as practically wise. The person of practical wisdom need not be formally schooled or a technical expert. She is an expert in the ability to know what needs to be done here and now, on the spot. Her expertise is about persons and places, tradition and the rhythms of community life, about what has a good likelihood of succeeding and what had best be left aside. Jane Jacobs was herself such a person, and she recognized kindred spirits from all walks of life, finding them among traders as well as guardians.

Uneasy Relationships: Traders and Guardians Together, and at Odds

Institutions that incorporate traders and guardians in pursuit of business success have difficult, contentious environments. Temperaments differ, and personal histories can interfere with clear thinking. Traders and guardians may clash with each other, forsake their responsibilities under pressure, or unwisely act the part of their counterpart, with traders guarding and guardians trading. Examples are not hard to find, and I will focus on three. The first draws on the history of the Republic of Venice; a second recounts the anonymous confession of a contemporary US risk manager in an investment bank; and a third traces the collapse of a Wall Street trading firm.

Venetians took pride in the city's republican form of government. Venice was led by a doge, or duke, who reflected, ostensibly, the will of the people. The doge was selected by a process that showed the trappings of democracy—the final candidate who emerged from a selection process needed to hear the full, public acclaim of the populace gathered in the Piazza San Marco—but concealed the deliberation and negotiation among the city's elite, and the most select of that elite, the Council of Ten.[20] Candidates were always drawn from a pool of the city's historic aristocracy; they were no strangers to wealth, commerce, and power. Indeed, it was just such familiarity that led the Council to hedge the doge, once installed, with restrictions on his freedom of movement, association and, of course, trade. These restrictions began with a contract and were reinforced by constant vigilance. Thus Doge Moro, ascending to his post in 1462, pledged in the formal document known as the *promissione*, among other things

> we cannot nor ought we to engage in trade, nor arrange for it to be done by any person in any way of any kind, either in or outside Venice, nor must we invest in any partnership; and we shall make our Dogaressa and our sons and nephews, whether or not they are living with us, swear that they will not engage in trade, nor arrange for it to be done by person in any way or of any kind either in or outside Venice, nor invest in any partnership. And similarly our daughters and nieces living with us are held and bound to the observance of all the foregoing. . .
>
> Moreover, we are obliged every two months to have the present capitulary and *promissio* of the Venetians clearly read to us in the right order. . .
>
> Moreover, we cannot nor ought we to go outside the Dogado [authorized places within the Venetian lagoon], unless by the wish of our Small and great Councils.[21]

The doge divested his investments, new investment was forbidden, and reminders of obligation were frequent. He could travel beyond Venice only with permission from the Council. In such fashion, the doge operated within the confines of his guardian role and avoided conflicts of interest. In Jacobs's terms, the doge was a guardian and hence not to be trusted in matters of trade and personal gain. Why all this caution and this bundle of restrictions? The Venetians were not naïve about power and its temptations, and they were tough in their dealings.

The records of the Venetian Republic attest to the need for regulations and stories of the inevitable efforts to subvert or avoid them. For example, after his death, Doge Agostin Barbaro was investigated for numerous instances of cooking the books, including underreporting wine received in tribute and selling it off via shell accounts. Venetian nobles proved no less susceptible to the temptation of self-aggrandizement than current businesspeople. Their venality prompted Domenico Morosini, himself a patrician, to excoriate the character and inclinations of his peers in arguing for a drastic reconstitution of office-holding. "In any republic," he argued

> there are many rich men, who are powerful and factious, and who are not worthy to hold offices, but who strive after those that they cannot justly obtain and attempt to gain them through devious means, so that worthy and meritorious men are most often rebuffed. Nothing is more dangerous and more destructive than this in a free republic. For men of thirst do not govern well. . . . Therefore, to guard against this evil, the magistracy should be divided.[22]

But Morosini's pleas went unheeded for then, as now, plutocracy guarded its privileges and resisted the sway of argument.

Jacobs would not have been surprised by either the outcome or the force of his claim. If modern politicians are cut from the same cloth as their Venetian counterparts, contemporary business faces similar problems in dealing with its leadership. Modern corporate organization devises its own answers to the problem of self-interested leaders and organizations that have commercial and guardian functions. Before pursuing my other two examples, I examine a typical modern answer.

Aligning Incentives

Just as the Venetian counselor Morosini did, so too do contemporary businesses feel the urgency of restricting their guardians. The Venetians hoped to accomplish their end by so restraining the exercise of personal interests that the Doge became, in effect, the embodiment of the republic, a paragon of good conduct and a light for all other cities to behold. A favorite tactic of modern businesses seems, at first blush, to stand at odds with that solution.

Corporate boards recognize the inescapability of self-interest by tying chief executive officer (CEO) compensation to corporate performance. In effect, the board says to the company's CEO, "do the best you can for the firm, show us results, and you will be well-rewarded." When self-interest is bound to the fortunes of the company, the leader's benefit is then the company's benefit, and vice versa. Personal gain—a bigger salary, more stock options, greater bonuses—accrues from corporate success. As a board links CEO compensation to improvements in a company's stock price, it "aligns" its own interests with those of the person charged to govern. Recognize and restrict self-interest, said the Venetians; recognize and unleash self-interest, responds the alignment theory.

This device has worked well, in cases, for its logic has power: who would not work hard for an organization that promises rewards commensurate with efforts? But there are traps as well. Boards, under pressure from stockholders and market analysts, may insist on a short-term focus, measuring progress by how much a company's stock has risen, quarter by quarter. This focus, in turn, can drive out any emphasis on a company's mission that can't be quantified in share prices, and it pushes questions of a firm's long-term prospects out of sight. Anxiety about failure to meet the expected benchmarks may prompt questionable choices that meet accounting standards but carry a trace of deception. In *Lights Out: Pride, Delusion and the Fall of General Electric* (2020), *The Wall Street Journal* reporters Ted Mann and Thomas Grypta trace the fall of General Electric from wealthy conglomerate to uncertain and much-diminished status. Top managers, fearful of missing their revenue targets, routinely used internal sales or the sell-off of a piece of a division's real estate portfolio at the close of a quarter to boost apparent profits, thus realizing a balance sheet gain, only to repurchase the property as the next quarter opened. Those sleights of hand disguised the truth about the firm's condition, both for internal management and outside investors and analysts.

Walling Off Functions

Below the level of the CEO and board, complex financial organizations segregate trading and guardian functions for the safety of both and often reinforce the segregation with the use of an in-house ombudsman. A young financial analyst, whose work required meeting with CEOs and chief financial officers (CFOs), told me how one of his meetings yielded inadvertent knowledge of a prospective merger. Such knowledge would be literal gold for his firm's traders, but he was troubled. He consulted his ombudsman, whose message was firm and clear: not a word to anyone on the trading side of the firm, and not a penny of yours for investment.[23]

Seeking counsel, as the young analyst did, presupposes a substrate of virtues, including honesty, which Jacobs saw as crucial. But pressures to deviate can be intense. In an anonymous piece published in *The Economist* of August 7, 2008, a risk manager reflected on what accounted for bank overexposure in the credit crisis. In effect, guardians and traders—risk managers and broker-traders—were at odds. There was money to be made, he wrote, and pressure was intense:

> The pressure on the risk department to keep up and approve transactions was immense. Psychology played a big part. The risk department had a separate reporting line to the board to preserve its independence. This had been reinforced by the regulators who believed it was essential for objective risk analysis and assessment. However, this separation hurt our relationship with the bankers and traders we were supposed to monitor.

> In their eyes, we were not earning money for the bank. Worse, we had the power to say no and therefore prevent business from being done. Traders saw us as obstructive and a hindrance to their ability to earn higher bonuses.

Too often, the risk manager confessed, his team gave in to the pressure, contributing to deep problems for the bank. Courage was lacking here but so, too, was something else: the risk team "had strong analytical skills, [but] were not necessarily good communicators and salesmen. Tactfully explaining why we said no was not our forte. Traders were often exasperated as much by how they were told as by what they were told."[24]

To recast this tension in Jacobs's terms, the traders and bankers hewed to the norms of the commercial syndrome, with some exceptions. They were ultra-competitive, full of energy and initiative, inventive in their creation of novel financial instruments, and keen for the security that lucrative deals provide the dealmakers. But they veered from some important principles of commercial self-regulation: they scoffed at thrift, wouldn't think of compromising with the risk managers, and confused enticing, short-term results with investment for productive purposes. Some put honesty at risk. Overall, their behavior suggests deficiencies in the moral principles common to both syndromes. Where was wisdom to be found?

The same question applies to the risk managers. They sought, via obedience and discipline, to serve, loyally, the better interests of the firm. By job definition, they were shunners of trade. But their rigidity—austere avoidance of largesse, ostentation, and leisure—won them no friends among the traders. They seem the very picture of the stuffed shirt, the person you wouldn't want to be tied to at the office party. They were lacking, at least, in the common virtue of friendliness, as were their counterparts among the traders.

As with alignment of incentives for CEOs, segregation of functions within the organization can help to mitigate the confusion of trading and guardian functions. Keeping them separate is crucial, Jacobs thought, for mixing the two would often produce "monstrous hybrids," citing the examples of criminal organizations, Marxist theory, and authoritarian governments.[25] But she did not despair at the possibility of harmonizing the two. "To seek harmony in the sense of oneness," says Kate, "is a profoundly false lead. But harmony can be sought by seeking to maintain each syndrome's own identity and integrity."[26]

The Chief Executive Role: Challenges of Accountability

But doesn't the very role of CEO of an organization pose another theoretical challenge to Jacobs's framework? Shouldn't a CEO be a guardian through and through? She must embody and represent devotion to the organization, dispense largesse, show prowess and power via membership on boards, and act as sage advisor to mayors, governors, and presidents.

And yet: the CEO, in acting on behalf of the organization, must be industrious and inventive, on the lookout for the novel, champion efficiency, and so on. These are trading acts and many biographies of corporate CEOs suggest that one must follow a trader's path, whether in marketing, finance, operations or technology to reach the ranks of leadership. If this is the case for the CEO role, how best to avoid the potentially disastrous mixing of the two syndromes in one?

The most common resolution of this question goes back to the Board and involves using guardians to "guard the guardian." For the modern corporation, this means vesting power in the board of directors, to whom the CEO is accountable. Who is fit to staff the board? Common practice matches like to like, filling boards with executives of comparable status and leaders drawn from the realms of business, politics, and, occasionally, academia. On the face of it, this is an astute solution. Board members will be made of stern stuff, expert, insightful, and tough. A board comprised of such talent should know the potential missteps and temptations that may beset a leader. They can offer guidance—guardrails, if you will—to ensure the safety of the firm. They have their own set of incentives—board compensation and personal reputation—to hold them to their tasks. Venice had its Council of Ten to remind the Doge of the conditions of his *promissione*; boards can do the same with corporate mission and goals. When a board operates with wisdom, courage, commitment to the organization, and detachment from the CEO's personal wishes, much good can result.

But poor judgment, timidity, self-interest, and personal loyalties can undermine good intentions and jeopardize good results. Boards can be club-like—most often, male-dominated—and the reluctance to penalize a member of the club can dull judgment and blunt resolve. A board can transmute from critical and accountable body to cozy, vest-pocket cabinet for the CEO.

The MFS Global Holdings Ltd. bankruptcy is a sad example. The firm was commanded by Jon Corzine, a former Goldman Sachs chairman and US senator from New Jersey. In financial circles, Corzine was a legendary figure, a man who had made a personal fortune as a trader at Goldman. His proficiency as a dealmaker likely propelled his political success, too. When MFS enticed him to be chairman and CEO, he assumed the roles on the condition that "he would 'report directly to the board.'"[27] He would be free to make deals unencumbered by checks and balances. This arrangement was far from the norm: typically, Wall

Street trading firms subject proposed trades to several levels of oversight and approval, beginning with the risk manager and progressing through the trading chief, chief risk officer, head of sales and trading, CEO and, finally, the board. By eliminating those intermediate levels, Corzine spoke only to the board and only from his own wisdom. When he made a $6.3 billion trade on European sovereign debt, the company collapsed into bankruptcy. Had the trade been subject to normal oversight, few believe it would have been approved. The Wall Street Journal quoted one MFS executive as saying "I could kick myself for not recognizing it sooner."

But recognition is one thing and action another. In the MFS case, the board would have benefited from a member who "dissented for the sake of the organization." This role spins a trader's concern—dissent for the sake of the task—in the direction of a guardian's duty to secure the organization. This is rare, but it can and has been done. The economist Albert Hirschman explored the possibility in *Exit, Voice, and Loyalty: Responses to Decline in Organizations, Firms and States* (1970). Confronted with the possibility of wrongdoing or serious disagreement with a proposed course of action, one might choose the exit option and head, quietly, for the door. Someone else might speak up and register disagreement and then either acquiesce or exit. A third option is to exercise voice and continue to work within the confines of the organization, seeking ways to alter its direction.

Choosing voice, either upon exit or while remaining in the organization is tantamount to dissent, and voicing dissent is not without cost: as many a whistle-blower can testify, ostracism and punishment often follow. Voicing dissent requires courage, one of the substrate principles, and practical wisdom, savviness about how best to speak: when, in what terms, to whom, and with what consequences. Lacking these virtues, neither trader nor guardian will be able to extricate an organization from the mess into which it has stumbled or been led.

An Ethics for Routinized Work and Gigs?

Jacobs provides a keen analysis of the moral underpinnings of work in which people, whether commercial traders or guardians, exercise agency. They are doers—designing, inventing, directing, producing, consulting, regulating—and this work has tangible effects and bears some stamp of ownership. The work can be difficult and not without frustration, but one may take satisfaction from the personal contributions made.

This is all well and good for those who enjoy a wide swath of freedom to operate in their work, but it does not touch upon the state of most who work for a living. Many are bound to a routine where the exercise of freedom and initiative is rare, if not prohibited. If this is so within the ranks of well-paid employees in large enterprises, it is even more the case in low-status and low-wage occupations. A person staffing a call center has a script to follow, a carefully crafted decision tree for responding to a customer. A person who works on contract for a firm knows her time is limited, as is her task. A ride share driver knows the temporary company of his fares but ties to his organization are ether-thin. Much, not all, temporary work, routinized work, contract work, and the gig economy offer little of the potential energy and delight which Jacobs saw possible in work.

Jacobs knew this: early in *Economy*, she had pointed out the difference between development work—brimming with ideas, touched, alternately, by failure and success—and production work. The latter must be briskly efficient; all the risk and fun are in the former. Finding ways to integrate elements of the two into one can be daunting.

Jacobs saw greater human possibilities in work. In *Economy*, she noted the way in which the sheer delight of discovery and invention drove much of development work. Innovation answered to questions born in wonder—What if. . .? Might we. . .? How can. . .?—and their realization was reward in itself, apart from economic benefits. One can love one's work for what it reveals about oneself as well as for what it yields. Aristotle had insight into this. "We exist in activity," he wrote, "i.e., by living and acting, and in his activity the maker is, in a sense, the work produced. He therefore loves his work, because he loves existence. And this lies in the nature of things: what a thing is potentially is revealed in actuality by what it produces."[28] We are what we make or trade or guard.

Jacobs's faith in human beings and their capacities ran deep. "We human beings come by creativity naturally," says Hiram in *Nature*. "People don't need to be geniuses or even extraordinarily talented to develop their work. The requirements are initiative and resourcefulness—qualities abundant in the human race when they aren't discouraged or suppressed."[29] How, then, to encourage work that will unbind initiative and support resourcefulness?

Jacobs, I think, would ask us to think carefully about the concrete conditions of work. What is the worker actually doing? With whom? In what environment? When these, and other very specific questions are asked, one might begin to think about the redesign of work and the work environment. It would also be crucial, and more difficult, to clarify what makes work "good." The late Pope St. John Paul II argued that good work has three characteristics.[30] It produces something that is needed by society. It develops the talents and capacities of the individual worker, an emphasis taken over from Aristotle, and it forges community among those involved in cooperative effort. On these criteria, many kinds of modern work disappoint: products are trivial, the work itself enervating, and the prospects for community faint.

Better design of work and organizations would help. Although Jacobs never wrote specifically about organization design, perhaps out of conviction that good organization would develop organically, I think her table of commercial virtue traits suggests some helpful design principles.

If an organization wants to foster "good work," it will produce worthwhile products and services, not ephemera. That is, it will *invest for productive purposes*. What is made or the service that is provided will respond to genuine need, not passing fancy. The organization will *be honest*, with its employees, partners, and customers. Honesty within the organization will be shown by the transparency of its hiring and promotion criteria and effective measures for allowing free communication among employees and supervisors. In turn, the organization should seek ways to allow for the exercise of *initiative and enterprise*. These will be exercised in different ways according to the nature of the organization, and some organizations will give more leeway than others in this regard. But all organizations should promote the exercise of voice and *dissent for the sake of the task*. (Those who manage sometimes find it hard to listen to those voices. In the summers between college, I worked a night shift cleaning the offices of a large multinational from 5:00 p.m. till 1:00 a.m. Each custodian was responsible for one floor, and each was charged to capture, for recycling, the silver-laden residual paper from a copying process. Recycling required a break from routine—the nightly cleaning, dusting, and vacuuming of all offices; sweeping and mopping common halls; cleaning a dozen toilets and washrooms—and a trip off one's floor. As a result, most ignored it. I suggested, via the suggestion box, that each custodian be equipped with a snap-on sack for his cart so that recycling could be done easily at shift's end. Visions of financial reward danced in my head: we were capturing silver, after all. The response? "We already have a process for recovering the paper." Yes, they did, but precious little was recovered. Managerial "knowledge" trumped local knowledge.)

Where to find contemporary organizations that embody these ideals for doing and valuing work? The recent development of B corporations offers some encouragement. As the introductory language on its website suggests, "Certified B Corporations are a new kind of business that balances purpose and profit. They are legally required to consider the impact of their decisions on their workers, customers, suppliers, community, and the environment."[31] To date, more than 3,000 companies representing 150 industries have achieved B corporation certification. As the numbers suggest, this kind of "good business" is enjoying fresh energy.

King Arthur Flour of Norwich, Vermont is a good example.[32] The company is employee-owned and an original B corporation member. It shares profits with employees, has significant commitments to its local communities, and posts its annual progress in the four domains measured by B lab—governance, workers, community, and environment—and sets new goals based on that assessment.[33]

B corporations are not a panacea. Large and well-established organizations are not about to downsize and reconceive their mission. But for nascent organizations, B corporations represent one-way in which good work can be realized in contemporary organizations. Surely there are many more. I can hear Jane Jacobs say, "Look around you. . ."

Notes

1 See www.bls.gov.

2 Jacobs, *Death and Life*, 50.

3 Jacobs, *Death and Life*, 14.

4 Jacobs, *Death and Life*, 32.

5 Jacobs, *Economy*, 74.

6 Jacobs, *Wealth*, chapter 13.

7 Jacobs, *Wealth*, 218.

8 Jane Jacobs, *Systems of Survival* (Random House, 1992), 5. Hereafter, *Survival*.

9 Jane Jacobs, "Systems of Economic Ethics, Part One," in Fred Lawrence (ed.), *Ethics in Making a Living: The Jane Jacobs Conference* (Scholars Press, 1989), 212.

10 Jacobs, "Systems of Economic Ethics, Part One," 212.

11 Jacobs, *Survival*, 52.

12   Jacobs, "Systems of Economic Ethics, Part One," 236.

13   Mary Ann Glendon, Learned Hand Professor of Law Emerita at Harvard Law School, takes up this suggestion *in A Nation Under Lawyers*, (Harvard University Press, 1994).

14   Jacobs, *Survival*, 121.

15   Jacobs, *Survival*, 121.

16   Jacobs, *Survival*, 25.

17   Jacobs, "Systems of Economic Ethics, Part One," 225.

18   Jacobs, "Systems of Economic Ethics, Part One," 270.

19   Jacobs, *Survival*, 83.

20   For a detailing of the election process, see John Julius Norwich, *A History of Venice* (Vintage Books, 1989).

21   David Chambers and Brian Pullan, with Jennifer Fletcher (ed.), *Venice: A Documentary History, 1450–1630* (Toronto: University of Toronto Press, 2001), 47.

22   Chambers, Pullan and Fletcher, *Documentary History*, 70–71.

23   Personal account from a former student.

24   "Confessions of a Risk Manager," *The Economist*, August 7, 2008.

25   Jacobs, *Survival*, chapter 6.

26   Jacobs, *Survival*, 106.

27   See *The Wall Street Journal*, November 23, 2011. The subsequent citation also draws on this article.

28   *NE*, Book IX, 259.

29   Jacobs, *Nature*, 33.

30   See https://www.vatican.va/content/john-paul-ii/en/encyclicals/documents/hf_jp-ii_enc_091981_laborem-exercens.html. This site has the full text of *Laborem Exercens*, a social encyclical that has much to say about work.

31   See https://bcorporation.net/ accessed October 10, 2019 at 2:37PM.

32   See https://www.kingarthurflour.com/.

33   https://www.kingarthurflour.com/about/mission/b-corp-report.

6

Sustaining "the Whole Precarious Contraption"

Education in the City

Education, Not Schooling

The penultimate chapter of *The Nature of Economies* bears the title "Unpredictability," and its themes recall Jane Jacobs's early characterization of the city as "wholly existential." An economy is the result of many actions, forces, and events. She introduces the metaphor of an "ensemble" to describe this process and entrusts its exposition to one of the symposium participants, Hiram. He is an ecologist who applies principles of evolutionary development—diversification, specialization, unexpected ramifications—to economics. No one person, no one thing, guarantees continuing economic vitality, and no one person has all-encompassing expertise. "Some members of the ensemble may come up with what's needed," asserts Hiram, "but they must depend on the rest of the ensemble—or the co-developments of other members and on many, many others in the ensemble, to keep the whole precarious contraption stable enough and expanding enough to assimilate corrections and bifurcations."[1] The economy demands constant gearing up, recalibration, iteration after iteration. This is not the work of a solo practitioner—how could it be? The whole human enterprise has no tidy order. Its order is contrived as needs be and never achieves stasis: the "contraption" is precarious but stable enough to make do as long as it evokes the contributions of willing collaborators.

People and organizations—human capital—are the creators, via co-development, of the needed work. But how does that capital itself develop? "Human capital [. . .] means skills, information, and experience—cultivated human potentialities—resulting from investments made by the public, by parents, by employers, and by individuals themselves."[2] By most accounts, the cultivation of human potentialities is the work and result of education. We count on schools to show the way to recognize and enhance a student's potential and guide its realization. But Jacobs's list of cultivators omits any explicit mention of a *formal* education system, of schools. To be sure, she credits "the public" for investments, but even that mention need not be construed as pointing to formal schooling. The public invests in museums and libraries, too, where much self-initiated learning, sometimes prompted by librarians and docents, occurs.

Considering the range of institutions Jacobs does survey, the omission of schools is surprising. A partial catalog of institutions she does consider over the course of her work includes city, state, and national governments; the police; the military; churches, temples, and synagogues; unions; tenant organizations; investment and commercial banks; retail businesses, small and large; large corporations of many stripes. Mention of education is scant. (There are traces of attention to it in *A Schoolteacher in Old Alaska*, an edited volume of her aunt Hannah Breece's journal, and in her preface to the Modern Library edition of Charles Dickens's *Hard Times*. University education gets rough treatment in both *Death and Life* and *Dark Age*; I will consider this below.) There are schoolchildren on the sidewalks of Hudson Street, but no comment on their schools or teachers. And so the question persists: why no consideration of the early stages of formal education? Was Jacobs slyly endorsing the quote attributed to Mark Twain of not letting schooling interfere with her education? I don't think so. While there is no systematic analysis of the institutions of primary and secondary education, or an explicit philosophy of education or teaching, Jane Jacobs was always keen on something else—learning—and alert to its domains.

The First Domain or Primary School: Parents, Family, and Community

In her final book, *Dark Age Ahead*, Jane Jacobs identified stress on the family as one of five portents of an impending dark age. That judgment casts light backward on the entirety of her work. Perhaps she felt that it went without saying in *Death and Life*: family is the primary school for the young (and a rough education for new parents). Its curriculum is comprehensive, forming body, mind, and spirit, and immersive, requiring imitation, initiative, and the absorption of lessons born of much faltering, occasional small triumphs, and disappointments. Failure and stress haunt this learning. Things fall apart more readily than they cohere.

Jacobs herself had benefited from the tutelage and encouragement of her father as a young learner. As Glenna Lang reveals in *Jane Jacobs's First City: Learning from Scranton* (NYU, 2021), young Jane Butzner was a precocious and self-directed learner. She read the *Encyclopedia Britannica* avidly; she engaged in dialogues on ethics and many other topics with her father; at the beginning of a school year, she would read the assigned textbooks and fret at the oh-so-slow pace of classroom instruction. Learning was a staple of the family diet.

As Jacobs surveyed the prospects of "families rigged to fail" in the second chapter of *Dark Age*, she concluded that an entire community was needed to provide the range of cultural knowledge—for instance, how to bank, how to avoid the temptations of drugs, how to tutor children, how to coach athletes, how to develop cross-cultural understanding and respect for difference—that society had presupposed was the remit of the traditional two-parent family.[3] Every family would need the bedrock of public institutions and their services—agencies that tend to roads and public health services, police and the judiciary, libraries, to name but a few—and these would be supplemented by private and not-for-profit enterprises—clubs, fraternal associations, churches and the like—all mediating structures of what we would call civil society. But more powerful even than the formal public institutions she names is another kind of support crucial to a family's success. Families would need a kind of subliminal support, something conveyed by means "thoroughly informal, thoroughly intangible, and probably the most important: speaking relationships among neighbors and acquaintances in addition to friends."[4] Jacobs had known this interlocking set of supports—family, local government, local community groups, responsible adults—in the Greenwich Village neighborhood where she and her husband, and those many others, raised their children; she saw it as well in Toronto, where the Jacobs's had moved in the wake of the Vietnam War. Long before "it takes a village to raise a child" became a catchphrase, Jacobs had seen the reality. In ways both formal and informal, the city was the primary locus for education, a school in its own right and with its own rites.

The faculty of this school are masters of what Michael Polanyi called "tacit knowledge."[5] Tacit knowledge is the accumulated understanding that accrues to a person by virtue of life experience—via work, parenting, or any number of activities. The human being, according to Polanyi, always knows more than they can say.

The "curriculum" of this "city-school" thus draws on the precious trove of cultural knowledge and wisdom that enables full participation in the community.

Tacit knowledge is fragile, dependent on individuals and groups who transmit and enact it. Jacobs was keenly sensitive to the loss of such knowledge; she noted the loss in several of her books. When longtime residents leave a neighborhood, local knowledge erodes. When the local economy falters, and young people abandon it for the sake of opportunity elsewhere, the thread between generations frays. Jacobs witnessed that fraying in slums that failed to "unslum" in *Death and Life*. Later, she saw it in the loss of vitality in Quebec's countryside as the pull of Montreal and Toronto drew the young away. Still later, she described it in her account of bypassed places in *Wealth*.

Tacit knowledge passes know-how on to the next generation but also carries something more in the process. It helps every "I" recognize the greater "we" that ensures a person's growth and development. The nesting of "I"s within a "we" is the heart of community. Primary school begins at home, flows into the streets, and prepares the young for entry into other "public" schools.

But what if streets offer no connection of the young and old, no mingling of would-be learners with accomplished tutors? What if transience, rather than rootedness, comes to dominate the city? And what if "the city" in which most live today bears little resemblance to early twentieth-century Scranton or late twentieth-century Greenwich Village? These are crucial questions, but I will defer them to later when we consider how and if Jane Jacobs's insights translate to our present circumstances.

Modes of Instruction in the "Primary" School

The primary educators—parents, extended family, friends—meet their students in widely different classrooms and without fixed schedules. This shapes the way in which they can teach. The 24/7 parents will instruct, tutor, advise, reprove, explain, demonstrate, and model good behavior. They offer emotional as well as physical sustenance and provide shelter within which children can explore and develop. "Instructors" at a second or third level—extended family to street acquaintances—play a much more limited role. They may sometimes function *in loco parentis*, but have a different ambit. Their interactions will be more casual and the timing unpredictable. In *Death and Life*, Jacobs called such people "public characters," known to all in a neighborhood and the source of tips, warnings, and practical advice.

At all levels, demonstration and example count for more than a straight lecture. "Preach the gospel," said St. Francis, "and use words when needed." When I interviewed Jane Jacobs in 1985, practical example was an emphasis. She underlined the importance of internships and work-based learning for adolescents. And for the primary school young, she extolled the virtues of individual tutorial work as opposed to the classroom instruction of what she called an "apprenticeship" model.

"There are," she asserted, "two kinds of education. One kind is apprenticeship. A lot of what we don't think about as apprenticeship education is just that. It's the commonest form of education."[6] She pointed to elementary school as an example, suggesting that the students who admire their teachers might themselves aspire to be teachers, and so they perform well. They are apprenticing, following the teacher closely and doing as she does and as she commands. (By contrast, she confessed, "I was a rebel in school."[7]) Apprentices learn the rules, color within the lines, footnote properly, check all the boxes. They always read the instruction manuals. This is early training for bureaucratic service, Jacobs noted. It can amount to "a substitute, very often, for not thinking."[8]

This is not to dismiss the importance of acquiring basic skills or the role that drill and repetition must play in early education: one doesn't come by alphabet and word recognition intuitively or absorb the multiplication tables from the ether. But it does suggest that education that follows the lead of the young learner, rather than dictating a marching cadence, better serves her education. This was certainly true in Jacobs's case. She had a keen appreciation of the loving attention she received from her father in her guided study.

At another point in our interview, she turned to a second form of education, "another sort of education and it's what upper class people, aristocratic eccentrics, people of leisure and people destined to rule have gotten throughout history. In every case where this is successful, the teacher is inferior, socially, to the pupils."[9] (Perhaps she had in mind the ancient example of Aristotle serving as tutor to Alexander the Great!) She saw the origins of liberal education in "that kind of education . . . [and it] can't be done by a teacher who regards himself or herself as superior."[10] When I told her that I detected similarities in what she was suggesting to the work of Ivan Illich, she recalled a discussion with him and how he had invoked John Holt as a third voice esteeming the learning potential of the young if only they are paid proper attention. Jacobs, Illich, and Holt were contemporaries in the New York of the 1950s and 1960s, and the convergence of their thought is remarkable.

Holt (1923–85) was himself the product of an elite education. He had studied at Phillips Exeter as an adolescent and at Yale for his undergraduate degree and had served in the US Navy during the Second World War. In the 1950s, he spent six years teaching elementary schoolin Colorado and Massachusetts. His enchantment with the unfolding of children's understanding and disenchantment with the educational system, which seemed to stifle or ignore a youngster's natural inclination to learning led him to write his first two books, *How Children Fail* (1964) and *How Children Learn* (1967).

Holt's reverence for the unfolding intelligence of the child shines in every one of his richly detailed observations of young children at play. For Holt, play was the open road to learning. Gesture and smile, grimace and yelps of delight, growls of frustration, and rat-a-tat repetition of words real and nonsensical were a child's means for engaging the world. In the revised edition of *How Children Learn*, Holt wrote of a child's games that "the spirit behind such games should be a spirit of joy, foolishness, exuberance, like the spirit behind all good games, including the game of trying to find out how the world works, which we call education."[11] But, he continued, "I am afraid that this is not what most people understand by the word 'education.'"[12] Although he taught in several schools, and lectured at Harvard's Graduate School of Education later in his career, Holt grew disaffected with formal schooling and championed homeschooling. His disaffection was fueled by his own experiences and the powerful critique of organized schooling developed by Illich.

Ivan Illich (1926–2002) contained multitudes. An Austrian by birth and son of a Catholic father and a mother who had converted from Judaism, Illich became a Roman Catholic priest after extended study at a number of European universities, including Florence, Salzburg, and the Pontifical Gregorian University in Rome. Fluent in several languages and with a polymath's gift, he was also an organizer, recognized for his outreach to the Puerto Rican community of New York City and named, at a young age, as vice rector of Puerto Rico's Catholic University. He established the Intercultural Center for Documentation in Cuernavaca, Mexico, an institution which began with a mission to teach missionaries about culturally appropriate evangelization and expanded to become a language training center open to all and the site of wide-ranging seminars with scholars and practitioners from around the world. Disagreements with the Vatican led him to resign the practice, but not the status, of his priestly role. While Mexico remained a home base, Illich traveled and lectured across the globe and published more than a dozen books.

In *De-Schooling Society* (1971), Illich argued that the Western institution of formalized education "confuse[d] teaching with learning, grade advancement with education, a diploma with competence, and fluency with the ability to say something new."[13] In subsequent works, he argued that this confusion affected other social institutions as well, from health care to national security and the economy at large. Illich, like Jacobs, was wary of how formal systems of education quickly separated students into those who could master the ropes and those who fumbled along. It measured a student's learning by mapping her ascent through the steps of a preordained and compartmentalized curriculum. Success on one level opened doors to higher levels: schooling begat more schooling.

By contrast, Jacobs and Illich saw the proof of student learning in the fruits of the learning itself, the student's growing confidence as a writer or fledgling scientist or craftsman, via supervised self-study, experiment, and practice. Learn the basics via drill, Illich suggested, then connect with accomplished practitioners or scholars and let a student's interest guide the trajectory of education. We must dis-establish school, Illich argued, because "the very existence of obligatory schools divides any society into two realms: some time spans and processes and treatments and professions are 'academic' or 'pedagogic' and others are not . . . education becomes unworldly and the world becomes noneducational."[14]

The de-schooling of society, which might sound like an anarchist's creed, was in the service, Illich maintained, of a richer notion of human life. It was a move toward what he termed, in his next book, *Tools for Conviviality* (1973), the "convivial." Illich chose the term "to designate the opposite of industrial productivity. I intend it to mean autonomous and creative intercourse among persons, and the intercourse of persons with their environment. . . . I consider conviviality to be *individual freedom realized in personal interdependence* [emphasis mine] and, as such, an intrinsic ethical value."[15] Note that Illich links individual freedom with interdependence. The person who learns on her own terms has first benefited, and continues to do so, from the example and tutelage of others. Autodidacts may drive their own learning, but that drive originates in the previous, and ongoing, work of others. Convivial learning is "conversational" learning in the sense that I invoked in explaining the subtitle of this book. Convivial learning is communitarian learning, the context in which the many "we's" nurture the emergence of many more "I's."[16]

But when "individual freedom" is untethered from "personal interdependence," rabbit holes wait to swallow the unwary.

If You Would "Teach," First Pay Attention

If the potential primary educators are many and their classrooms and labs various, what makes for a good instructor? The best education occurs, Jacobs suggested, when a teacher attends to the learning of the *subject*, the particular student before him, rather than to the subject *matter* to be taught. The difference in emphasis is at once simple and profound: pay attention to this learner, how she learns, where she may stumble. Think about how to spark comprehension and fan it into a blaze. This is, to use an overworked phrase, truly "student-centered" learning, which, while recognizing general intelligence, is keen to the varieties of aptitudes, inclinations, and dispositions which lead to learning.

But to foster student-centered learning, the good tutor must be self-aware and capable of self-direction. The preface to *Death and Life* offers a primer. There, Jacobs advised, "the scenes that illustrate this book are all about us. For illustrations, please look closely at real cities. While you are looking, you might as well also listen, linger and think about what you see."[17] We should parse these three sentences carefully. "All about us"—Jacobs doesn't say "all about you," placing the reader apart, but joins the reader to the whole, "us," the city. Learning occurs in and through what we share in common. Look, listen, linger, think: these are discrete functions and need to be integrated. So begin by looking, but don't stop there. Sights are important but incomplete: you need sounds—the blare of traffic, the snatches of talk on the street, the cries of the sidewalk huckster or even, paradoxically, silence. To take all that in, and make sense of it, requires patience. So you need to linger, to stick around. What one sees and hears is important, but seeing and hearing are not knowing. The tourist Instagrams his way through the city, using its sites as his own set of props and backgrounds. Understanding the city takes time, putting the phone away, finding a place to sit down and think. "Think" about what's seen: thinking and understanding are not the mere accumulation of sensations and feelings but result from questioning, comparing, and judging. The hop-on bus in New York or any large city offers general orientation and a panorama of the environs, but the rider needs to step off, not simply watch the scene pass by. An afternoon coffee taken at the bistro or bodega, and a seat on a bench, may be the path to thinking about what's been observed and understanding some piece of it.

The prefatory instructions of *Death and Life* presuppose someone who will be inquisitive, reflective, and embedded in the textures of city life. Still, one could be all these things but remain captive to error, misconception, and prejudice.

To understand the city, one must know oneself. As Jacobs writes in the preface to *Systems of Survival*, "if you do not already recognize a bias you may have absorbed from education, experience, interests and ambitions, perhaps you will discover one here. The precept 'know thyself' includes knowing the scales with which one weighs actions and attitudes in the great world of work outside oneself."[18]

These two prefaces, separated by more than twenty years, reveal Jacobs's abiding concern with a particular kind of knowing, which we have seen in the discussion of *Systems*, what Aristotle called "practical wisdom." He differentiated practical wisdom from both technical knowledge and the realms of theory. In his commentary on the *Nicomachean Ethics*, Martin Oswald writes that practical wisdom "tends to imply wisdom in action, and hence a moral intelligence"[19] while technical knowledge is that "which enables a person to produce a certain product,"[20] whether that be a good, like shoes, or a service, like the healing proffered by a physician. By contrast, theoretical knowledge is engaged in "for its own sake, or rather for the attainment of truth. It is a contemplation of nature in its widest sense."[21]

Practical wisdom commands attention even if it wins faint academic praise. Knowing what should be done in any particular circumstance requires arriving at judgments that incorporate the facts as they can be known, the presuppositions of the people engaged in debate, and a clearly articulated goal that commands assent. Jacobs's own experience of civic engagement was often trying. Both in New York and Toronto, her presence and judgments were much sought after and brought a steady train of advocates to her door. She had long and wearying experience of contentious public hearings. They were full of people of varying judgment, who bristled with opinions and convictions, and championed an extraordinary range of projects. While she prized the knowledge of the thoughtful person close to the scene, Jacobs knew the difference between informed judgment and self-satisfied agitprop. This surely underlies her invitation to pause and reflect upon oneself.

As for her own biases, I suspect that Jane Jacobs knew that her own experience with formal education, from know-it-all elementary school teachers to a condescending Oxford don to an authoritarian dean at Columbia, colored her attitude toward educational systems. Every one of us struggles to get beyond our customs, preoccupations, and biases. Jacobs certainly saw this struggle in her aunt Hannah Breece, whose journal Jacobs edited and published as *A Schoolteacher in Old Alaska* (1995). She regretted the tone of cultural superiority which pervaded her aunt's journal. But she found much to admire in her aunt's bravery, her ingenuity in devising new modes for teaching, her savvy dealing with remote administrators, and her respect for the contours of a native culture so different from her own. While learning how to teach among indigenous peoples, Breece was also learning how colonial systems work and how to work through and around them. Like her niece, Hannah Breece was a woman of practical intelligence and a generalist, not a specialist.

But as Jacobs wrote, ruefully, in her introduction to the Modern Library edition of Charles Dickens's *Hard Times*, "as barriers between various intellectual 'turfs' continue to loom higher and more obdurate, generalists have become an extinct species in academic life and an endangered species outside it, in spite of growing realization that in the actual, complex world information from many different fields bears on most problems or situations."[22] Dickens, she said, feared the eclipse of humanistic knowledge by scientific methods. The first character we meet in *Hard Times*, the headmaster Thomas Gradgrind, insists that schooling be based on nothing but facts and forbids his children and pupils, access to myth, story, and fable. But facts alone, and their kindred statistics, can ignore, said Jacobs, "unquantifiable realities, subtleties, and common sense."[23] Life, after all, as the French philosopher Gabriel Marcel wrote, "is a mystery to be lived, not a problem to be solved." Or, to put it in Jacobs's terms, the mystery resides in the explosion of what she called "problems of disorganized complexity" in *Death and Life*, which may not be wrestled to the ground with scientific tools alone.[24] Where will the insights of the person of practical wisdom be credited?

Teaching, Learning, Knowing

What I am describing as Jacobs's unstated philosophy of education underlines the relationships among teaching, learning, and knowing. Teaching may or may not lead to learning, for learning depends upon an array of interlocking factors. How well does the teacher know his material? Can he "perform" in such a way as to evoke comprehension in the student? Is the student prepared, cognitively and affectively, for what is required? Further difficulties: if "knowing" is the outcome of successful teaching and learning, what outcomes are being measured? The philosopher Gilbert Ryle famously distinguished between "knowing that" and "knowing how," but one should also ask about knowing "why." Thomas Gradgrind's philosophy in *Hard Times* identifies "knowing that," propositional knowledge, as the one true knowledge and assumes that adding one proposition to another will serve the student in whatever she needs to know. Facts alone count. Marshal them and yoke them together. Independent curiosity, feeling and longing to know more, or other, has no place. As I write this morning, Mercury transits the sun. I "know," via the *New York Times*, that such transits are rare, that the angle of transit may ascend or decline, and that all of this has something to do with orbits and planetary angles. This is a tidy set of propositions, about which I marvel, but about which I know precious little. Knowledge of facts and propositions has obvious value but measuring learning by this standard alone leaves too much out. The "how" and the "why" recede or disappear.

Jacobs's idea of apprenticeship education engages all three kinds of knowing. Her first mention of it in our interview might read as a dismissal of those "goody two-shoes" encountered in grade school, whose hands were always in the air at every question, eager to serve as classroom beadle. But as our conversation unfolded, she returned to apprenticeships in a positive light. She thought there should be more of these, that they should be intentional, not implicit as in the grade school example, and they should provide compensation for the person offering the apprenticeship opportunity: it's real work, she said, deserving of compensation. I think she foresaw a wide range of apprenticeships, art and shop to be sure, but also opportunities in crafts and the professions. Further, learning via apprenticeship covers all three kinds of knowing. The apprentice learns *how* to blow glass or to write 500 words for a deadline or to manipulate the strained shoulder by imitative, supervised practice. She learns *that* the fire must burn at this intensity, that good writing always keeps the reader in mind, that this conjunction of muscles in the shoulder flexes and arcs in these motions safely and in others injuriously. The beauty of the glass, the enlightenment of the reader, the healing of the shoulder are three answers to the question of *why*.

The apprentice model also offers a version of the tutorial method which Jacobs prized. Jacobs knew that her preferred model was privileged. Not every child has a diligent father like hers. Not even the great and powerful, like Alexander the Great, can find an Aristotle today. Nor can the sustained tutorial work of Oxford's colleges be a model for a large urban system. But apprenticeship means learning by doing at the instruction and example of a master. New businesses sometimes make use of mentors provided by SCORE, the Service Corps of Retired Executives.[25] It's not hard to imagine a similar, sustained program for secondary schools. I am willing to bet that some systems have already implemented programs along these lines. Such programs would also provide intergenerational connections to supplement familial ties.

Principles of Jacobsian Learning and Some Corollaries

Jane Jacobs left no blueprint for schooling, nor did she evince any interest in outlining an educational system. But she did leave many hints about what contributes to learning. And as the preceding suggests, learning is not confined to a classroom, nor is it realized only in formal contact between teacher and students. We get closer to her concern when we talk about the learning of cities themselves. This is not a fanciful anthropomorphism. If cities are the developing, organic communities that Jacobs sought to understand, then cities "learn" in many places through many different people and at many levels. The list of learners includes parents, children, and students, but also neighborhood residents, elected officials, leaders of neighborhood associations, nonprofit organizations, and members of the business community. The persistence of city problems reflects two realities. Problems in human living are recurrent and unpredictable: their solution has to be lived through. And the solutions bring new challenges in their wake, requiring further learning. In the spirit of *Systems of Survival*, I offer the following table (Table 6.1), with comments. I will be talking, by analogy, about the city and how it learns as well as about actual teachers and students.

Respect the Phenomena

The old adage has it that for a man with a hammer, everything looks like a nail. To a butcher, a cow is a set of cuts, to a dairy farmer quite another thing. Throughout her work, Jacobs insists on seeing, then understanding, what's given. Writing

Table 6.1 Principles of Jacobsian Learning.

Principles	Corollaries
Respect the phenomena	Learning requires many strategies
Honor received wisdom with the gift of questions	Give weight to local custom and wisdom but ask "why?"
Think historically	Be alert for processes and functions
Experiment constantly and variously	Welcome failure for its capacity to instruct
Know the particulars	Theory should follow the facts
Welcome the exception as a spur to thought	Don't fall under the spell of patterns
Embrace good theory but don't accept it uncritically	Beware the guardian credentialer!
Invite collaboration	Development depends on co-development
Converse	Someone else can see my biases and lacunae

of Muhammed Yunus, the Nobel Prize-winning economist, she noted that his insights into the power of microlending occurred when he withdrew his head from "clouds of handed-down learning . . . [and] observed the work going on around him."[26] The blinkered redevelopment official who saw Boston's North End as a slum could not see, let alone understand, what Jacobs saw and understood: freshly painted doors, bustling street life and happy families pointed to a healthy neighborhood. When one begins to understand the city as a problem in organized complexity, not a mess begging for imposed order, then one appreciates "the kind of problem a city is."[27] Scale modelling doesn't help us understand the city, as she commented at the Great Cities of the World conference in Boston.

Respect for the given phenomena also requires knowledge of the learner's capacities. Advanced courses in number theory make a wonderful mystery of one's and two's, but a child playing with blocks and balls can learn rudimentary arithmetic. The resident whose street is clogged with trucks and cars may not know the algorithms of the transit planners, or the apps that drive traffic, but she knows whereof she speaks and stalls. We should begin with what is known to us, said Aristotle in the *Nicomachean Ethics*, before we ascend to more general knowledge. Observe, listen, and think locally, alongside the resident experts, Jacobs would argue, before consulting the anointed experts.

Learning Requires Many Strategies

Blanket invocations of "the spirit of Jane Jacobs" to cover any and all situations are not at all in keeping with her legacy. In my Google news alert tied to Jacobs, I can count on several such invocations each week, whether from small towns, far-flung suburbs, or global megalopolises. But what will do to stimulate the life of Worcester, Massachusetts necessarily differs from what is needed in rural Vermont or in Delhi, India. One out of eight US citizens now lives in California; thinking about the highway-ramp laced interchanges of Southern California cities needs must differ from thinking about the Central Valley environs, and San Francisco, let alone Eastern or Midwestern cities.

Honor Received Wisdom with the Gift of Questions

In keeping with respect for the phenomena at hand, Jacobs prizes the local, "cultural" knowledge embedded in persons, practices, and institutions. In discussing the dynamics of "unslumming" in *Death and Life*, she highlighted, as we noted, the role of "public characters." "They seem to think that their neighborhood is unique and irreplaceable in all the world, and remarkably valuable in spite of its shortcomings. In this they are correct, for the multitude of relationships and public characters that make up an animated city street neighborhood are always unique, intricate and have the value of the unreproducible original."[28] But public characters are not infallible oracles.

Give Weight to Local Custom and Wisdom but Ask "Why?"

Since every individual and organization wears some blinders, one needs to be humble and cautious. So to the fervent, long-term resident who says "we must keep the neighborhood the same!" one should feel no qualms in asking "can any neighborhood stay ever the same? Should it? Isn't adaptation a feature of life?" and so on. One-sided questions are rhetorical poses. In Boston's West End, questions ran only one-way, or no way. Planners saw the West End as a slum even though its residents lived, happily, in what they knew to be a down-at-the-heels environment.

Questioning wisdom goes for teachers and students in actual classrooms, too, and responsibilities run both ways. The teacher must be more than the caretaker of the inheritance, the student more than an auditor. Teachers bear responsibility for creating an atmosphere that welcomes questions. Students must commit to asking them. Every student can recognize a teacher hostile to questions; every teacher dreads the silence that blankets a room of unresponsive students. Wisdom thrives on questions.

Think Historically

Paying attention to the phenomena and receiving local wisdom implicitly affirms this principle. Jacobs believes that there is absolutely nothing new under the sun: only God creates *ex nihilo*. Human progress depends on the gradual accumulation of insights, the generation of "new" approaches indebted to past achievements and the prospect of continuing adaptations. Learning should look to origins, but the historical quest for origins rarely terminates in a singular person or event. How then to proceed?

Be Alert for Processes and Functions

History reveals indebtedness in the train of processes and functions that lead to current phenomena. At the Great Cities of the World conference in 1980, Jacobs scoffed at the purported originality of the Faneuil Hall redevelopment. Not so, she rejoined, pointing to antecedent work by different hands in different cities. And the genealogy of cities unfurled at the end of Chapter 5 of *The Economy of Cities* makes the point vividly. History binds and determines only when it is ignored. Taken into account, it frees person and city to imagine different futures.

Experiment Constantly and Variously

This principle applies to formal classrooms and to the classroom writ large, the city itself. Every good teacher—the reflective, self-critical, and observant person described above—is alert to the multiple and unfolding variables that animate a classroom. He makes frequent assessments of individual and collective comprehension, reads and responds to the emotional climate, and calibrates his efforts accordingly: more of this, less of that, perhaps some of this.

So, too, with the city. The existential, contingent unfolding of city life always yields new problems. Their answers should not be taken off-the-shelf, "canned and presumed knowledge of kinds which we erroneously imagine can save us from future decline or forgetfulness."[29] This is a hard process, one that will test a city's government and its coffers. Cities bear the significant risk of experimental failure. But a failed experiment yields knowledge, too—"not *that* way"—and may reveal new questions and avenues of approach. The different avenues bear trying. This will require enormous patience and political courage since failure carries economic and electoral costs.

Know the Particulars

In classrooms, knowing the particulars of one's students requires tact and grace. No teacher should aspire to the role of surrogate parent, but she must be prepared to acknowledge, if not fully understand, the circumstances that trail invisibly behind students as they enter the classroom. This is difficult and delicate, but essential. Cities require a similar preparation. If you would act responsibly, said Aristotle, know the particulars of the circumstances in which you act. Toronto is as different from New York, as ancient Athens was from Sparta. Place matters as do methods, materials, intent, and consequences. How much is too little, what is just right, here and now? What means should be chosen? Any adult who was well-raised, thinks Aristotle, knows that she should "do the right thing," but the doing, the performance, is always situated, concrete, unique in the moment. So, too, Jane Jacobs: knowledge of the particulars has pride of place and theory can wait, or follow. "There is no substitute for knowing the particulars."[30] In the wake of such knowledge, let theory begin to follow the facts discovered.

Welcome the Exception as a Spur to Thought

The unexpected result is a boon for the good teacher. The demonstration of an apparent anomaly—a chemical reaction that fizzles rather than oozes, a piece of music played slightly off-key, a poetic stress that violates a pattern—can foster a student's insight. In a city, the unexpected prosperity of a scruffy neighborhood may be an object lesson for those promoting economic development if they are sufficiently attuned to the phenomena before them. Conversely, the failure of a well-funded and attractive neighborhood to catalyze further investment and lure more residents should be the incentive to ask why.

Exceptions disrupt patterns. While patterns comfort, they can also deceive since thought relaxes in that very comfort. While Jacobs sought patterns, she feared the tendency to see patterns where they did not exist or were identified too quickly or without sufficient attention to time, place, and circumstances. This underlies her sustained criticism of planning. Too often, she thought, it forced formal, top-down templates upon the contours of the lived environment. Hold the templates, which answer previous questions, not the ones posed by the current situation, she would insist. Understand what is happening on the ground. Ask what works and fails here and now, whether that accords with or challenges prevailing hopes and theory. Recognizing the exception forces one to reconsider assumptions. Why doesn't this fit? What have I been assuming and, therefore, missing? It is no coincidence, I think, that Jane and Bob Jacobs delighted in doing puzzles as a pastime.[31]

Embrace Good Theory but not Blindly

Jacobs was wary of looking to provenance as a guarantee of quality. She was skeptical of theory bred in universities, schools of education, think tanks, and government commissions that purported to offer comprehensive and well-articulated guidance but which often seemed remote from concrete circumstances and begrudging of contrary information or experience.

The defenders of established theory, the current wisdom, tenaciously resist challenges to its explanatory power, as Thomas Kuhn famously demonstrated in *The Structure of Scientific Revolutions* (1962).[32] Established theory, wrote Kuhn, provides the taken-for-granted view of "the way things really are." But reality plays havoc with theory. Kuhn saw good theory as the best, current account of "the real thing," a sturdy but not fault-free holding place. As discrepant examples and anomalies accumulate, the defenders strive mightily to save the theory via exceptions, codicils, and the like. But the repair job finally yields to a new and more satisfactory account, a new "paradigm."

For Jacobs, good theory is perspicacious, humble, and alert to anomalies: it thrives on sustained questioning of the data and welcomes correction. The work of Thomas Piketty is an excellent example of such theory. Piketty's *Capital in the Twenty-First Century* (2014),[33] a data-rich argument about the sources of economic inequality and a provocative case for a global wealth tax, was both fervently acclaimed and fiercely disputed. Piketty took neither the praise nor the criticism personally: he invited others to join in discussion and provided his data online.[34] He wanted to get things right. Jacobs would have approved.

Invite Collaboration; Converse

From a young age, Jane Jacobs sought conversation partners. Some of these, as Glenna Lang relates, were imaginary: "She had started with Thomas Jefferson but grew bored with him because he seemed most interested in abstract ideas. Ben Franklin, in contrast, asked good, down-to-earth questions."[35] Both as writer and citizen, Jacobs prized conversation and collaboration. Like Piketty, she did not shy from the confrontation of differing opinions and personalities. Her own writing reveals the power of what she terms co-development. One need only consult the notes and acknowledgments which accompany her later work to discern how her own biases and lacunae were corrected. Monologues and soliloquies might be of interest to her as art forms, but not as forms of civic life.

The nine principles I have sketched overlap and intersect. They are implicit in the "habits of thought" Jacobs identified as crucial for understanding cities in the closing pages of *Death and Life*.

I think the most important habits of thought are these:

1. To think about processes;
2. To work inductively, reasoning from particulars to the general, rather than the reverse;
3. To seek for "unaverage" clues involving very small quantities, which reveal the way larger and more "average" quantities are operating.[36]

The principles are also on extended display in a letter I received from her in March of 1985. I had asked about her method of working and how she found her way into and through a topic. "Here is what I do," she replied

> When I start exploring some subject, I hardly know what I think. I'm just trying to learn anything I can about it. Rather than reading systematically, which is possible only if you know what you want, I read as omnivorously as I can manage, in anything that interests me. I often even don't know why I'm interested in some facet or other, and all I can say about that is that from experience I've learned to trust myself when I'm interested. (The experience from which I've learned that is being interested but saying to myself No, no, come off it, stop wasting time, this is beside the point, and then learning much later as I begin to put things together, that it wasn't beside the point at all and my subconscious, or something, was trying to tell me something.)

> As I read and also notice things concretely, patterns from this information begin to form in my mind. Also, I learn that what I thought originally was "the subject" is not necessarily the subject, or is only an alley or sideshoot of it—that there is a lot else to it, or underneath it. So I make outlines as I go along, but they keep changing and what I end up with bears little relation—or relation only in small part—to what I was starting with, I thought. Very messy. This is also very uncomfortable. I don't like all this confusion. I only keep at it because, hard and uncomfortable though it is, it is worse to stay in such confusion. I tend to think: I would never have gotten into this if I knew what I was getting into, but then it's too late.

> Back to the patterns. They begin to show up, of their own accord, just out of the material itself. I am very suspicious of them. I try to find stuff to disprove

them, and when they don't hold up, I discard them. Often in doing so, I learn something else, so the process, while sometimes disappointing—hey, it sounded like a great idea but it wasn't—is not wasted. In principle, this process is exactly the same as when I look at other people's patterns or conventional beliefs, and jettison them because they don't hold up. A simple example is the section called Specious "causes" of City Growth, beginning on p.140 of The Economy of Cities. I apply the kind of thinking to be found there to my own notions, when I get them.

If a pattern or idea holds up, instead, and further exploration or examples, insofar as they appear, only reinforce and amplify it, then I begin to trust it, although I keep on the lookout for contradictions.[37]

Omnivorous reading, outlining, hypothesizing, and revising, seeking patterns but remaining skeptical, probing a pattern and discarding it, all in the service of finding "a piece of the truth." This is learning all the way down.

The Kind of Problem a University Is

A casual inquiry on Google—how many colleges and universities are there in New York City?—elicits a long list of institutions public and private, small, medium, and large, narrowly focused (Swedish Institute of Massage Therapy) and broadly comprehensive (CUNY, Columbia, Fordham et al.) A similar query about Toronto yields a list more moderate in length but of similar range. Had she chosen to do so in either city, Jane Jacobs could have strolled for months along halls of higher education or completed the university study so rudely interrupted by the Columbia dean. Something about the university gave her pause.

Perhaps it had to do with the nature of the institution and its purposes. To use the framework of *Systems of Survival*, we might ask whether colleges or universities are guardian or trader institutions. The case for guardian status is strong: the university seeks to create and transmit knowledge; it is zealous in protecting that knowledge—its intellectual property—and its physical property; it strictly regulates membership; it loves ostentation, reflected in faculty robes, commencement rites, and other traditions; its hierarchy towers layer upon layer. All of these aspects, in Jacobs's terms, are the traits of guardians. But the university has another face that looks like a trader's. It champions free intellectual inquiry; its scholars cooperate across departmental, institutional, and national borders;

it values intellectual honesty; its scientists thirst for the new. Surely, these are trader traits. So where does the university fit?

When Jacobs first mentions colleges and universities, she was not worried about a conceptual "fit" but a physical one. In the latter pages of *Death and Life*, while reflecting on how the New School for Social Research successfully integrates with its street neighborhood, she writes, "big universities in cities, so far as I can see, have given no thought or imagination to the unique establishments they are. Typically, they either pretend to be cloistered or countrified places, nostalgically denying their transplantation or else they pretend to be office buildings. (Of course, they are neither.)"[38]

"Of course"—contemporary university halls are not the halls of the monastery, that Western Ur-college, nor are they the urban oasis with sheltered greens and commons, as if Amherst, Massachusetts should be tucked into a corner of Boston or New York, and not a set of office buildings competing for scarce space. But still: what are they?

Jacobs does not answer that question in *Death and Life*. But her series of negations suggests what she thinks they might be. The college or university should be a place open physically to the city, a seam, not a border, to use the language of *Death and Life*. Intellectual openness to the city is even more important. It should engage the questions posed by the city, becoming a partner in conversation with its citizens, not a treasury restricted to the few. It should stake out and defend a mission and identity consonant with its openness, not defer to interests not properly its own.

On these criteria, Jacobs finds the modern urban university wanting. It does not welcome the city physically—gates, fences, and security kiosks mark its edges—but more importantly, on her account, it seems a reluctant conversation partner and beholden to the dictates of the market, not its mission. Why is this so?

"Cloistered" and "countrified" places are favorite guardian locations. Even though the university has elements of both systems, as we have noted, Jacobs argued that the guardian mindset tends to drive out, or suppress, the trader cast of mind in the university. She notes that scholars and researchers may be of either cast. One of her characters in *Systems* notes that Fidel Castro was trained as an economist, and thus should have been sensitive to the give-and-take of economic life, but, as another interlocutor rejoins, Castro brought his guardian mentality to a task that required commercial savvy. "Education does not guarantee a cast of mind appropriate to the training," he concludes.[39] Similarly, as we saw, Jacobs suggested that Muhammed Yunus became an insightful economist in spite of his formal training by attending to the give-and-take of the small economies bubbling around him and ignoring the "clouds of handed-down learning." His insights grew in clear and open air as he observed small relationships of production and exchange at ground level.

If distance from engagement with the city is one failing of the university, responding too eagerly to the requirements of the modern market is another. The earliest precursors of the university, the monasteries, kept knowledge alive and flowering for high purposes. Knowledge was to be preserved for its own sake but also as the vehicle for educating succeeding generations and growing the store of what was known. All this for the glory of God and the welfare of the community. But different gods rule our days.

In *Dark Age Ahead*, Jacobs decried the university's flight from education to the arms of the market by embracing "credentialing," the view that sees the university's mission as providing a ticket to success in the modern economy, post-graduation. "Credentialing," she writes,

> not educating, has become the primary business of North American universities. This is not in the interest of employers in the long run. But in the short run, it is beneficial for corporations' departments of human resources, the current name for personnel departments. People with the task of selecting successful job applicants want them to have desirable qualities, such as persistence, ambition, and ability to cooperate and conform to be a "team player." At a minimum, achieving a four-year university or college degree, no matter in what subject, seems to promise these traits.[40]

Jacobs did not originate this critique. Ever since Clark Kerr, then the chancellor of the University of California, described the "multiversity," a moment and coinage that Jacobs acknowledges, critics inside and outside of the university have worried about the drift away from its original mission. In *The Uses of the University* (Harvard, 1963), Kerr noted that "the university started as a single community—a community of masters and students. It may even be said to have had a soul in the sense of a central animating principle. Today, the large American university is, rather, a whole series of communities and activities held together by a common name, a common governing board, and related purposes."[41] This situation is a fact to be acknowledged, not a prompt for restoring the original ideals. As society grew more complex, so too did its needs and ambitions, and the multiversity was a logical outgrowth. It extended the boundaries of its curricula and assumed unforeseen dimensions. When John Henry Cardinal Newman was championing *The Idea of a University*, argued Kerr, he had in mind a humanist project with an accent on teaching, but the modern research university was already aborning in Germany. The multiversity was its present incarnation.

Critics of the university as an "ivory tower" misread the current situation. It cannot stand apart. If anything, the university is more embroiled in society than ever before. But the terms of that connection are what gave Jacobs pause.

Higher education became not an end in itself but the portal to economic security. Jacobs identified an underlying, powerful, cultural dimension to this development. "From the 1950's on," she wrote in *Dark Age*, "American culture's gloss on the purpose of life became assurance of full employment: jobs. Arguably, this has remained the American purpose of life."[42]

If jobs won by graduates are the primary measure of the university's success, then higher education's other purposes—the search for knowledge, the intellectual development of its students, contributions to resolving the problems of city, state, nation, and globe—are ancillary. Students, Jacobs suggested, came to universities to be "on speaking terms with wisdom,"[43] but found themselves spoken to, and of, in the various professional dialects of the multiversity. They were tuition units, student credit hours, customers, patients, and clients while enrolled, valued alumni (as potential donors) when successfully graduated. To be sure, many university communications staff at expensive institutions will tirelessly speak of their campus as providing a"transformative" experience. But it would not take a cynic to recognize the transactional aspects of that experience.

What might Jane Jacobs see as a fitting mission for the modern university? Speculation, all we have, might get a base from her "negations." It should not be a cloister, not a country retreat, not a fancier, extended, and pricey training for corporate and government life. Negations take us only a few steps. We might also infer something of higher education's ethos, or spirit. It will have something to do with the cultivation of wisdom, as well as the development of capabilities, in the student. It will have something to do, as well, with helping a culture stay true to its best features, those things which have helped it to endure and flourish. The portending dark age, which Jacobs feared, masks a culture where deep meanings and collective commitments have receded. Stemming that recession poses a challenge and requires an education that no college, no university, no single institution can provide.

The Treasure-house of and for All: Knowing, Enlarging, and Transmitting the Culture of the City

Can the pursuit of jobs be a sufficient motive power for guiding and sustaining a culture? Jacobs's sardonic observation seems to suggest that it cannot, that there must be more to life than devoting attention to "getting and spending." But invoking the preservation of culture as a task for the university, and education generally, raises a vexed set of questions. "Culture" entails a broadly shared set of meanings, practices, and beliefs, an intellectual, affective, and political "commons." The idea of such a commons is under broad attack, spurred, paradoxically, by an insistence on culture as a restricted, not shared domain. "My" culture replaces "our culture."

There is no small truth in the emphasis on multiple cultures. Cultures are the storehouses of personal and communal identity. A person finds a first identity through the culture of her family: she is a daughter, perhaps a sibling and cousin and niece and granddaughter. Other cultures—those of the neighborhood, of race and ethnicity, of religion, to name a few—will further shape her development. The import of each will vary according to her unique circumstances and the interplay of these influences. The behavior she exhibits, the language she uses, her habits of personal conduct, and the customs she observes will all bear the imprint of her cultures. These cultures are largely given, inherited, not the result of choice. As a child, one has no choice about one's family, or race and ethnicity, or, likely, religious affiliation. Choice comes later.

None of these cultural influences is a full determinant of her character, let alone her destiny. Paradoxically, they contribute to individuation. The person comes to be as the unique fullness of many different parts, irreducible to none of them. Important choices loom for each, including one suggested by Jacobs: what relationship will I take up to my larger community, my country, say, the larger world beyond the many given, local, and familiar cultures which I inhabit?

This is a fraught question, on several counts. In the United States, some would dispute that there is an American culture; others would dismiss it as not worth preserving, and still others might invoke some version of it—America First! America the Great!—without much reflection. Those who doubt the possibility of a common culture might assert that each must claim his own culture, incorporating whatever strains of identity each prizes. Those who dismiss it may see American culture as a compendium of error, ignorance, hate, broken promises, greed, manipulation, and violence and as too white, too male, too exclusive. Why bother to sustain that culture? It's not mine; it's not worth preserving. I have no stake. I do me, you do you.

This lonely hyper-individualism, or its threat, is not a problem newly recognized. In the nineteenth century, Alexis DeTocqueville staked the success of the American experiment to the vitality of local forms of association, which enriched the young country's life. Americans were farmers and churchgoers, small merchants and active members of town meetings and other local groupings. They were never just "citizens," distinguished by their membership in the state, as their revolutionary French counterparts saw themselves. Associations offset the threat of an atomized society where only citizenship counted.

But those ties have attenuated as society has grown more complex. In their landmark study of the mid-1980s, *Habits of the Heart* (1985), Robert Bellah and his colleagues pointed out the erosion of association and community as "lifestyle enclaves" segregated by race or income or professional standing or all of these in combination supplanted communities which had mixed people of different statuses, religions, races, and aspirations.[44] Robert Putnam and David Brooks have taken up these themes in their work.

Jane Jacobs wrote and thought with a conviction that argued the need for a "we," a community, to emerge from the very different I's and small we's, of family, race, ethnicity, and income and professional differences. She did not minimize the difficulties inherent to that formation or the persistence of dissent about its meaning and prospects. But she knew there was a world larger and older and richer than the world anyone inhabits at the present moment and that playing a part in its unfolding is the task, and joy, of citizenship or, better, neighborliness. Her analysis of cross-use, of what we might call "getting out of our comfort zone," occurs in *Death and Life*; it has psychological as well as sociological point. "Differences," she writes, "not duplications, make for cross-use and hence for the person's identification with an area greater than his immediate street network. Monotony is the enemy of cross-use and hence of functional use."[45] To transpose terms: if I should limit the world to my slice of it, my lifestyle enclave, or my set of political beliefs and personal relationships, I will become a monotony unto myself. The development of personal identity requires continuing engagement with difference. Both person and culture grow as a result.

Jane Jacobs found this identity despite difference in her experience of Canada. Let me quote, at length, from our interview, rather than summarize and superimpose.

> Canada doesn't have a melting pot myth. It has a mosaic myth and image. There's an historic reason for that: it was necessary for coming to terms with the French in Quebec. The English *wished* to assimilate them but it didn't work and any time efforts were made in that direction, trouble ensued.
>
> This is not just a lot of talk. When we first came here, we rented a house which was next to a daycare center, run by a group of nuns, mainly for children of immigrants. When I was out cutting the grass or something, the kids would come and introduce themselves tome—and these were just little kids, three and four years old—"I'm Marie, I'm Romanian. I'm Joe. I'm Korean . . ." the way all this was said they were proud of this, it was part of their identification. American children would have picked up already on being ashamed that their parents were not American. I asked the nuns about this and they said, "Oh, yes, that's true. They're very proud of where they come from." I asked them, what do you do about that? They answered, "It's fine. It's good for self-esteem and respect of their parents." You can be a Canadian and hang on to your ethnic things and that's considered being a *good* Canadian.
>
> When I became a Canadian citizen the immigration judge asked me various questions to see if I knew where I was! Then she asked, "Do you like it here?" I said, "Yes" and she asked "Why?" I said I liked the way people are not ashamed of their origins. She told me that she was an immigrant herself. She had had a big fight when she first came here during the war, when she wanted to speak her language, which was Polish, with other Poles in the factory where she worked. Because of wartime fear of spies, they had a rule that you couldn't speak your own language. She was outraged at this: she did speak her own language; she was warned against doing this; she was fired; and she took up the fight and helped establish that anyone could speak their own language, anywhere, without penalty. I thought, "Isn't this great! They have an immigration judge who fought for immigrants' rights." I don't think that would be so apt to happen in the United States: they'd want someone who was great on Americanization . . .
>
> Another thing that's different: I got a little mimeographed sheet when I was applying for citizenship. It stated what the chief duty of a Canadian is—I thought this was so nice: the chief duty of a Canadian is to get along well with your neighbors.[46]

To be proud of one's origins and yet to find oneself part of a whole much greater than one's personal story: this is the healthy tension of being a person in community. Creating and preserving such a civic culture is crucial; its challenges are profound.

Notes

1 Jacobs, *Nature*, 19.
2 Jacobs, *Nature*, 56.
3 Jane Jacobs, *Dark Age Ahead* (Random House, 2004),35.
4 Jacobs, *Dark Age*, 35.
5 For an account of Polanyi's thought, see lse.edu/Economic-History/Assets/Doc uments/Research/FACTS/reports/tacit.pdf.
6 Keeley, "An Interview with Jane Jacobs," in *Ethics*, 9.
7 Keeley, "An Interview with Jane Jacobs," in *Ethics*, 10
8 Keeley, "An Interview with Jane Jacobs," in *Ethics*, 10.
9 Keeley, "An Interview with Jane Jacobs," in *Ethics*, 10.
10 Keeley, "An Interview with Jane Jacobs," in *Ethics*, 10–11.
11 Holt, *How Children Learn*, (Dell, 1970), 34.
12 Holt, *How Children Learn*, 34.
13 Ivan Illich, *De-Schooling Society* (Harper & Row, 1971), 1.
14 Illich, *De-Schooling* Society, 24.
15 Ivan Illich, *Tools for Conviviality* (Harper & Row, 1973), 11.
16 What then to make of the development of the internet, something that neither Jacobs nor Illich nor Holt envisaged? On the face of it, the internet would seem to foster just the kind of independent learning that all three championed. But the seeming alignment is tenuous. Like Illich, Jacobs and Holt presuppose a community of learning characterized by "personal interdependence." But free soloing often rules the day among internet "researchers." Who needs guidance? Everyone can and should judge for themselves.
17 Jacobs, *Death and Life*, xxiv.
18 Jacobs, *Survival*, xii.
19 Aristotle, *Nicomachean Ethics*, 312.
20 Aristotle, *Nicomachean Ethics*, 315.
21 Aristotle, *Nicomachean Ethics*, 315.
22 Jane Jacobs, "Introduction: Dickens as Seer," in Charles Dickens (ed.), *Hard Times*, (Modern Library, 2001), xvii.
23 Jacobs, "Introduction: Dickens as Seer," xviii.
24 Jacobs, *Death and Life*, 429.
25 See www.score.org.

26 Jacobs, *Survival*, 169–170.

27 Jacobs, *Death and Life*, 418.

28 Jacobs, *Death and Life*, 279.

29 Jacobs, *Dark Age*, 6.

30 Jacobs, *Death and Life*, 441.

31 A puzzle-in-process lay atop one of their tables on one of my visits.

32 For an account of Kuhn's work, see https://plato.stanford.edu/entries/thomas-kuhn/#pagetopright.

33 Thomas Piketty, *Capital in the 21st Century* (Harvard University Press, 2014).

34 For connections to Piketty's work, see https://history.parisschoolofeconomics.eu/en/research-projects/.

35 Glenna Lang, *Genius of Common Sense* (Godine, 2012), 28.

36 Jacobs, *Death and Life*, 440.

37 Personal letter, March 1985. Copy available in the Jacobs Collection at The Burns Library, Boston College.

38 Jacobs, *Death and Life*, 267.

39 Jacobs, *Survival*, 128.

40 Jacobs, *Dark Age*, 44–45.

41 Clark Kerr, *The Uses of the University* (Harvard University Press, 1963), 1.

42 Jacobs, *Dark Age*, 57.

43 Jacobs, *Dark Age*, 47.

44 Robert Bellah, et. al., *Habits of the Heart: Individualism and Commitment in American Life* (University of California Press, 1985).

45 Jacobs, *Death and Life*,130.

46 Keeley, "An Interview with Jane Jacobs," in *Ethics*, 26–27.

7

Further Conversations with Jane Jacobs

Jane Jacobs offered her final analysis of the present age in *Dark Age Ahead* (2004). In the years since its publication, and the nearly two decades since her death, the present age has come to look very different. Income inequality has widened across countries and continents. With increasing numbers of extreme weather "events," an already simmering earth seems ready to boil over. The world experienced financial crisis in 2008–9 and beyond. Technology transformed many aspects of life, often at the expense of established work; those well-positioned by virtue of education and advantageous social connections often prospered, but many more found their jobs lost or whittled down, with a corresponding shrinkage of income. Political, religious, racial, ethnic, and gender differences threatened already stressed societies with lasting fractures. And then came the plague which touched us all.

The Covid pandemic enveloped the globe in 2020. Hospitalizations, and deaths from the virus, reached startling heights, prompting historians to recall the catastrophic Spanish flu of 1918. Doubt and fear spread as elderly nursing home residents died apart from family contact and brave caregivers, nurses, aides, and doctors succumbed to the virus. In cities, pedestrian traffic dwindled and those who dared to walk the streets beelined to the opposite side when another walker approached. In those few establishments that remained open, flow signs directed customers and patients to stand six feet apart. Schools, libraries, restaurants, theaters, and houses of worship shuttered. One had to wonder: what will become of cities now, and in the aftermath?

The title *Dark Age Ahead* might lead some to suspect that Jacobs had foreseen the future and despaired. But that would be a mistake. Jacobs never played at prophecy. If she were with us, what might she say about our present circumstances? We can't know, of course, although we do know that she would reject the oracle's role. We can imagine some lines of her thinking: what to notice, what to fear, what to do. We can imagine her urging us to pay attention, as best we can, to what's before us; wonder about how it got this way; vary our angle of approach; think about what we have perceived; and only then, speak of what may be the case. Perhaps we will have nothing to say as the problem stiffly resists our questioning. In that case, she would urge us to stay silent or, better, seek a wiser head. Jacobs insisted that we speak only about what we know. She favored circumspection over hasty action. Where people's lives and hopes were at stake she was reluctant to prescribe, unlike the planners she castigated. Jacobs thought that many planners hated the city, seeing in its disorder the makings of a school for scandal or the scruffy school of hard knocks; and that their recommendations showed their contempt for ordinary people. By contrast, Jacobs averred, "I think you should stay away from prescriptions for anything that you don't love."[1]

As the preceding chapters have shown, Jacobs never confined her interest to cities and their planners or the circumstances of mid-century New York City. *Dark Age* demonstrated her broad and abiding concern with the human prospect. Her methods—concrete, inductive, historically minded—remained a constant, whether she was seeking to understand how economies grow or falter, how human beings craft a life together, or worrying about science veering toward pseudo-certainty, or cultures fading away. Cities remain the background for these challenges and the proving ground for possible responses.

In Jacobs's spirit, what follows are suggestions and suppositions, not prescriptions. The suggestions will often borrow from good work currently underway, cadging bits and pieces from multiple sources. Just as early cities borrowed practices, goods, and techniques from each other, I play the magpie in searching for good ideas. Sometimes I will substitute hope and further questions for suggestions. When I point to examples and invoke other thinkers, the point is not to choose up sides or settle scores.

But to be historically minded, as Jacobs was, we must first acknowledge the profound changes in the contemporary urban context. While this notice will take us far from American shores and the New York of the early 1960s, it is helpful to revisit *Death and Life* to take new bearings.

Since its publication, champions, as well as critics, of *Death and Life* have erred in several directions. Some uncritical champions disregarded her warnings— that she was writing about *great American cities* with each of those three words important—and applied her thought, willy-nilly, to provincial outposts, far flung across the globe, to American settlements of middling size with "great" hopes, and even to towns and villages. (The careful reader may be inclined to chastise me with falling into the same traps: Worcester? Rochester? Imperial Venice? I hope to redeem my examples with the analysis that follows.) Her analysis was elastic, but one size did not stretch to fit all. Some critics seized upon just this point: they argued that what she wrote applied only to the Greenwich Village of the late 1950s and to the New York, and perhaps only Manhattan, of that era. It was all too particular, local, grounded. Another kind of criticism built upon this: the city she described is now a chimera, the happy dream of another era when American cities loomed large. To these critics, Jane Jacobs's work, especially in *Death and Life*, was a period piece.

Critics were right about some of this. The contemporary lover of cities does regard a world very different from 1950s New York with America ascendant. And, as we noted previously, relatively few Americans live within the bounds of a great city; they are more likely found in its extended region of suburbs and towns. Great though American cities may be, today's world cities dwarf them in size and complexity of problems. Consider the data. No US city ranks among the top ten, population wise, worldwide; Mexico City is the largest city in North America, with New York and Los Angeles next in line. China encompasses more than one hundred cities with a population greater than a million: Shanghai, at 24 million inhabitants, is the world's most populous city. Africa's fifteen largest cities range from 2.8 million to the 20.4 million of Cairo and 21 million of Lagos. India's ten largest cities range from 3.1 to the 18.4 million of Mumbai. As historians, geographers, and economists have long noted, the twenty-first century is the urbanized century. Across the world, the city draws people from the hinterlands with the perceived, shimmering prospect of education, work, hope, and opportunity. Can Jane Jacobs's work speak to *these* cities, their leaders, and the hopeful millions? Or was Lewis Mumford's smirking judgment, offered at the time of *Death and Life*, confirmed: she offers "home remedies" for urban cancer?[2]

If Jane Jacobs's work can speak to changing situations in this moment and in the future, it will not speak with the voice of the confident consultant who has "seen this all before" and can sum up what needs to be done. Hers is a colloquial voice, one that poses questions; listens carefully to local lore; sifts wisdom from the chaff of foolishness, ill will and mistake; and ventures to encourage—"Why not? Let's give it a try!"—rather than disparage. Despite her misgivings about some forms of scientific analysis, Jane Jacobs knew that expert knowledge is important. She knew that statistical analysis—recall her *American Economic Review* article—is a powerful method of "observing," a technical counterpart to what an ordinary person sees. She knew that science, which hewed close to the phenomena—witness her interest in biomimicry in *The Nature of Economies*—was crucial, never more so than in helping to situate the conversation about cities in matters of environment and climate. But in the conversation of cities many other voices needed a hearing, whether these were lay or expert voices.

In two of her final three books, Jacobs chose the conversational idiom, rather than straight exposition, to structure her argument. While this puzzled some of her readers, she accounted for the choice in the preface to *Systems*: "I am convinced we need continual but informal democratic explorations on the part of people who must thread their ways through governmental, business, or volunteer and grass-roots policies, or must wrestle with the moral conflicts and ethical puzzles that sprout up unbidden in all manner of occupations."[3] Note the emphases: continual, democratic, informal. Throughout her life, Jacobs had been a discerning interlocutor with people of all stripes. She would employ formal language where needed and didn't fear to joust with experts, but she also knew the power of ordinary speech and extraordinary observation to propel an argument. For her, the conversation of cities was not an exclusive seminar, since problems emerge without announcement, all over the place, unwelcome as weeds popping up through a sidewalk crack. They needed to be grasped, by those closest to hand; they would not be studied into submission.

Let me suggest four conversation starters, suggested by current, "unbidden," puzzles and problems that we might explore with the help of Jane Jacobs's thought. Jane Jacobs helps us (1) think about cities, and other, smaller places, and how they may promote human flourishing; (2) see how many and small public spaces may become a welcoming home for persons; (3) understand how to get our hands dirty in growing economies from the ground up; and (4) appreciate the kinds of politics and culture we must collectively create.

What Does Every Person Need to Flourish? How Can Cities Promote That Flourishing?

In the introduction, I suggested that Jane Jacobs, who disdained titles and honors, might be a philosopher unawares. My initial questions here point in that direction, and I have Aristotle in mind.

In the first book of his *Nicomachean Ethics*, Aristotle pursues the question of the highest good sought by human beings. Like Jane Jacobs, Aristotle begins his inquiry close to street level, examining everyday assumptions about what constitutes the highest good. Popular opinion replies that the highest good is happiness, which all seek, and Aristotle agrees, although he tosses aside the most popular opinions of what happiness consists of. Most say pleasure is happiness, but that can't be the highest good: animals enjoy pleasure too. Although we have an animal nature, we have higher capacities for speech and reason, and they must be involved in our happiness. Others say honor, but Aristotle notes its fragility: honor depends on those who confer it, and we have a sense, says Aristotle, that happiness must be something the realization of which we control. It's not a gift bestowed by others who may turn fickle. Pushing beyond popular opinion, Aristotle discovers a formal element in happiness: it is a "final" good, one superior to other, lesser goods, and one which, when attained, fully satisfies the seeker and puts an end to further search and questioning. A brief demonstration of Aristotle's argument, a staple in my introductory philosophy classes, might run like this: "why do you study? To achieve a degree. But why do you seek a degree? So as to get a job and begin a career. But why do you want a job and career? To realize my potential and support a family. But why do you want these things? Because they will make me happy." Only a fool, says Aristotle, would continue the questioning past this point and ask "but why do you want to be happy?" The answer is self-evident. Happiness is the good we seek, and all other goods are incidental to its attainment.

But Aristotle was not satisfied by his formal definition of happiness as a final good. He thought it a skeleton in need of fleshing out. And so he inverted the discussion: if happiness is the highest good attainable by a human being, it represents human fulfillment or perfection. Perhaps, then, we can enflesh our formal definition by asking, "what are human beings made for? What constitutes our perfection or fulfillment?" (Aristotle actually phrases the question differently—what is the *function* of the human being?—but the sense is well conveyed by asking about fulfillment or perfection.) Human beings must be made for more than simply taking up space: plants do that. Nor can pleasure, as explained earlier, suffice: animals experience that. No, says Aristotle, human happiness is to be found in the perfection of our highest potential, the rational element. Happiness is to be found in the rich domains of thinking and the leisure of the contemplative life.

Aristotle scholars would remind us that Aristotle also championed the superiority of practical wisdom, an intellectual capability quite particular and bound to the here and now, far from the realm of theory and contemplation. Which does he ultimately favor? That is a matter for scholars to contest, but

Jane Jacobs, perhaps more than any other urban thinker, knew and practiced practical wisdom.

Despite her use of Plato as a model in writing the dialogue of *Systems of Survival*, Jane Jacobs was an Aristotelian soul. I will have more to say about this below but, for the moment, I want to perform an "inversion" of questions based upon her work. One might suppose that the best question to ask, using her insights, would be "how should human beings of the twenty-first century address the problems of the city?" Instead, I propose we ask "what do cities of the twenty-first century need to promote the fullness of human flourishing?" This second question presupposes the priority of the person. Cities will be good cities to the extent that they can nurture and sustain the best in human beings.

But this position requires answering a prior set of questions: what *is* human flourishing? Or, in other terms, what do human beings need to achieve their potential? And how might cities contribute to that? Although Jane Jacobs never addressed that question explicitly, her work is full of suggestive hints.

Jacobs's answers to these questions would begin with the fundamental premise: that from birth to death, across time and cultures, the person is a relational being. While we talk casually about "writing the next chapter of our lives," no one comes into life via self-authorship. No one traverses the terrain from crawling to toddling to purposeful striding without the hands and props provided by others. No one speaks a language entirely her own, although personal styles and idioms will emerge. "No one": "I" am the shared creation of many we's. What have others provided? What shall I provide for others like myself? Who and what do I need?

Six Basic Needs: Care, Learning, Friendship, Civic Friendship, Work, and Beauty

Every person needs *care*, in many dimensions. Family should be the chief provider of early care, but help in that process is crucial. Jacobs's second chapter in *Dark Age* underlined the terrific stresses which beset the contemporary family and the many transformations family life has undergone and will undergo. Intergenerational ties have weakened. Families are often spread across the globe. By comparison, my American boyhood was rich with extended family ties: cousins, aunts and uncles, grandparents were close at hand. But not everyone so benefited, then or now. My own children's childhood had few relatives close at hand. Where family ties are stretched or remote, local association ties—to schools, churches, synagogues, and mosques, to teams and clubs—are vital. But these, too, need public support. As a corollary: the city, by means private and public, must find resources for the care of persons in family. To neglect or scant these family needs courts greater problems. Jacobs knew the burdens and costs of providing care. Care for the person is a collective responsibility; city practices, budgets, and policies must reflect this.

Every person needs the *opportunity to learn* and support in pursuing that opportunity. Despite the absence of explicit attention to school systems, Jacobs's work is replete with the conviction that the city itself embodies the greatest opportunity to learn. From the sidewalks of 1960s New York, the place where children learned how to be with each other and with adults, receiving lessons in elementary civics, to the indispensable tutelage of formal and informal mentors, Jacobs celebrated the city as a collective learning community. The urgency of knowing pervades the human condition—the philosopher Bernard Lonergan, SJ speaks of the unrestricted desire to know which is lodged in every heart, which prompts one question after another—and the city answers to that deep yearning. Cities of the twenty-first century are rightly concerned with providing the technical skills and training that will enable people to succeed in an ever-changing economy, but they will fail their people if they do not attend to the equally urgent, and existentially prior, desire to learn which isn't exhausted by technical or professional knowledge. This desire cannot be fulfilled through formal education alone. Jacobs would ask how cities can encourage the unfolding of dense networks of human learning. This points to a related need.

Every person needs *friendship*. If someone were to have wealth and health, professional achievement, and every kind of good fortune but lack friendship, said Aristotle, we could not call that person happy "since man is by nature a social and political animal."[4] The need for friendship, and the consequences of its absence, permeate Jacobs's work. Friendship within the family nudges the child through adolescence and toward maturity and creates bonds among siblings; friendship on the streets of New York, Toronto, and elsewhere creates a web of security. Friendships forged out of alliances in responding to a community's needs are the basis of democratic self-governance that Jacobs saw everywhere at risk. Aristotle was a realist about friendships, distinguishing friendships of utility and pleasure, the most common forms, from friendships grounded in mutual pursuit of virtue. Jacobs's cities are full of the former two, and a place where the latter also may, occasionally, flourish.

Following Jacobs, and in consonance with the principle of subsidiarity discussed in an earlier chapter, cities should seek ways to foster *civic friendship* and generally devolve responsibility for decision-making to the locales most affected. Boston experimented with this in the 1970s under the leadership of Mayor Kevin White. White created "Little City Halls" across Boston's neighborhoods. The idea was to provide access to city services close to one's home and provide on-the-spot solutions to local problems. While subsequent mayors made some use of them, it was left to a recent mayor, Marty Walsh, to promote them once more. Other cities have created similar programs. Such devolutions do not eliminate conflict, nor are they always successful, but they can become an effective means of eliciting broad engagement with civic life.

Civic friendship requires the real, effective presence of citizens, people with work to do for the sake of the city, writ large, and for themselves as citizens. On the face of it, one might think that such friendship would have a natural ally in the interconnected world of social media. After all, social media promises access to the broadest of public arenas with the enjoyment of voice for all. But this promise has proved disappointing and sometimes dangerous. Social media have unintended atomizing effects. While the vocabulary of social media promoters adopts the language of friendship, the reality is different. Social media touts friends and friend groups, group chats, affinity groups, and crowdsourcing: it can assemble a mob in a flash. But mobs are not communities and the temporary assembling of the like-minded has nothing to do with friendship. Indeed, it threatens the very possibility of friendship as group after group draws exclusionary boundary lines. Friendship presupposes welcome and draws people together. Friendship has staying power.

Every person needs *work* to anchor their relationship to the world. Jacobs understands work broadly: there is work to do at home and within retirement as well. To be sure, the foreground focus of *Economy, Wealth,* and *Nature* rests on the commercial undertakings of individuals, of businesses large and small, and of governments, but the deep background focus reveals more. There is the work each person undertakes in formal learning; the work undertaken by caregivers, most of them women, in family life; the work of mentors in imparting skills and perspective; the work of elders in binding generations and transmitting the legacy of a culture. We want to make something of ourselves and we do that in the company of others. Many hands make for many different kinds of work.

Personal agency in work is important; make-work, assigned by another, is not the work we need. Jacobs's insistent critique of planning in cities, of planning for economic development, and of rigid scheduling in education is also a call for encouraging freedom for the person, sometimes alone but often in concert with others, to "do the work."

Every person needs the nourishment that *beauty* provides.[5] This is not solely a matter of pretty streets and striking architecture, thrilling as these may be. In *Death and Life*, Jacobs had warned against regarding the city as "a work of art"[6] and argued that to regard it so led to bad results. Beautiful buildings and artful configuration of streets that were ignorant of history, local usages, and functions do little to enhance a city's life. They might be useful as "chess pieces,"[7] which could be configured to catalyze activity, but they were not valuable in themselves.

By inviting a rich diversity of peoples and perspectives, cities are home to the makers of beauty. They incubate artists and their art. Cities can support multiple choral groups and orchestras, theaters, lofts, galleries, and workshops. If human beings need work, if we are *homo faber*, doers and makers, we are also *homo ludens*, delighting in being at leisure, playing and enjoying the creations of others. Natural beauty has its own needs. Water, green spaces, and topography need protection for the abiding enjoyment they offer. An environment bereft of the many expressions of beauty that human beings create, or silently regard, will not serve our deepest needs.

How, then, to promote human flourishing? Be clear about what a human being is. Begin with reverence for the mystery of the human person, Jacobs suggests. Know that each of us needs care, opportunities to learn and work, the ties of friendship, and the delights of beauty. With that knowledge, begin to think about places. Acknowledge, to vary a famous Jacobsian phrase, the kind of mystery persons are.

How Can We Fashion Places in Which We Will Feel at Home?

A set of questions for this question: why places? What makes them special? ("You can put that any old place.") Why not cities themselves? Come to think of it, aren't cities themselves "places"? Further: why the criterion of feeling "at home"? Aren't places sought to escape the boredom or routine of home?

These are all good questions. I chose "places" because that focus, rather than the city as a whole, helps to avoid the peril of overgeneralizing Jane Jacobs's work that I have warned about, and criticized, earlier. I have noted her caution against applying lessons learned from great cities to small cities or towns or suburbs. Yet despite size differences, each of these may be full of "spaces" that may qualify as "places." A focus on places takes us to the level where people live and move, in megacities as well as in small and middling-sized cities and even towns. Put perhaps too simply: we live locally, no matter how large or small the encompassing municipality. Everyone's patch deserves careful attention. We can seek to identify, create, or preserve thriving places in all habitations, great and small.[8] With appropriate caution, Jacobs's insights may be applied without being overgeneralized.

But if attention to place draws us back to particular locales, it also draws on the deep pools of meaning explored by the thinkers we introduced in the first chapter, Mircea Eliade and Christian Norberg-Schulz. Dwelling gives one a place in the world, a relationship to earth and sky, to a receding past and a beckoning future, a fixed point in a whirling world. Poets know human beings need this: Yeats prayed that his daughter be "like a flourishing linnet tree/Rooted in one dear perpetual place";[9] even Odysseus the great wanderer, sought to come home to Ithaka.

Jacobs's sense of what makes for a welcoming place was finely tuned. She voiced it early in *Death and Life* in her discussion of parks. For parks to be successful, she observed, they must be intricate, sunny, centered, and enclosed. Those features correspond to what Norberg-Schulz emphasized in exploring the importance of paths, centers, and shelter in the human settlement. Space that is intricate but centered, tied to the elements (the sun), and offering security (enclosure) can become a place we can call home. (Perhaps every home-like place must blend, in one form or another, the elements of earth, air, fire, and water.)

A good place, a home-like place, gathers people. This may seem obvious, but Jacobs was appalled by the way designers and planners failed to appreciate this. She thought they were preoccupied with form and function: what is this space for? Shopping? Transacting business? Serving as just a throughway? The focus on function ignored the subjective experience of the city-goer for the sake of the plan. Jacobs cited Kevin Lynch, whose early work, *The Image of the City* (1960),[10] was among the first to draw attention to this experience. Lynch and Jacobs treasured the ordinary person's perceptions and experiences. This was not the stuff of high theory. The feelings and expectations of the person might be quite simple: "People's love of watching activity and other people is constantly evident in cities everywhere," Jacobs wrote in *Death and Life*.[11] But this simple delight in others, a not-surprising characteristic of a person born into relationship with others, should not be underestimated. Quiet and subtle ties to a larger world are born of such engagement. Plans for a space that seek to "optimize" the shopping "experience" or routinize the often arcane transactions of business and government might be reasonable goals for a planner, but people are more than shoppers, customers, or citizens. Good places draw on deeper human yearnings.

Making good places will differ according to local culture, conditions, and scale: a piazza in Verona, Italy will differ from a town square in Portsmouth, NH, or a market in Malaysia. The Project for Public Spaces (PPS), inspired by the work of William H. (Holly) Whyte and Jane Jacobs, does exemplary work in place-making.[12] Over the thirty years of its existence, in locales as different as Flint, Michigan; Perth, Australia; and Mexico City, PPS has helped make "place" happen. It consults with the local population and presents a five-step place-making process, described as "place-led, community-based"[13] blending the hopes and insights of local people with experts who work to assist the design of new, or renewed, places. Their process moves from defining the place and its stakeholders, through evaluation of the space and tagging its issues, to a vision of the place. Experiments and an iterative process of retesting and refining ideas lead to longer-range improvements that complete the cycle. Its methods are geared to fine observation—via behavior-mapping and time-lapse photography, for instance—but only applied where feasible and helpful. One could read its publication, *How to Turn a Place Around* (2021), as a kind of Festschrift for Whyte and Jacobs.

Good places are good for business, too: wherever people gather, possibilities for exchange multiply. Commercial exchange, as Jacobs knew, gives people a reason for leaving the comfort of their familiar surroundings and venturing up-, down-, or cross-town; while shopping no longer needs physical space, whenever it does occur, people gather. Whatever commerce may be at hand will help to vivify a place, but it will not exhaust a place's potential for greater life still. Economic innovation is something that people must do, Jacobs reminded us, not a gift bestowed from above or beyond.

How Can the Economies of Places "Sprout Up" Rather Than Wait for Something to Trickle Down?

During a 1970s performance by an experimental theater group, the cast dispersed throughout the auditorium, pausing at different rows and whispering, "you can't do anything in the world without money." For a restive, left-leaning audience, the message was confirmation of its worldview: however much one might disdain filthy lucre, money, and moneyed interests, ruled the day.

Jane Jacobs would have altered the script. She would say "you can't do anything in the world without capital—human capital." Money is, of course, one form of capital, and our thinking often defaults to equating the two. As we noted in exploring her economic thinking, Jacobs saw the potential peril of money. "Big" money, dispensed from afar and on high, might ruin an economy, by provoking a cataclysm rather than encouraging new undertakings. Still, if economic development is to occur, money will out. Capital must be available. To borrow the terminology of the accountants, we should ask about its sources and uses.

Economic sprouts may get a first watering from what Jacobs occasionally called "love capital." Personal financial accounts—savings, credit cards, loans— and those of family and friends are often the first funding source for new ideas. It's possible that no formal agreements are signed for the term of the loan: it's about love, after all, and while strangers depend upon contracts, friends rely upon each other. "When people are friends," said Aristotle, "they have no need of justice."[14]

Borrowing on one's credit card(s) and arranging personal financing is the bet the entrepreneur places on himself. Enamored of an idea, the innovator gauges that the risk is worth the reward. Capital investment at this level—personal, friends, and family—is not insignificant. A recent study of what economists call the "tinkering economy" estimated its value for 2017 at $47 billion, a figure, they noted, which exceeded the R&D expenditures of all major corporations.[15]

Especially for the tinkerers, sweat equity looms large. It was sweat capital, Jacobs observed, that powered the gradual remaking of the North End when Boston lenders were skeptical and scant. Jane and Bob Jacobs were no strangers to this capital: early photos of their Hudson Street building in New York show them with sleeves rolled up, ready for the work to be done with their hands.

To these local, small-scale, and hypothetical examples, let me add three organizations that Jane Jacobs identified during our 1985 interview that she thought especially promising. Their history has not been without challenges and, in one instance, failure, but their histories are instructive.

I have already written about the Muhammad Yunus's Grameen Development Bank, a pioneering microfinance organization. Its origins were small and personal, loans made by a professional person to local villagers. Yunus, a university-trained Bangladeshi economist, saw the plight of the poor villagers, who were forced to rely on extortionate small loans to fund their simple enterprises day by day. In response, he developed lending circles, comprised of villagers, the great majority of them women, to offer the funds at more reasonable, though still high, rates. In the original model, no paperwork was involved: a loan applicant needed to provide five character references. Lending to neighbors, rather than to strangers, provided acute insight into creditworthiness and powerful social leverage for repayment. Over the years, repayment rates have been notably high. Who knows better than the poor the importance of repaying loans and carefully stewarding funds?

The Bank is not without its critics, with complaints ranging from high interest to faltering micro-enterprise results which prompt desperate borrowers to take serial loans just to pay back original loans,[16] but its achievements have been remarkable and replicable. Born in Bangladesh, Grameen now has a US presence.

Accion International[17] was founded in 1961 "to empower the poor with the knowledge and tools to improve their lives." Over the nearly sixty years of its existence, Accion has pursued that goal in diverse and increasingly sophisticated ways. At its inception, Accion looked much like the Peace Corps, placing trained volunteers with poor communities in Venezuela to assist in community-chosen projects. During the 1970s, Accion pioneered microlending, beginning in Recife, Brazil. (Its website states, "To our knowledge, these were the first loans that launched the field of microcredit.")[18] Accion extended its lending across Latin America in the following decades and began a US program in 1991. It has developed joint programs in China and provided opportunities in Myanmar. African lending began in 2000, including a partnership with "the leading regional bank in West Africa," and lending in India began in 2005. It established a Center for Financial Inclusion in 2008, a Venture Lab in 2012, and "the first global fintech fund for the underserved, the Accion Frontier Inclusion Fund" in March 2017.

This overview suggests the elements crucial to Accion's success. It follows the lead of the local community, acting as facilitator, not dictator. It learns as it goes, placing its local, microwork in the context of larger concerns and the macro environment. It is willing to partner with a range of organizations, different in scale and expertise, and it is unafraid to undertake new projects in new cultures. It has courage, the gift of its people, for the long haul. Even as Accion's efforts and expertise enlarge, it remains rooted in its original vision.

When an institution strays far from its origins, trouble can ensue. Such was the fate of The South Shore Bank of Chicago, founded in 1973 and later known as ShoreBank. It became insolvent in 2010. When I spoke with Jane Jacobs in 1985, she praised the work of Mary Houghton, one of its founders, in bringing lending to poor and troubled neighborhoods. The bank enjoyed wide acclaim among elected officials, both local and state, as well as among civically minded banks. It developed branches in several Midwestern cities and in the Pacific Northwest. Throughout its ascent, South Shore Bank hewed close to its original mission.

"But," writes Sheila Bair, the former head of the Federal Deposit Insurance Corporation, "in the early 2000s, ShoreBank started going astray. It . . . did not focus enough on the basics of running a bank. It made poorly underwritten loans and forayed into trendy areas beyond its core mission. For instance, it started making microloans in remote developing economies."[19] (By contrast, note that Grameen and Accion lent locally.) Politics hurt too: some saw the bank as a "Democratic" organization in a time of Republican rule. And the recession of 2008–9 brought catastrophe to its loan portfolio. As it struggled to underwrite its portfolio, the Bank arranged $150 million of private equity funding, but the federal refusal of TARP funds (Troubled Asset Recovery Program) sealed its fate.

South Shore Bank's successes bore the stamp of effective cooperation across sectors. Lending addressed local problems and drew on local expertise; political leadership knew a good thing and removed obstacles; the Federal Deposit Insurance Corporation (FDIC) guaranteed depositors' funds. Its failure was precipitated by poor judgments, accelerated by the external shock of the recession, and guaranteed by the absence of TARP funds. The bank's demise demonstrates the simultaneous power and fragility of subsidiarity in action: the power of the FDIC sustained the bank in its heyday, the refusal of the government to extend itself further spelled its end. Economic development that begins at ground level thrives when reinforcing partnerships thrive and government knows how, when, and in what manner to assist.

If Grameen, Accion, and Shore Bank seem remote examples, let me point to several closer to my home. My examples, I am sure, have counterparts everywhere. They suggest, but do not exhaust, examples of economic development in a Jacobsian mold.

Clark University of Worcester, Massachusetts demonstrates the power of partnership, interlaced among different sectors and actors, in fostering economic development.[20] Clark lies in Worcester's Main South neighborhood, a low-income area troubled, historically, by crime, addiction, and the decay of housing. In

1984, as the university welcomed a new president, Richard Traina, Clark began a partnership with the local community that continues to this day and which has yielded great results for all parties. In concert with local community members, Clark joined a ground-level working group that resulted in the formation of the Main South Community Development Corporation (MSCDC).

Early efforts to upgrade neighborhood housing stock and to foster economic opportunities were bankrolled by Clark. A subsequent and ambitious University Park Partnership would attract federal funds from the Department of Housing and Urban Development (HUD), as well as private investment, and issued in educational opportunities for both adults and high school students, many of whom received tuition scholarships to attend the university. Clark opened a university-supported middle and high school, University Park Campus School, in 1997. Subsequent developments, led by MSCDC, included renovations and new construction on streets adjacent to the university, with plans for more.

Many kinds of capital influenced the success of the MSCDC and the Clark partnership—money from the university, money from HUD, tax investment credits purchased by Clark alumni, block grant funding from the city of Worcester. But surely human capital counted most. At the creation of the MSCDC, doubt and uncertainty held hands with hope. The persistence of all parties for more than forty years is a triumph of love, sweat, money, and determination.

That quartet of factors also accounts for the success of another engine of local economic development, Haley House of Boston.[21]Established in 1966 as a house of hospitality in the tradition of the Catholic Worker movement, serving homeless and destitute men, Haley House broadened its services to provide meals for the elderly and a food pantry. Its expanded focus grew from paying careful attention to its immediate neighborhood and to city-wide developments in Boston. It strove for self-reliance: for a number of years, it maintained an organic farm in Central Massachusetts, then created an urban farm in Roxbury, whose produce helps the soup kitchen operation and introduces the young to urban gardening and sustainable practices. As an initial response to gentrification of its South End neighborhood, a process that was emptying single-room occupancy dwellings, Haley House raised funds for acquiring a row house and preserved it for the sake of its elderly, fixed-income residents. Today, it manages 100 units of housing in the South End and has made efforts in social enterprise, employment, and transition from incarceration. Not all of these have been consistently successful. It suspended, then reconceived and reopened, operation of a community café and catering service in Dudley Square, Boston. Haley House has faced setbacks before—chronic shortages of funds, opposition from neighbors—but its human capital has seen it through.

Clark and Haley House have been entrepreneurial in pursuing their missions with good results. What about the individual entrepreneur? The *New York Times* has reported on the work of Jukay Hsu and David Yang, whose company, Pursuit, is "a small yet innovative player in a growing number of nonprofits developing new models for work force training. Their overarching goal is upward mobility for low-income Americans and the two-thirds of workers without four-year college degrees."[22] Hsu and Yang want to provide middle-class income for their graduates, a goal that has been elusive for most job training programs. But, as the Times reports, their graduates earn an average of $85,000, far above their pre-training average of $18,000. Jane Jacobs had argued, early on, that "cities grow the middle class,"[23] providing a chance for expansive and enriched lives. That seems elusive today, with commentary focused on inequality, noting the failure of cities in this regard as incomes tend to bifurcate between the very rich and the poor. The success of companies like Pursuit, and the ongoing efforts of Community Development Corporations to elevate their members will be crucial for tending sprouts into fully grown local economies and, perhaps, creating a new kind of middle class.

What Kinds of Politics and Culture Are Needed to Realize Good Places and Encourage Economic Development?

Good places and promising economies depend upon politics and culture. Their relationship can be symbiotic: a good place, as we have noted, already floats upon an undercurrent of economic life, and this, in turn, can steer people toward the civic realm where friendships may develop and common purposes be discovered. But the symbiosis is not guaranteed. Where the civic realm is already diminished, ordinary politics, the formal machinery of government and offices, reigns, and it may be at odds with, or simply ignorant of, specific places and unfolding economies. Local culture may be eroded or, worse, erased. "Empire," Jacobs told me, was the English "version of economic life,"[24] and local communities might feel themselves in the position of colonies: far from the effective concern of the central government and valued only for their usefulness to central purposes.

The erosion of culture was always a prominent theme in Jacobs's work, but it loomed especially large beginning with *The Question of Separatism*. Writing about "bypassed places"[25] in *Systems*, she noted the cultural forgetfulness that afflicted regions thrown out of kilter by distant city economies. Practical knowledge, skills, and techniques persist through tutelage, repetition, and stewardship. But those who would tutor, instruct, and mentor, need pupils and apprentices: when the young, seeking greater opportunity elsewhere, leave, so, too, does the future life of the community. In *Dark Age*, she noted that "cultures take purposes for themselves, cling tenaciously to them, and exalt them to the purposes and meanings of life itself,"[26] but her subsequent listing of these purposes, from Rome—rule the world—to contemporary America—get a good job—hardly brims with hope. Her mid-twentieth-century contemporaries, Paul and Percival Goodman, had identified, not without irony, "The City of Efficient Consumption" as one incarnation of the American higher purpose.[27] On this view, the department store was the crucial institution of the city, ease of access to it was of paramount importance, and status-envy the motive that powered relentless purchasing. In this century, Michel Kimmelman, writing in the *New York Times* of Hudson Yards, the city's enormous real estate project, incorporating luxury dwellings, the very high end of retailing, and some modestly priced residences, observed:

> And while those apartment buildings look to be less enormous than the supertalls that have gone up so far, stepping down toward the river, the whole site lacks any semblance of human scale. With its focus on the buildings' shiny envelopes, on the monotony of reflective blue glass and the sheen of polished wood, brass, leather, marble and stone, Hudson Yards glorifies a kind of surface spectacle—as if the peak ambitions of city life were consuming luxury goods and enjoying a smooth, seductive, mindless materialism.[28]

It may be that the Goodmans were correct—everyone wants the stuff the department stores peddle—but surely local government should see the limitations of preoccupation with getting and spending. Hudson Yards, continues Kimmelman, "gives physical form to a crisis of city leadership, asleep at the wheel through two administrations, and to a pernicious theory of civic welfare that presumes private development is New York's primary goal, the truest measure of urban vitality and health, with money the city's only real currency."[29] Hudson Yards lies not far from Hudson Street, Jane Jacobs's original neighborhood; this is a "neighborhood" she could not save but would certainly rue.

But the larger question remains: how can we sustain a civic culture when commercial culture dominates our attention? Much as we might complain, with Emerson, that "things are in the saddle/And ride mankind,"[30] still we go on acquiring, not worrying overmuch. Catalogs stream through our physical mailboxes, tracking, and scratching at our desires. Ads fringe our screens large and small. We listen anxiously for the quarterly reports on consumer spending, a putative sign of the economic health of society at large, rarely pausing to recollect that the consumer is *us*, reduced to a function in the market, neither friend or spouse or parent or neighbor or citizen. We might say, with Pogo, that community and culture have met the enemy and it is us.

"A culture is a vast and obdurate entity, difficult to divert from a mistaken course upon which it has set," wrote Jacobs in *Dark Age*.[31] How, then, to create a culture counter to the dominant commercial culture? Jane Jacobs, I think, would say that is the wrong type of question. She would point to evidence of existing counter-cultures and begin by asking what they have in common. What do healthy cultures do? What makes them possible? With these questions in hand, we can begin to think forward to the tasks of encouraging their numbers to multiply. The cultures that Jacobs celebrated for their vitality, or mourned for their demise, shared the following five characteristics.

First, they were intergenerational, connecting the young with their elders and the present community with its past. *Death and Life* is replete with examples of this from the minding of children in the streets by near neighbors to the accounts of parenting and coaching. But a culture cannot become stagnant if it hopes to endure: if there are no opportunities at hand for the next generation, the young will look elsewhere as we saw in Jacobs's discussion of migration from town to city in *Quebec* and *Systems*. Thinking about the threats posed to the multiform families of the twenty-first century, she looked, hopefully, to "parents, elders or schoolmasters"[32] as guardians and transmitters of the culture.

Second, they preserved, cherished, and articulated a cultural story. "Where there is no vision, the people perish" (Proverbs 29:18). Jacobs would push this further: where there is no story, there are no people. Stories ground cultural identity, with enormous consequences for politics. There is no better example than the one she cited in *Quebec*. Exploring the secession of Norway from Sweden, she identified the importance of two Norwegian folklorists, Moe and Asbjornsen, in unearthing folktales and reviving the Norwegian language.[33] As the stories were brought to life and published, Norwegians began to recognize themselves as a distinct people. These were their roots. The stories fostered a sense of a common heritage. Folk art helped to create a national politics.

Third, they celebrated places important to that story. Cultures are concrete: they abide *somewhere*. Important places will differ: here a street, there a monument, there a historic district, further on a church or synagogue or mosque.

Fourth, they embodied practical knowledge, a how-to-do attitude as well as common wisdom, a why-to-do attitude, connected to the story. A culture of inventiveness, such as characterized several of the cities described in *Economy* and elsewhere, spreads know-how in many directions. Skills transfer, new applications emerge, new ventures arise. Common wisdom provides the framework that guides the new: "Now that we've done this, what's the next thing that needs doing?"

Fifth and finally, they depended upon the willing disposition of friends, neighbors, and strangers to discuss matters on which they well might disagree. The fora for such discussions were many: Jane Jacobs knew of teach-ins and drop-by conversations, formal public meetings, and organized street protests and rallies. Conversation developed on sidewalks and porches, in cafes, school halls, in the bleachers and on plazas and, on occasion, in the considered testimony of the committee room. To be sure, the conversations were not always gentle, and sometimes downright impolite, but people were talking.

If we use these criteria to search for what would constitute healthy cultures today, two things are apparent.

First, they are most often microcultures, living on streets or neighborhoods or in small cities or towns. They can take root in many different soils—ethnic heritage, avocations, religious belief—and many of these roots may tangle, to their mutual enrichment. Their small size does not make them irrelevant to fostering a broader, healthy culture. Jane Jacobs would think no other way: the health of the culture at large depends upon its hospitality to thriving local cultures. The mystic and philosopher Martin Buber wrote in *Paths in Utopia* (1949), that the real essence of community is to be found in a community of communities.[34] Like Jacobs, Buber saw a community as an organism, developing on its own terms. Like Jacobs, he prized organizational power exercised in subsidiary fashion: just what's needed, no more, no matter the level of organization. While we often think of the state as a policeman, Jacobs and Buber knew that a healthy state should serve as a host and a catalyst for the flourishing of its people.

But there is a problematic dialectic here, a tension to which both thinkers were sensitive. For a community can welcome or exclude. Jacobs once told me that she was wary of easy talk of "the *common* good" since one could push that to an extreme and unduly restrict freedom or impose viewpoints. Communities can be so specific in their constitution as to shun the world or rule out the desirability of "other" worlds. Nativist or isolationist sentiments in the United States, Europe, and elsewhere display this tendency. If one insists on a single, governing monoculture in which our identity is specified as "citizen," personal freedom will be at risk. Insist on exclusive, "only ours" communities and sectarianism of various stripes—religious, ethnic, racial, political—will emerge.

Second, microcultures may pop up anywhere, given the right conditions. Jacobs would expect no less: what can restrain all that exuberant human inventiveness or dam that rush of human capital? As I write this morning, a *Boston Globe* article highlights "third spaces," free public spaces that pop-up to offer free amenities and gathering spots. The article highlights the work of CultureHouse,[35] a place-making organization based in Somerville, Massachusetts.[36] Another good example of third spaces is the makerspace movement.

Makerspaces combine a variety of users—skilled craftspeople, designers, youngsters, retirees, rookies, and veterans—in a space mixing technology high and low, raw materials, and a surprising assortment of odds and ends. A visitor might find wood lathes, glass-blowing equipment, 3D printers, and laser cutters cheek by jowl. Space may be leased on monthly or annual bases; many facilities are open all day, every day. Makerspaces often start up in places forgotten or in disuse: old warehouses, garages, office buildings gone empty. They depend upon practitioners. They run on dues and rental charges, but the zeal of practitioners to pass along neglected skills provides powerful emotional sustenance. They welcome the young and the community at large.

In my city, Worcester, Massachusetts, there were two prominent, public makerspaces, Technocopia and Worcshop, which displayed the movement's salient characteristics. A collective CV of the organizations showed an astonishing eclecticism, a league of roboticists, chemical engineers, elementary school instructors, carpenters, iron forgers, agriculturalists, fashion designers, and many others. Both sites had repurposed sections of old buildings, one close to downtown, the other at the city's edge. Both welcomed the public and invited the attention of the young. But only one survived.

Several smaller makerspaces remain, often nested within schools and college. But Technocopia, the surviving public makerspace, is the kind that offers special promise. Such public makerspaces may function, to use Jacobs's term, as seams, welcoming people in, rather than borders, shunting people away. A makerspace that draws the public in at street level; that becomes a place for off-site offering of high school or college classes; that carves a spot for casual tinkering, open to the very young, that echoes the more demanding and technical tinkering that goes on in back rooms; that reflects, in display, some aspects of the city's making and trading business history—such a makerspace might address the most elusive aspects of civic culture.

Makerspaces are not without problems. As the journalist Will Holman points out, there are questions about their efficacy in breeding sustainable businesses, about their necessary presence in dense areas and absence in rural areas, and about their funding models.[37] The demise of Worcester's Worcshop, which had relocated to a small semi-rural town, underscores Holman's point. But the promise of makerspaces, I think, remains great.

If cities can nourish the kind of vital micro-communities that I have been describing, they may begin to foster a "fourth space," a vibrant "political" space. Some, especially the technological enthusiasts, think we have achieved this already. Isn't that, they would argue, what the internet provides, a digital commons open for all, a forum for free speech? Some of this is true, I think, but the kind of political space I am thinking of has a different, ancient precedent, and one with strict rules of conduct. I am thinking of ancient Greece and the city of Athens.

The ancient Athenians' public space was, "the Agora [. . .] a large public square, humming with human activity—shopping, gossip, dramatic performances, military and religious processions—and surrounded on all sides by buildings, including many of the key institutions of Athenian democracy."[38]

A vital, heterogeneous, public space, the Agora was a salon for the *polis*. Demarcating its boundaries, writes the philosopher Simon Critchley, were "marble stones about three feet high called *horoi*. These defined the horizon between public and private space, preventing the encroachment of the latter into the former."[39] While Jane Jacobs would have no truck with much of Athenian society—its aristocracy, marginalization, and exclusion of women, its slavery—she could not help but be buoyed by the possibilities of an *inclusive* Agora. There, people would *meet* face-to-face, would *do* a variety of things, and be held

Figure 7.1 The Agora, Athens, 2023. Acropolis in high background. Author photo.

accountable for what they say. Critchley, citing Deborah Tarn Steiner's work in *The Tyrant's Writ* (1994), writes

> the historians and dramatists of the classical period repeatedly stated that a
> democracy depends on the ability of citizens to speak freely and declare their
> will out loud. As Steiner wrote, "It is logos and not writing that exists at the
> heart of democratic Athens's self-definition and the good speaker—not the

writer—who keeps popular government on course." Speech is the hallmark of the democrat.[40]

In the Agora, one had to account for one's claims in speech and in person. Arguments had to be made, evidence offered and contraries considered. And here, the most pointed differences with the internet emerge. In the Athenian Agora, there were no hiding places to shelter trolls. In the allegedly free, because open to all, space of the internet, reasoned speech has a hard time. Word snippets, memes, video, images, memes, not speech, command the most attention. In the Agora, the citizen was in the midst of fellow citizens; on the internet, anonymous friends and foes and bots do duty for interaction. On the internet, you may scream without consequence; in the Agora, speech was consequential.

Can we imagine what a contemporary American Agora would look like? This is a difficult question. For one thing, the online world pulls us away from the public square. For that small percentage of people who suffer from agoraphobia, the online world offers a welcome version of public contact where they might live "alone together" as Sherry Turkle has phrased it. Some others use the anonymity to hide and snipe without immediate, physical consequences: trolls enjoy the shelter which the internet provides "speech."[41]

It might seem an ardent fantasy, then, to hope for a public place animated by many different people and their purposes, a scramble of races, ethnicities, ages, and gender, a site for commerce, education, entertainment, and a place for neighborly conversation. Where to find such places? As Jane Jacobs would say, you just have to look for them.

Eric Klinenberg has done just that. In *Palaces for the People* (2018), he identifies a range of institutions which embody one, or several, of the aspects of a new Agora. The public library is his lead example, an institution which nurtures young and old and exposes them to each other, provides shelter, hosts activities relating to the life of the community and its history, loans books, to be sure, but also loans tools and museum passes.

Libraries are not alone. On the sidelines of playing fields for their children, young parents create some of the social ties that used to develop on street corners and local shops. As Klinenberg writes,

> Social infrastructure is crucially important, because local face-to-face interactions—at the school, the playground, and the corner diner—are the building blocks of all public life. People forge bonds in places that have healthy social infrastructures—not because they set out to build community, but because

when people engage in sustained, recurrent interaction particularly while doing things they enjoy, relationships inevitably grow.[42]

As in economic development so, too, with the development of social infrastructure: it is a doing, not a well-conceived plan dreamed apart from a community and imposed from without. It emerges from many small, repeated interactions with people like, and unlike, ourselves.

Courage and imagination, not fantasy, will create the kinds of social infrastructure we need. I can imagine a kind of civic makerspace where, say, a community displays and dramatizes parts of its history; where ancestors and elders, in person or on video, bring the story to life; where a storefront becomes a classroom where the rudiments of rhetoric, argumentation and debate are taught, modeled, and demonstrated; where such instruction yields a framework for public discussion guided by amity, generous listening, a commitment to facts, and a willingness to bend one's mind and heart to persuasion; where local food and drink draw people to a common table.

There is a famous Francisco Goya etching titled *The Sleep of Reason Produces Monsters*. The image shows a sleeping artist whose dreams are bedeviled by bats and owls. In our fraught times, we may seem closer than ever to Goya's fearful title, as opinion flies free of the tethers of fact, slogans replace argument, and the passions put a stick to reason. But the monsters can be caged. The public square belongs to us.

On what may we hope to rely in meeting these challenges? (This is a subhead which needs treatment like the others)

A first answer to this question might invoke money, technical skills, smarts, and political will. That is a potent mix, but it is not a solution All of these are necessary, but not sufficient, conditions for bringing renewed life to places. Human beings are neither "selfless geniuses or angels,"[43] Jacobs cautioned in *Wealth*. City failures—human failures, finally—trace to "short sightedness, folly, overspecialization," as well as to bad luck.[44] Money and smarts and will, if the combination is to succeed, require something more fundamental.

In the penultimate chapter of *The Nature of Economies*, Jacobs reveals that something more. One of the characters, Kate, has been worrying about threats to habitat. What factors might prevent habitat destruction? "Very well," she says, "we have aesthetic appreciation, fear of retribution, awe expressed as veneration, persuasiveness, and corrective tinkering and contriving,"[45] a list to which another character adds "we have the sense of morality—another gift of consciousness . . . consciousness of right and wrong behavior is a very ancient and widespread trait."[46] What we need, in other words, are people who appreciate beauty, who know and respect the numinous, who hold to the line when normal consciousness of right and wrong needs the shadow of punishment—there are no angels, here—and who are brave enough to try, and try again. We need, in short, the collective enactment of a virtuous life.

This is no sentimental bromide. To collectively live the virtuous life is hard work but the very stuff of a healthy community and culture. A culture is a "whole precarious contraption,"[47] requiring constant attention, adjustment, and experimentation, as one of the interlocutors in *The Nature of Economies* says about continuing co-developments which fuel prosperity. There is no "app for that" and to cede the health of a culture to the ministrations of technicians and formal officeholders is to lose something preciously human. Like economic development, culture must be "done" and we must be the doers. "Any culture," Jacobs writes in the last page of *Dark Age Ahead*, "that jettisons the values that have given it competence, adaptability, and identity becomes weak and hollow. A culture can avoid that hazard only by tenaciously retaining the underlying values responsible for the culture's nature and success."[48]

But Kate's discussion in *Nature* also brings to full cycle an argument launched in the closing pages of *Death and Life*. There, Jacobs identified the ruinous consequences of a seemingly benign sentimentalizing of nature. "Owing," she writes

> To the mediation of cities, it became popularly possible to regard "nature" as benign, ennobling and pure, and by extension to regard "natural man" (take your pick of how "natural") as so too. Opposed to all this fictionalized purity, nobility and beneficence, cities, not being fictions, could be considered as seats of malignancy and—obviously—the enemies of nature.[49]

Once maligned, cities became fit candidates for redemption. The redemption would be accomplished by infusing "natural" elements—in reality, Jacobs argued, suburban facsimiles of nature, tidy and domestic—into urban environments. And this approach evoked the most scathing vituperation of *Death and Life*: it was "schizophrenic," "insipid, standardized, [a] suburbanized shadow of nature—apparently in sheer disbelief that we and our cities, just by virtue of being, are a legitimate part of nature, too."[50] *Human nature* blossoms in the conversation of cities, not through its shrubs, bushes, and ornamental plantings.

The other elements of Kate's list surface repeatedly in Jacobs's work. Jacobs celebrated the courage, loyalty, and friendship that animate successful neighborhoods. She saw the connection between "esthetic curiosity,"[51] the delight of improvisation and the inventions that issue from them. She was reverent before the deep unknowns: "development still embodies mystery. Why should there be a force driving the universe toward intricacy and away from simplicity?"[52] wonders one of the interlocutors in *Nature*. She was reverent, too, in considering our place in the world we have inherited and the one we will not see. We "owe immense debts to the past . . . we can only pay these debts by making gifts to the future."[53] Gratitude is the tribute reverence pays to the future. Jane Jacobs paid that tribute throughout her life and work.

Notes

1　Keeley, "An Interview with Jane Jacobs," in *Ethics*, 20.

2　See *The New Yorker*, December 1, 1962, 148.

3　Jacobs, *Systems*, xiii.

4　Aristotle, *Nicomachean Ethics* (New York: Macmillan, 1962), Book I, 15.

5　See, for instance, Dana Gioia on this topic at https://www.firstthings.com/media/ why-beauty-matters.

6　Jacobs, *Death and Life*, 372.

7　Jacobs, *Death and Life*, 167ff.

8　In this regard, see Jennifer S. Vey and Nate Storring (eds.), *Hyperlocal: Place Governance in a Fragmented World* (Washington, DC: Brookings Institution Press, 2022).

9　W. B. Yeats, "A Prayer for My Daughter," in *The Collected Poems of William Butler Yeats* (Macmillan, 1977), 185.

10　Kevin Lynch, *The Image of the City* (Cambridge, MA: MIT Press, 1960).

11　Jacobs, *Death and Life*, 37.

12　See www.pps.org.

13　Kathy Madden, *How to Turn a Place Around* (Project for Public Spaces, 2021), 133.

14　Aristotle, *Ethics*, Book 8, 215.

15　See https://www.marketplace.org/shows/marketplace-morning-report/03112019 -markets-edition/.

16　On the problems with microfinance lending, see, for instance, Aneel Karnani, "Microfinance Misses Its Mark," https://ssir.org/articles/entry/microfinance_misses _its_mark.

17　For Accion, see www.accion.org.

18　See www.accion.org (accessed December 3, 2019).

19   Sheila Bair, *Bull by the Horns* (Free Press, 2012), 285.

20   Although I am a Worcester resident, and a former adjacent neighbor to Clark, my comments are derived, largely, from a HUD case study found at www.huduser.gov/portal/casestudies/study-05252017.

21   See www.haleyhouse.org.

22   See Steve Lohr, "Income Before: $18,000. After: $85,000. Does Tiny Nonprofit Hold a Key to the Middle Class?," https://www.nytimes.com/2019/03/15/business/pursuit-tech-jobs-training.html.

23   Jacobs, *Death and Life*, 282.

24   Keeley, "An Interview," in *Ethics*, 2.

25   Jacobs, *Systems*, chapter 9.

26   Jacobs, *Dark Age*, 55.

27   See Percival and Paul Goodman, *Communitas: Means of Livelihood and Ways of Life* (Columbia University Press, 1947).

28   See Michael Kimmelman, "Hudson Yards is Manhattan's Biggest, Newest, Slickest Gated Community: Is This the Neighborhood New York Deserves?," https://www.nytimes.com/interactive/2019/03/14/arts/design/hudson-yards-nyc.html.

29   Kimmelman, "Hudson Yards."

30   Ralph Waldo Emerson, "Ode, Inscribed to William H. Channing." https://www.poetryfoundation.org/poems/45874/ode-inscribed-to-william-h-channing.

31   Jacobs, *Dark Age*, 5.

32   Jacobs, *Dark Age*, 5.

33   See Jane Jacobs, *The Question of Separatism: Quebec and the Struggle over Sovereignty* (Random House, 1980), chapter 3.

34   See Martin Buber, *Paths in Utopia* (Beacon, 1958).

35   See https://culturehouse.cc/ and https://www.bostonglobe.com/2024/08/16/opinion/culturehouse-third-places-boston/.

36   See https://culturehouse.cc/#mission.

37   On Makerspaces, see Will Holman, "Makerspace: Towards a New Civic Infrastructure," *Places Journal*, November 2015, https://doi.org/10.22269/151130 (accessed March 29, 2019).

38   See "Athens in Pieces: We Know Socrates' Fate. What's Ours?," *New York Times*, March 20, 2019, http://www.nytimes.com/2019/03/20/opinion/athens-democracy.html. In *Paths in Utopia*, Buber also notes the absence of the Agora in contemporary society.

39   Critchley, "Athens."

40   Critchley, "Athens."

41   Sherry Turkle has been the most thoughtful commentator I have encountered on the challenges to conversation in our situation. See *Alone Together: Why We*

Expect More from Technology and Less from Each Other (2011) and *Reclaiming Conversation: The Power of Talk in a Digital Age* (2015).

42 Eric Klinenberg, *Palaces for the People: How Social Infrastructure Can Help Fight Inequality, Polarization, and the Decline of Civic Life* (Crown, 2018), 5. Jacobs knew Klinenberg's earlier work exploring the differing fates of elderly Chicagoans during a heat wave.

43 Jacobs, *Wealth*, 208.

44 Jacobs, *Wealth*, 178.

45 Jacobs, *Nature*, 130.

46 Jacobs, *Nature*, 132.

47 Jacobs, *Nature*, 139.

48 Jacobs, *Dark Age*, 176.

49 Jacobs, *Death and Life*, 444.

50 Jacobs, *Death and Life*, 445.

51 Jacobs, *Wealth*, 222.

52 Jacobs, *Nature*, 23. For a profound meditation on reverence, see Paul Woodward, *Reverence: Renewing a Forgotten Virtue* (New York: Oxford University Press, 2001).

53 Jacobs, *Quebec*, 122.

Appendix

For Further Reading

Anderson, Darran. *Imaginary Cities: A Tour of Dream Cities, Nightmare Cities, and Everywhere in Between.* Chicago, IL: The University of Chicago Press, 2015.

Barnet, Andrea. *Visionary Women: How Rachel Carson, Jane Jacobs, Jane Goodall, and Alice Waters Changed Our World.* New York: Harper, 2018.

Feeney, Mark. "City Sage." *The Boston Globe*, November 14, 1993.

Fishman, Robert. *Urban Utopias in the Twentieth Century: Ebenezer Howard, Frank Lloyd Wright, Le Corbusier.* Cambridge, MA: MIT Press, 1982.

Flint, Anthony. *This Land: The Battle over Sprawl and the Future of America.* Baltimore, MD: John Hopkins University Press, 2006.

Flint, Anthony. *Wrestling with Moses: How Jane Jacobs Took On New York's Master Builder and Transformed the American City.* New York: Random House, 2009.

Glaeser, Edward and David Cutler. *Survival of the City: Living and Thriving in an Age of Isolation.* New York: Penguin Books, 2021.

Goldsmith, Stephen A. and Lynne Elizabeth (eds.). *What We See: Advancing the Observations of Jane Jacobs.* Oakland, CA: New Village Press, 2010.

Gratz, Roberta. *The Battle for Gotham: New York in the Shadow of Robert Moses and Jane Jacobs.* New York: Nation Books, 2010.

Ikeda, Sanford. *A City Cannot be a Work of Art: Learning Economics and Social Theory from Jane Jacobs.* New York: Palgrave macmillan, 2024.

Jacobs, Jane. *The Last Interview and Other Conversations.* Brooklyn, NY: Melville House, 2016.

Krieger, Alex. *City on a Hill: Urban Idealism in America from the Puritans to the Present.* Cambridge, MA: Belknap Press, 2019.

Laurence, Peter. *Becoming Jane Jacobs.* Philadelphia, PA: University of Pennsylvania, 2016.

Meijling, Jesper and Tigran Haas (eds.). *Essays on Jane Jacobs.* Stockholm: Bokförlaget Stolpe, 2019.

Mennel, Timothy, Jo Steffens, and Christopher Klemek (eds.). *Block by Block: Jane Jacobs and the Future of New York.* New York: Municipal Art Society of New York, 2007.

Norberg-Schulz, Christian. *Existence, Space and Architecture.* New York: Rizzoli, 1971.

Norberg-Schulz, Christian. *Genius Loci: Towards a Phenomenology of Architecture.* New York: Rizzoli, 1979.

Norberg-Schulz, Christian. *Meaning in Western Architecture.* New York: Rizzoli, 1974.

Rein, Richard K. *American Urbanist: How William H. Whyte's Unconventional Wisdom Reshaped Public Life.* Washington, DC: Island Press, 2022.

Sim, David. *Soft City: Building Density for Everyday Life.* Washington, DC: Island Press, 2019.

Starr, Kevin. *Coast of Dreams: California on the Edge, 1990-2003.* New York: Vintage Books, 2004.

Strauss, Anselm. *Images of the American City.* New York: Routledge, 1961.

Whyte, William H. *City: Rediscovering the Center.* Philadelphia, PA: University of Pennsylvania, 2009.

Bibliography

Acemoglu, Daron and James A. Robinson. *Why Nations Fail: The Origins of Power, Prosperity, and Poverty.* New York: Crown, 2012.

Alexiou, Alice Sparberg. *Jane Jacobs: Urban Visionary.* New Brunswick, NJ: Rutgers University Press, 2006.

Allen, Max (ed.). *Ideas That Matter: The Worlds of Jane Jacobs.* Owen Sound: The Ginger Press, 1997.

Aristotle. *Nicomachean Ethics.* Translated by Martin Ostwald. New York: Macmillan, 1962.

Bair, Sheila. *Bull by the Horns: Fighting to Save Main Street and Wall Street from Itself.* New York: Free Press, 2012.

Bairoch, Paul. *Cities and Economic Development: From the Dawn of History to the Present.* Translated by Christopher Braider. Chicago, IL: The University of Chicago Press, 1988.

Banerjee, Abhijit and Esther Duflo. *Poor Economics: A Radical Rethinking of the Way to Fight Global Poverty.* New York: PublicAffairs, 2012.

Banerjee, Abhijit and Esther Duflo. *Good Economics for Hard Times.* New York: PublicAffairs, 2021.

Bellah, Robert, Richard Madsen, William M. Sullivan, Ann Swidler and Steven M. Tipton. *Habits of the Heart: Individualism and Commitment in American Life.* Berkeley, CA: University of California Press, 1985.

Bonhoeffer, Dietrich. *Letter and Papers from Prison.* New York: Macmillan, 1978.

Brooks, David. *Bobos in Paradise: The New Upper Class and How They Got There.* New York: Simon & Schuster, 2000.

Buber, Martin. *Paths in Utopia.* Boston, MA: Beacon Press, 1949.

Calvino, Italo. *Invisible Cities.* New York: Harcourt, 1974.

Chambers, David and Brian Pullan. *Venice: A Documentary History 1450-1630.* Toronto: University of Toronto, 2001.

Critchley, Simon. "Athens in Pieces: We Know Socrates' Fate. What's Ours?" *New York Times,* March 20, 2019. http://www.nytimes.com/2019/03/20/opinion/athens-democracy.html.

Cronon, William. *Nature's Metropolis: Chicago and the Great West.* New York: Norton, 1991.

Crowley, Roger. *City of Fortune: How Venice Ruled the Seas.* New York: Random House, 2011.

Easterly, William. "Planners vs. Searchers in Foreign Aid." *Asian Development Bank*, January 18, 2006.

Eliade, Mircea. *The Myth of the Eternal Return*. Princeton, NJ: Princeton University Press, 1971.

Eliot, George. *Middlemarch*. New York: Modern Library, 1984.

Ellul, Jacques. *The Meaning of the City*. Grand Rapids, MI: Eerdmans, 1970.

Gans, Herbert, *The Urban Villagers: Group and Class in the Life of Italian-Americans*. New York: The Free Press, 1982.

Glaeser, Edward. *Triumph of the City: How Our Greatest Invention Makes Us Richer, Smarter, Greener, Healthier and Happier*. New York: Penguin Books, 2011.

Glendon, Mary Ann. *A Nation Under Lawyers: How the Crisis in the Legal Profession is Transforming American Society*. Cambridge, MA: Harvard University Press, 1994.

Gopnik, Adam. "Street Cred." *The New Yorker*, September 2016.

Graham, Wade. *Dream Cities: Seven Urban Ideas that Shape the World*. New York: Harper Collins, 2016.

Hirschman, Albert O. *Exit, Voice, and Loyalty: Responses to Decline in Firms, Organizations, and States*. Cambridge, MA: Harvard University Press, 1970.

Holt, John. *How Children Learn*. New York: Pitman, 1967.

Hughes, Susan. *Walking in the City with Jane: A Story of Jane Jacobs*. Toronto: Kids Can Press, 2018.

Illich, Ivan. *Deschooling Society*. New York: Harper & Row, 1971.

Illich, Ivan. *Tools for Conviviality*. New York: Harper & Row, 1973.

Jacobs, Jane. *Cities and the Wealth of Nations: Principles of Economic Life*. New York: Random House, 1984.

Jacobs, Jane. *Constitutional Chaff: Rejected Suggestions of the Constitutional Convention of 1787, with Explanatory Argument. / Compiled by Jane Butzner from the Notes of James Madison ... Major William Pierce ... Dr. James McHenry ... Rufus King ... and the Honorable Robert Yates*. New York: Columbia University Press, 1941.

Jacobs, Jane. *Dark Age Ahead*. New York: Random House, 2004.

Jacobs, Jane. "Introduction: Dickens as Seer." In *Hard Times*, xi–xx New York: The Modern Library, 2001.

Jacobs, Jane. *The Death and Life of Great American Cities*. New York: Vintage Books, 1961.

Jacobs, Jane. *The Economy of Cities*. New York: Random House, 1969.

Jacobs, Jane. *The Nature of Economies*. New York: Random House, 2000.

Jacobs, Jane. *The Question of Separatism: Quebec and the Struggle over Sovereignty*. New York: Random House, 1980.

Jacobs, Jane. *A Schoolteacher in Old Alaska: The Diary of Hannah Breece*. New York: Random House, 1997.

Jacobs, Jane. "Strategies for Helping Cities," reprinted in Samuel Zipp and Nathan Storring, *Vital Little Plans*. New York: Random House, 2016.

Jacobs, Jane. *Systems of Survival: A Dialogue on the Moral Foundations of Commerce and Politics*. New York: Random House, 1992.

Kanigel, Robert. *Eyes on the Street: The Life of Jane Jacobs*. New York: Alfred A. Knopf, 2016.

Keller, Evelyn Fox. *A Feeling for the Organism: The Life and Work of Barbara McClintock*. New York: Freeman, 1983.

Kerr, Clark. *The Uses of the University*. Cambridge, MA: Harvard University Press, 1971.

Kimmelman, Michael. "Hudson Yards is Manhattan's Biggest, Newest, Slickest Gated Community: Is This the Neighborhood New York Deserves?" https://www.nytimes .com/interactive/2019/03/14/arts/design/hudson-yards-nyc.html.

Kleinenberg, Eric. *Palaces for the People: How Social Infrastructure Can Help Fight Inequality, Polarization, and the Decline of Civic Life*. New York: Crown, 2018.

Lang, Glenna. *Jane Jacobs's First City: Learning from Scranton, Pennsylvania*. New York: New Village Press, 2021.

Lang, Glenna and Marjory Wunsch. *Genius of Common Sense: Jane Jacobs and the Story of the Death and Life of Great American Cities*. Boston, MA: Godine, 2012.

Lawrence, Fred (ed.). *Ethics in Making a Living: The Jane Jacobs Conference*. Atlanta, GA: Scholars Press, 1989.

Le Corbusier. *The City of To-morrow and its Planning*. Cambridge, MA: MIT Press, 1971.

Lohr, Steve. "Income Before: $18,000. After: $85,000. Does Tiny Nonprofit Hold a Key to the Middle Class?" https://www.nytimes.com/2019/03/15/business/pursuit-tech -jobs-training.html.

Lynch, Kevin. *The Image of the City*. Cambridge, MA: MIT Press, 1959.

Madden, Kathy. *How to Turn a Place Around: A Placemaking Handbook*. Project for Public Spaces, 2018.

Marketplace Morning Report (NPR). "$40 Billion Worth of Tinkering." https://www .marketplace.org/shows/marketplace-morning-report/03112019-markets-edition/.

Marshall, Alfred. *Principles of Economics*. New York: Macmillan, 1920.

Marx, Leo. *The Machine in the Garden*. New York: Oxford University Press, 1964.

Mumford, Lewis. "Mother Jacobs' Home Remedies." *The New Yorker,* December 1, 1962, 148.

Norberg-Schulz, Christian. *The Concept of Dwelling*. New York: Rizzoli, 1985.

Norwich, John Julius. *A History of Venice*. New York: Vintage Books, 1989.

Rossiter, Clinton (ed.). *The Federalist Papers*. New York: New American Library, 1961.

Rotella, Carlo. *The World is Always Coming to an End: Pulling Together and Apart in a Chicago Neighborhood*. Chicago, IL;: The University of Chicago Press, 2019.

Smith, Adam. *The Wealth of Nations*. Indianapolis, IN: Hackett, 1993.

Smith, Henry Nash. *Virgin Land: The American West as Symbol and Myth*. Cambridge, MA: Harvard University Press, 1950.

St. John Paul II, Pope. *Laborem Exercens.* https://www.vatican.va/content/john-paul-ii/en/encyclicals/documents/hf_jp-ii_enc_14091981_laborem-exercens.html.

Turkle, Sherry. *Alone Together: Why We Expect More from Technology and Less from Each Other.* New York: Basic Books, 2011.

Turkle, Sherry. *Reclaiming Conversation: The Power of Talk in a Digital Age.* New York: Penguin Books, 2015.

Warsh, David. *Economic Principals: Masters and Mavericks of Economic Thought.* New York: Free Press, 1993.

Warsh, David. *Knowledge and the Wealth of Nations: A Story of Economic Discovery.* New York: W.W. Norton, 2007.

White, Morton and Lucia. *The Intellectual Versus the City.* Cambridge, MA: Harvard University Press, 1962.

Woodward, Paul. *Reverence: Renewing a Forgotten Virtue.* New York: Oxford University Press, 2001.

Zipp, Samuel and Nathan Storring (eds.). *Vital Little Plans: The Short Works of Jane Jacobs.* New York: Random House, 2016.

Zukin, Sharon. *Naked City: The Death and Life of Authentic Urban Places.* New York: Oxford University Press, 2010.

About the Author

Richard Keeley became friends with Jane Jacobs over the last twenty years of her life. He served as Director of Boston College's service-learning program, PULSE, from 1975–91, and it was this connection that piqued Jacobs's interest in the university. Keeley organized several campus conferences featuring Jacobs and her thought, most notably a two-day event, *Jane Jacobs: In Conversation* which brought together architects, economists, journalists, the former mayor of Toronto, and city activists from Boston. His overtures prompted Jacobs's donation of her papers to the Burns Library at Boston College. Keeley's published work on Jacobs includes an interview and two essays in *Ethics in Making a Living: The Jane Jacobs Conference* (Atlanta) as well as a contribution to *Ideas that Matter* (Owen Sound, Canada). He concluded his career at Boston College as Senior Associate Dean for Undergraduates in the Carroll School of Management and as Director of Programs for the university's Winston Center for Leadership and Ethics, which now features an annual Jane Jacobs Lecture.

Index

Agora
  in ancient Athens   167
  lack of in contemporary cities   169,
      173 n.9
Aristotle
  on friendship   153, 155
  on happiness   151
  Jacobs as Aristotelian thinker   83,
      106, 152
  on practical wisdom   106, 108, 127,
      128
  on sociality of human being   90

Backward cities   73
Bairoch, Paul   93 n.9
Banerjee, Abhijit and Esther Duflo   80,
      94 n.31
Boston College   68, 100, 104, 106, 107
Burnham, Daniel   22, 29

Calvin, John   18
Calvino, Italo   11
Canadian Cities and Regions
  Montreal   33, 84–5, 122
  Quebec   84, 122, 143, 164
  Toronto   24, 70, 84, 121–2, 127, 134
Capital   36
  challenges faced in securing capital for
      cities   86–9
  discriminatory lending   51
  factor of production   68–9
  human capital   92, 119, 158, 161–2, 166
  lack of in the West End   37
  lending circles   80
  "love capital"   39
  redlining   79
  time and capital costs   79
Cities and nature
  city as natural to the human
      being   171
  supposed opposition of the two   171

Corzine, Jon   113–14
Covid   56
Cox, Harvey   19
Cronon, William   22
Cultural amnesia   61

Das Kapital   86
Desrochers, Pierre   92 n.4

Easterly, William   89
Economic development in cities
  gift resources   74–5
  government and economic
      development   79
  "strategies for helping cities"   68, 82,
      104 n.35
  thing theory of development   38, 97
Economic theory
  Cities and the Wealth of Nations   30,
      67, 72–3, 77, 85, 98
  The Economy of Cities   67–70, 72, 75,
      77, 99, 133, 137
  initial reception of Jacobs's economic
      thought   67–8
  The Nature of Economies   67, 119, 171
  new growth theory   68, 92 n.2
  problem of accounting for continuing
      growth   68–9
Ellerman, David   92 n.4
Exit, Voice, and Loyalty   114
Eyes on the Street (book)   103

Federalist #51   30
Fishman, Robert   24
Four factors promoting thriving
      neighborhoods, "eyes on the
      street"
  importance of context   42
  requires neighborhood not a single
      street   47
  safety   41

Friendship
    civic friendship   152, 154, 165, 171
    in city neighborhoods   11, 38, 63
    and a complete life   153, 155

Gans, Herbert   37
Gentrification   48, 50, 52
Glaeser, Edward   69
Gopnik, Adam   43–4
Graham, Wade   26 n.29
Grass roots economic development
    Accion International   159–60
    Clark University (Main South
        Community Development
        Corporation)   160–1
    Grameen Development Bank   88,
        174–6
    Haley House   161–2
    Japanese bicycle industry   76
    Poverty Action Lab   80
    South Shore Bank failure   160
Great Cities of the World Conference   35,
    67, 146
Greenwich, Connecticut   46
Greenwich Village   42, 59

Hirschman, Albert   114
Holt, John   123–4
    play as education   124
Howard, Ebenezer   23–4, 50
Hudson Street   36, 41, 47, 49

Illich, Ivan   124–5
    convivial learning   125
    de-schooling society   125
The Intellectual versus the City   20
Invisible Cities   11

Jacobs's philosophy of education
    apprenticeship   103, 123, 129
    credentialing eclipsing learning   139
    family and community as "primary"
        school   120–1
    university education   137–40
Jefferson, Thomas   20, 135

Kanigel, Robert   41
Keller, Evelyn Fox   91
Kinds of urban neighborhoods   80

Lang, Glenna   34, 121, 135
Le Corbusier   24, 50, 61
Lonergan, SJ, Bernard   100

The Machine in the Garden   21
Main, Ted and Thomas Grypton   111
Makerspace   166–7, 170
Marshall, Alfred   90–1
Marx, Leo   22
Metropolitan regions
    a loose definition   84
    regions workers abandon   85
    supply regions   73, 85
MFS Global Holdings Ltd   113–14
Moral ecology   39, 57, 99
Mumford, Lewis   23, 36, 149
myths of city origins
    Mircea Eliade   12–13
    Jacques Ellul   16–18

Naked City   49
Nature's Metropolis   22
Norberg-Schulz, Christian   13
    encountering others in the city   56
    kinds of landscapes   15
    paths, centers and shelters   156
Nowlan, David   70

Piketty, Thomas   86–7, 135
Polanyi, Michael   121
Polis   57
Porter, Michael   69
Poverty Action Lab   80

Racism and discrimination   51
Ricardo, David   71
Rochester, NY   28–9, 148
    Kodak   31–2
Romer, Paul   68–9
Rotella, Carlo   38

St. Augustine   18
St. Thomas Aquinas   107
    and influence of Aristotle   18
Sartre, Jean-Paul   28
Scheinkman, Joseph   69
Schleifer, Andrei   69
Schumpeter, Joseph   49
Scranton, PA   121–2

Smith, Adam   76
Smith, Henry Nash   21
Subsidiarity
    defined   80
    in relation to local government
        assistance   87–8
    South Shore Bank   160
Sunbelt Cities   88
Systems of Survival
    raiding and trading   99–101
    guardian and commercial
        syndromes   111–13, 115, 117, 123
    monstrous hybrids   112
    restraining guardians: Venice   108–10
    restraining guardians: in
        corporations   110–11, 113

Tacit knowledge   121–2
Transactions of decline   88

*Urban Utopias in the Twentieth
    Century*   24

Venice, Italy
    early economic development   72–4
    economic consequences of the
        Serrata   81
    economic stagnation today   81
Virgin Land   21
Vital Little Plans   29, 67

Wall Street   36, 46, 59, 98, 108, 111
Warsh, David   68, 70
What makes for "good work"
    B corporations   117
    criteria for "good work"   116
    development work *vs.* production
        work   115
    human fulfillment   115
Weil, Simone   91
White, Morton and Lucia   20, 50
Whitehead, A. N.   52
Why Nations Fail   81
Winthrop, John   19–20
Worcester, Massachusetts
    Harding and Millbury Streets   52–5,
        58, 60
    I-290 and neighborhood loss   53
    Main South Development   160–1
    proximity to commerce
        not a guarantee of
        development   62
    within the Boston region   84
    Yellow Pages   97
Wright, Frank Lloyd   21, 24

Yunus, Muhammed   139

Zipp, Samuel and Nathan Storring   29,
    67
Zukin, Sharon   49

www.ingramcontent.com/pod-product-compliance
Lightning Source LLC
Chambersburg PA
CBHW061735270326
41928CB00011B/2241